Watching Television

Hermeneutics, Reception and Popular Culture

Tony Wilson

Chapter 3

Polity Press

First published in 1993 by Polity Press
in association with Blackwell Publishers Ltd.
First published in paperback 1995.

Editorial office:
Polity Press
65 Bridge Street
Cambridge CB2 1UR, UK

Marketing and production:
Blackwell Publishers Ltd
108 Cowley Road
Oxford OX4 1JF, UK

Blackwell Publishers Inc.
238 Main Street
Cambridge, MA 02142, USA

ISBN 0 7456 0722 5
ISBN 0 7456 1636 4 (pbk)

A CIP catalogue record for this book is available
from the British Library and from the Library of Congress.

Typeset in 10 on 11 pt Garamond
by CentraCet, Cambridge
Printed in Great Britain by
T. J. Press (Padstow) Ltd

This book is printed on acid-free paper.

Contents

Illustrations

Acknowledgements

I would like to acknowledge the friendship and intellectual sustenance given to me over many years by members and associates of the John Logie Baird Centre (Universities of Glasgow and Strathclyde): John Caughie and Colin MacCabe, as my Ph.D. supervisors, are particularly to be mentioned. Grateful thanks are also due to my first teacher, Connie Balides (presently of the University of Wisconsin, Milwaukee), in Australian phraseology, a 'real battler' for the cause of popular culture.

More recently, the film and media group in the division of humanities at Griffith University have been stimulating and helpful friends and co-workers, despite what Sartre might have called a certain (and I hope temporary) 'co-efficient of adversity'. I look forward, if with a little trepidation, to addressing the concerns of this book in a series of lectures to be shared with my rigorous friend and colleague, Dr Jane Crisp.

I would also like to acknowledge the UK research assistance during 1991 freely provided by Gordon Sindan from the damp and windy Scottish town of Ayr, while I sat in front of a wordprocessor in an overheated Australia (not too distant from another, but sub-tropical and doubtless postmodern-ist, Ayr, Queensland). The flow of programme support material convinced me that the English-speaking world has indeed become an electronic village. In the international marketing of serial texts, while Australia's Channel Ten sells *Neighbours* to the BBC, Channel Nine buys Independent Television News's daily *World News*. The same episode of *Drop the Dead Donkey* was broadcast during 1991 on Thursday nights in the UK (Channel Four at 10.00 p.m.), and on the following Tuesday night in Australia (SBS at 7.00 p.m.).

Thanks are due to my employers at Paisley College for generously agreeing to the three months' unpaid study leave which allowed this book to be commenced, and to Nick Smith for capably taking over my teaching. Also to the Brisbane River, which mediated so efficiently between the author and two hot summers at Griffith University that the book could be completed within the temporary respite from a near deregulated flow of student assignments. I'm grateful to John Thompson of Polity Press (and the anonymous reviewers of my manuscript) for helpful comment on earlier drafts of this book, and patience over the finishing thereof. And in this text on identification and distanciation, I must acknowledge the work of Dr Myra Macdonald in so variously heightening my sense of irony.

Finally, Simone Levy, Picture Co-ordinator at Channel Four, was unstinting in her efforts to provide the stills from which many of the images in this book are drawn. My appreciation, also, for interest and assistance from L. W. Bird, Senior Account Manager of Du Pont Carpets, Cosima Dannoritzer of Clark Production, Stephen McCrossan of Scottish Television and Adrian Figgess of the BBC (while regretting that the BBC alone felt it necessary to charge substantial copyright fees). Helen Jeffrey, on behalf of Polity Press, prepared the way for the reader, editing the final manuscript with understanding and precision.

Notes on Television Programmes

When reference is made to a programme, its transmission channel, time and date (or period) of transmission is given: for example, *Fat Man Goes Norse* (C4, 7.15, 9.8.87–30.8.87). All transmission times are 'p.m.' unless indicated otherwise. Numerals giving the date of transmission follow the sequence day, month, year.

Abbreviations for transmission channels are as follows:

C4   Channel Four (UK)
ITV   Independent Television (UK)
BBC1   British Broadcasting Corporation Channel 1
BBC2   British Broadcasting Corporation Channel 2
C9   Channel Nine (Australia)
ABC   Australian Broadcasting Corporation
SBS   Special Broadcasting Service (Australia).

Transmission dates for television programmes referred to in the book range from the mid-1980s in the UK to 1991 in Australia. I have been fortunate to experience British broadcasting at its most innovative and varied, and, subsequently, Australia's contribution to that tradition of experiment, the Special Broadcasting Service at its best.

Introduction

You need to be *completely* informed. You need to know *the whole story*. Always rely on *National Nine News*. *National Nine News*, the unchallenged leader.

National Nine News Network, Australia

I

In recent years film and television studies have been characterized by a developing concern with research into audiences. 'Discussions about the television audience', as Seiter remarks, 'have proliferated.'[1] This emerging interest did not derive its energy from speculating, solely on the basis of films and television programmes themselves, about how audiences were supposed to react. Rather, it attempted (and continues to attempt) to establish how *real* audiences view television programmes and make sense of them. And within the 'messiness' (Ang) of everyday life, these audiences are recognized as possessing a complex membership of different gender, class, generational and racial groups.

Histories of media theory run the risk of reducing that history to a set of oppositions between text-centred and audience-centred research. *Watching Television* attempts to negotiate between those oppositions. Nevertheless, one might say that prior to the comparatively recent interest in audiences, within earlier structuralist analyses texts determined the audience's consumption. That is, where a film or television programme addressed its spectators or viewers with a dominant set of social representations (for example, a patriarchal conception of men and their 'appropriate' activity), the audience, it was argued, would consume those representations unproblematically. As far as a critical understanding of the film or programme's view of society was concerned, since the intended audience did not engage in this, neither did the real one.

During the 1980s the growth of empirical studies of the audience in psychology and sociology undermined this easy theorizing. Accusations that television produced violent behaviour needed investigating. Feminists and ethnic groups asserted the possibility of difference, of active viewers producing their own meanings from a text. An increasingly audience-centred theorizing rejected its structuralist predecessor, an abandonment both wide-ranging and enthusiastic. Structuralism, it was suggested, argued for a limited and damaging account of the pleasures of viewing: at the centre lay the resolution of psychic conflict. In structuralist theory the audience uncritically adopted the text's apparently coherent view of the world and forgot its own limited and fragmented experience. Here, an account of viewing was offered as a process which resolved the tension between aspiration and reality, between cultural prescription and ability to proceed in the world. For ninety minutes the spectator could behave with the patriarchal virtuosity of a James Bond. The pleasures of an audience were those of an individual who, untroubled by contradiction, enjoyed a coherent unity of outlook.

The audience-centred research which followed structuralism, on the other hand, sought to establish both that there were ineliminable differences between the cognitive perspectives associated with the real viewer and those of the programme or film and that these differences produced a variety of readings. The text has a meaning 'in accord with codes of perception that it does not control'.[2] These differences also opened up the possibility of rebelling against the images of life promoted by the film or television programme, as images in contradiction with an audience's experience.

Dominant cinema has the 'ability to place the spectator in the position of a unified subject'.[3] Television 'maps out fictions, little dramas of making sense in which the viewer as subject is carried along'.[4] In statements like these, according to an audience-centred perception of what went before, structuralist media theory ignored an important distinction. It failed to separate the 'implied' audience, the audience to which a text appeared to be addressing itself, and the 'empirical' audience, the real audience with which it was in fact communicating. 'There was no question of relating the work to ... the actual readers who studied it, since the founding gesture of structuralism had been to bracket off such realities.'[5] But, those who felt they took the audience more seriously argued, 'real readers are subjects in history, living in given social formations, rather than mere ("inscribed") subjects of a single text'.[6] Real 'readers' (viewers) arrive at the text (film or television programme) equipped with their own knowledge and accounts of experience, and can use them not only to produce new interpretations but to resist the text's 'positioning'.

The structuralist account effaced the distinctiveness of the reader's experience as a historical and social individual, 'as already constituted in other discursive formations and social relations' prior to engaging with the text.[7] For those whose centre of attention has shifted to real audiences, it is the specificities of these 'formations' which always produce different readings of, and sometimes act as the source for resistance to, the dominant ideologies of sexism, ageism or racism inscribed within the text. A sense of one's own identity, capabilities and experience can allow one to reject accounts of living produced in film or television. In the Conclusion I discuss the way in which the distance between television's images of age and how older viewers think of their own day-to-day lives allows them to rebel against the media in a UK television audience response programme. In this way cultural 'sedimentations' in the experience of a viewer of a particular class, age, gender and racial background allow critical readings of the ideological identities offered by film or television to emerge. Feminists, in particular, articulate 'contradictory desires that challenge master narratives'.[8]

For audience-centred theorists, then, the structuralist conception of the ideological subject was, in significant respects, reductionist. It denied the specificity of the individual's experience and the function of that experience in providing the individual with an emerging awareness of contradictory versions of reality. The male viewer who identified with James Bond was, for structuralism, freed from any hint of contradiction between the cultural prescriptions of patriarchal ideology and real-life inadequacies. The worker accepted dominant accounts of how things were which 'removed' the subjective consciousness of exploitation by reducing it to the status of delusion. The viewing subject was constituted as coherent, unaware of contradictions arising from tensions between the delusory freedom and equality espoused by bourgeois ideology and unequal realities which were materially constraining.

An audience-directed horizon of understanding the text–viewer relationship argues that all readings are productive of new meaning, invariably of ideological significance beyond that already given in the film or programme. In invoking the possibility of a rich and varied response to a work, the hermeneutic philosophy to which I refer below (section III) reminds us of this possibility in the case of television. The passage of time can allow an emerging history of a work's reception, testifying to its qualities as a source of varied response. Institutional efforts, for instance through the use of continuity announcements, to close down the range of possible readings can signify an apparent exercise of unwarranted power.

The meaning most easily attributed to a text by its intended audience is said to be the 'preferred reading' of a film or television programme (a phrase upon which I offer further comment below). Even this 'may be inhabited differently by subjects', producing different interpretations.[9] An investigative drama can be enjoyed by an audience as an investigative drama in a wide range of different experiences of its enigmas and their resolution. To suggest otherwise will truly 'close' the text, denying the necessity of an audience's reading it through the discourses associated with his or her particular cultural and historical situation. Structuralism, on the other hand, marginalized as unimportant the (apparent) differences which existed within viewers' experiences or between those experiences and the text's account of the world.

Audience-centred theorizing asserts that contradiction is present in everyday readings of dominant film and television. Its concern is with a 'real' audience subscribing to perceptions of society distinct from those of the text or maintaining a half-suppressed awareness of experiences incompatible with a dominant media account of the way things are. It asserts the need to realize such readings are genuinely contradictory. An audience's appropriations of meaning which conflict with its everyday experience permit progressive moments of viewing or spectating to emerge where a dominant ideology can be challenged. Political action demands, in this sense, a subject-in-contradiction where oppositional thought resides, if not in the text, at least in the discourses brought to its reading and in subsequent perceptions of its meaning.[10]

My argument in this volume is that the appropriation of meaning from a film or television text involves the experience of difference and distance at the heart of the familiar and recognizable. Here, contradictions may be discerned between the ideologies of text and viewer. The structuralist paradigm concluded (with some difficulty) that the individual who 'recognizes' ideology 'hailing' him or her, who 'turns around' in response to its address, had been 'interpellated' into the ideologically constructed position of unified 'subject' and subsequently identified him- or herself in these terms.[11] Recognition is of the same. I shall be suggesting that structuralism did not take sufficient account of the complexities of 'recognition' and identification. For recognition is rather an awareness of both similarities in and differences between self and textual subject, between ways of existing and understanding the world. Recognition is of the familiar and its limits.

II

Watching Television examines the relationship between television programmes and television audiences. In asserting the polysemic status of television textuality, it seeks to integrate a study of programme form with an investigation of forms of viewing. At a philosophical level, it replays concepts such as 'illusionism' and 'identification'. The frequent, if brief, quotations from preceding works are intended to underwrite the very idea of a phenomenological revision of media analysis.

This reworking of meanings is an investigation of 'reading formations' (Bennett), of audience activity and the texts which prompt it. I make use of a range of concepts – 'social role', 'cognitive horizon' and 'life-world', among others – to investigate the interaction between these visual texts and viewers. The result is not simply theoretical but practical: the ability to generate close analyses of both text and context of reception. For as Newcomb indicates in his early essay, television has its own specificity: it is not simply 'a transmission device for other forms'.[12] *Watching Television* provides, I hope, a philosophical underpinning and justification for current enthusiasm with ethnographic research, although that research itself requires systematic scrutiny. As Nightingale remarks at the outset of an important paper, a 'thorough re-appraisal of what "ethnographic" means is long overdue'.[13]

My emphasis is on neither programme nor audience, for I attribute equal importance to the activities of both in constructing televisual meanings. The 'work is performed and achieves being through reading'.[14] Central to my account is an attempt to 'unpack' the ideas of 'identification' and 'distanciation', which, while important in television (and film) studies, are notoriously subject to ambiguity and alteration in their meaning. Buckingham thoughtfully notes in *Public Secrets* that the concept of 'identification' 'has barely been theorised in relation to television'.[15] Caughie, equally, points out that in media criticism words like 'identification' 'appear quite frequently, but largely they have been appropriated as given categories rather than debated in their specificity for television'.[16]

Television invariably engages its audience within the 'horizon of everyday life' (Dahlgren). Unlike film, its popular forms of soap opera, situation comedy and game show celebrate 'ordinary' people and the 'ordinary' experience of a viewer. Its varieties of speech differ, therefore, not only on the basis of their truth value but in disclosing a range of abilities to address everyday viewers in ways they can recognize as familiar. For reasons of finance and censorship and to attain its particular cultural identity, television (much more than film) affirms the mundane and 'known'. My opening chapter considers the medium's use of the 'familiar' to construct the everyday world – the 'life-world(s)' – of the intended audience. Here the importance of a phenomenological investigation of viewing experience is suggested. But, of course, the familiar may also be politically objectionable, constructed from the discourses of oppression. The book's final chapter reflects upon the possibility which is permanently open to real viewers to resist this 'familiar' communication, distancing themselves from its terms of ideological address. The 'culture of the greatest number can at any epoch distance itself, make a place for itself, or establish its own coherence in the models imposed upon it'.[17]

The first chapter also provides a phenomenology of the viewers' interests and their readings of the text or programme as 'relevant' to those concerns. For in a life-world interpretations of experience are generated by such perceptions of mundane relevance. 'The practical horizon of the lived world (*Lebenswelt*) indicates the point of departure and the point of arrival of hermeneutical activity.'[18] The phenomenological analysis I offer indicates that viewing is to be considered primarily 'practical'. Being a member of a television audience means generating role-related, interest-driven narratives, varying in content even amongst viewers of the same programme. Often these stories are used to bring together and make sense of events within a text, with an audience supplying speculative information of its own to remove problematic gaps. Inferences 'serve to "fill out" the narrative, increasing coherence and interest through beliefs about the motives and thoughts which lie behind the characters' actions'.[19] But television's stories may also be reread by a viewer as a way of making sense of experiences within his or her life-world outside the immediate context of watching television.

Following this introduction to the phenomenology of watching television, my second chapter begins a discussion of 'identification'. Identification is a particular way of existing in and knowing the world. For a viewer to identify with a character, the former must appropriate one (or more) of that individual's social roles with its associated point of view on events, the 'horizons of understanding' with which that subject regards a situation. When identifying with the private investigator Hazell, for instance, the audience 'plays' at being a detective, asking appropriate questions. The viewer, like Hazell, understand occurrences in terms of their relevance to solving the crime.

But to play is to be (almost) always in motion : and in identifying the viewer moves within and between roles, 'inhabiting multiple and mobile identities that fluctuate from situation to situation'.[20] In regarding identification as a mode of both existence and awareness, my account draws attention to what I have called ontological and epistemological aspects of this complex process. This analysis of identification is mapped on to the phenomenology of the first chapter.

In Chapter 4 I suggest that identification is supported by experiencing television's images as 'veridical'. For an audience, veridical images allow a (near) transparent disclosing of the apparently real, of individuals who seem to be involved in the roles, relationships and restrictions of everyday living. These images constitute the televisual equivalent of filmic illusionism, with camera work and editing effaced so that viewers forget they are watching a constructed media artefact. Seeming to perceive the world and its subjects, the audience views individuals in the text as possible focuses for identification.

Television's mechanisms of identification, of aligning its intended viewer with a character or presenter, include both visual and verbal strategies ; these are examined in detail in Chapter 5. To a degree these are similar to those used in film (for instance, the point-of-view shot). But as a medium where spoken discourse is particularly central, television's positioning of its audience is significantly verbal.

III

Much of the conceptual geography in *Watching Television* derives from phenomenology and hermeneutics. While some indication of this philosophical 'anchor' is given in early chapters, it is not examined in detail since my emphasis is on the study of television. The 'hermeneutics' referred to within these pages is distinct from Barthes's 'hermeneutic' code, the text's construction of enigma. The *text*'s hermeneutic code, says Barthes, poses 'a question as if it were a subject which one delays predicating'.[21] Such a code consists of those visual and verbal strategies which might be used by a film to develop puzzles (for example, the motive for a bank robbery) which it later resolves. Hermeneutics, on the other hand, attempts to describe the reader's active response to the experience of uncertainties of meaning found, for one reason or another, in the text which he or she is viewing. Invariably, but in ways which are empirically complex, this response will be to construct sense-making narratives.

Philosophically, the book shares the audience-centred critique of structuralism noted above, implicitly defining post-structuralism as a unified and historically located position if only around a perception of the main theoretical blunder it seeks to transcend : the omission of the (actual) reader. Unlike Fiske, for whom 'developments in structuralism . . . go under the name of post-structuralism', my view of the relationship between these two theoretical areas is one of criticism and difference rather than continuity.[22]

Thus *Watching Television* distances itself from a structuralism in which consciousness is passively determined by the social and cultural (here, film and television). Structuralism was always less plausible in the case of television than film. The individual engaging with the former amid the distractions of domesticity 'is not as monolithically constructed, as a result of the fragmentation of the viewing experience'.[23] The environment of the home, not normally closed off in silent, cinematic darkness, is a source of interventions and associations with experience which can be at odds with many dominant texts.

Methodological agreements among recent studies of the continuous serial suggest there is an emerging paradigm for work on 'soaps', a growing research consensus whose 'normality' is constructed around certain rules and standards. Central to these rules is the requirement that, in analysing the processes of viewing, an equal regard be paid both to text and to audience, to the 'real' as well as the implied audience of the programme. Hobson's *Crossroads* (1982) and Ang's *Watching 'Dallas'* (1985) contain substantial analyses of discussions with audiences, as does Buckingham's *Public Secrets* (on the BBC's *EastEnders*, 1987). Seiter's edited collection, *Remote Control* (1989), is a series of reflections on audience behaviour providing useful evidence for the nature of identification and audience speculation about textual content to which I refer. Allen's *Speaking of Soap Operas* does not rely upon audience interviews. Nevertheless, it too claims to be interested in a 'reader-oriented poetics of the soap opera'.[24]

While clearly empirical, such work on the audience is not thereby excluded from being philosophically based. This is an issue I shall discuss in the body of the text. It is sufficient here to note that both Allen's and Buckingham's analyses use investigatory tools belonging to phenomenology and hermeneutics or to the literary investigations associated with this philosophy, that is reader response studies of how audiences perceive texts to have meaning. Allen relies upon a phenomenological concept in writing of the soap opera's 'horizon of expectations', its audience's assumptions about what they can expect to see and hear.[25] Buckingham's account of the relationship between viewer and text implicitly acknowledges the hermeneutic idea of the 'projection of meaning' : 'viewers constantly test their own and others' predictions against the evidence provided by the programme in their attempts to get it right'.[26] At this point the analysis of television converges with Radway's study of consuming popular written fiction, *Reading the Romance*. For this literature is also said to require the intended reader or viewer to 'supply a narrative projection'.[27]

In a further accord between the empirical and the philosophical, Schroder's references to the viewer's 'commuting' between involvement and distanciation in his 'The Pleasure of *Dynasty*' bear a close relationship to a philosophical understanding of reading as 'play'.[28] For the phenomenologist Ricoeur, reading is the 'playful metamorphosis of the *ego*'.[29] Similarly, the hermeneutic philosopher Gadamer regards the relationship between text and reader as characterized by an 'ease of play', a 'to-and-fro movement' in which the latter moves back and forth over the text in a holistic construction of its meaning.[30] 'The work of art is the playing of it . . . The work is what is played by the players it plays.'[31] Play elicits a truthful meaning for the text.

A close interest in theorizing about the audience and its behaviour (as well as the text) is clearly central to research into the 'soapie' and, I would hold, into television more generally. *Watching Television* may be read as a consideration of whether this emerging paradigm of research procedure, implicit within investigatory practice directed at the continuous serial, can be used more generally throughout television studies. Thus, while much of what follows may be applied to film, the discussion principally concerns television. Reader response theory and the phenomenological hermeneutics of viewing investigate the audience's construction of meaning for a text, rather than viewers' attitudes to the content of a programme once it is found meaningful. From this perspective, while some earlier accounts of television paid attention to audience reaction, they did so inadequately. Uses and gratifications theory and behaviourist studies both engaged in an empiricist and arbitrary separation of audience use or need from its understanding of a text. For an anti-empiricist phenomenology of reading, it is a mistake to assert that an audience can perceive a programme as possessing a fixed and unproblematic meaning, to which they *then* 'react' in different ways. Rather, determining the sense of a text and 'reaction' are inextricably and mutually related. There are no meanings, intrinsic or otherwise, beyond those supplied by readers : 'the work of art is not an object that stands over against a subject for itself'.[32] Looking and what it reveals are always directed by the interests of the individual in question.

Uses and gratifications theory, in particular, envisaged an extrinsic and distinct existence for the meaning of the text, on the one hand, and audience response, on the other. In this theory it is what the viewer does with the text which is emphasized at the expense of considering the programme itself. It is perhaps for this reason that the theory gave methodological houseroom to the suspect assumption of a text of unproblematic meaning to which viewers separately react in varying ways. As Fiske wrote, describing 'escapist needs in the media audience', 'we need to go further than merely labelling these needs escapist . . . Semiotic analyses of the programme can also show us what we are escaping *to*.'[33] There is need for detailed consideration not only of a programme but of how a viewer goes about assembling its meaning.

The last decade, then, has brought the demise of such important text-centred approaches to the construction of meaning as structuralism and uses and gratifications theory. Brunsdon is surely correct in seeing 'the transformation of English and literary studies since the 1960s' as consisting of 'the elevation of the act of reading over the text, as the point of meaning production'.[34] A semiotically active audience, endowing a text with meaning, is central to 'the enabling theses of contemporary cultural studies' (Mellencamp). This is a worldly audience inextricably located within, and drawing upon, horizons of understanding constituted by the experience of day-to-day living. If it was the case in 1989 that, as Silverstone remarks, 'it is precisely this integration [of television] into the daily lives of those who watch it which has somehow slipped through the net of academic scrutiny', then *Watching Television* seeks to join the growing number of books and articles addressing that failure.[35] Like them it maps out the conceptual grids it perceives as necessary to engage with 'audience talk'. Along with Radway, I object 'to the privileging of speech or writing as production', the 'conflation of cultural production with the moment of enunciation alone'.[36] Instead, my theoretical alignment is with a postmodernist assertion of an audience 'in play', whose differences as readers establish themselves in a capacity to read a text in an infinite variety of ways. It is in consumption, as well as in the text, 'that originality and creativity are to be found'.[37]

Watching Television sets out to capture philosophically something of the 'infinite, contradictory, dispersed and dynamic practices and experiences of television audience-hood enacted by people in their everyday lives . . . the complexity and the dynamism of the social, cultural, psychological, political and historical activities that are involved in people's engagements with television'.[38]

IV

This book is intended for a diversity of readers, not all of whom will have prior acquaintance with film and television studies or 'continental' philosophy. In the first two chapters I have attempted to explain my use of phenomenological and hermeneutic concepts of analysis. However, I am conscious that, for the reader not accustomed to the terminology of (post-)structuralist literary and media theory, these may present some difficulty. Structuralism, at least in the version which took root in *Screen*, produced an 'increasingly inaccessible prose style'.[39] To readers coming to film and television studies for the first time, it is worth saying that I use the word 'text' to refer equally to film and television programme (unless the context makes it clear that only one of these is intended. Similarly, 'reading' is used as a synonym for either viewing television or spectating in a cinema.

In this context two other terms should be mentioned : 'discourse' and 'subject' (or 'subject position'). 'Discourse' forms part of a process of communication ; it is possible to have both visual and verbal discourses, as in television. To refer to a character or presenter as a 'subject' occupying a 'subject position' in a text is to regard that individual as possessing a set of ideological assumptions with which (often without reflecting upon them) he or she interprets the world ; these constitute his or her 'position'. These terms have a history of complex use.[40] In referring to individuals or characters as 'subjects', I do not intend to imply that they bear a passive relationship to ideology or social organization, that they are 'subject-ed'. 'Subject' is a relational concept : subject and ' "object" are not fixed terms but indicative of a relationship between two elements'.[41] A textual subject communicating with the (implied) television viewer in direct visual address is also the object of the latter's glance.

My references to 'ideal reader', 'implied reader' and 'intended reader' are to one and the same person. This is the individual addressed (implicitly or explicitly) by a text and always distinct from the 'empirical', 'real' or 'actual' audience.

Technicalities such as a text's 'preferred meaning' (see note 9) or a television programme's 'segments' (see Chapter 3, note 91) are briefly examined when they first occur. 'Life-worlds' (constituting the individual's familiar daily environment) and 'horizons of understanding' (the individual's familiar cognitive assumptions) are discussed in Chapter 1. The concept of 'ideology' (notoriously difficult) is analysed in the Conclusion. Dominant ideology is written into action, misinforming its direction and purposes, existing implicitly within the rules, roles and relationships which guide its everyday routines. It is articulated in the familiar and unproblematic horizons of existence. Dominant ideology sets the task both of its discovery and of its resistance ; it is, in the broadest sense, disenfranchising. For Ricoeur, the term denotes a set of ideas which, while integrating a social group, may often do so in a way which supports ultimately unjustifiable relationships of authority or dominance.

Notes

1   Seiter, 'Making Distinctions in TV Audience Research', p. 61.
2   De Certeau, *The Practice of Everyday Life*, p. 170.
3   MacCabe, 'Realism and the Cinema', p. 232.
4   Heath and Skirrow, 'Television', p. 58.
5   Eagleton, *Literary Theory*, p. 109.
6   Willemen, 'Notes on Subjectivity', p. 48.
7   Morley, 'Texts, Readers, Subjects', p. 162.
8   Mayne, 'Response', p. 232.

9   Morley, 'Texts, Readers, Subjects', p. 167. The 'preferred' reading of a programme or film may be said to be the interpretation supported by those textual features whose organization and relationship appear designed to be read in this way, as a result of their complex and harmonious integration. (For instance, in a *film noir*, the organization of lighting, camera angles and shadows around the *femme fatale*.) (Cf. Hall, 'Encoding/decoding', p. 134.) There may be more than one preferred reading of a single text. Familiar both to UK viewers and those in Australia, the 'classic' BBC television situation comedy *Porridge* opens itself both to an 'innocent' and to a more prurient 'adult' reading, neither of which is privileged over the other. The very possibility of 'multiple' preferred readings of its humorous treatment of events within the closed world of a prison is a prerequisite of its transmission in mid-evening television as 'family' viewing. In this context a reductive analysis of 'preferred reading' would be one which limited the reference of the concept to a single interpretation of the text.

10 I have not considered psycho-analytic versions of structuralism. Many argue that, like structuralism, they are an inadequate attempt to anticipate, with a description of textual activity, the processes engaged in by actual readers. They represent 'a tendency to substitute for semiotic transactions a mere redistribution of (psychic) quantities' (Fletcher, 'Melodrama', p. 4). I leave others to argue for a reading of psycho-analytic approaches which engages with the complexities of the day-to-day awareness of actual audiences.

11 L. Althusser, 'Ideology and Ideological State Apparatuses', *Essays on Ideology*, p. 48.

12 Newcomb, 'Towards a Television Aesthetic', p. 480.

13 Nightingale, 'What's "Ethnographic" about Ethnographic Research?', p. 50.

14 Grondin, 'Hermeneutics and Relativism', p. 50.

15 Buckingham, *Public Secrets*, p. 82.

16 Caughie, 'Television Criticism', pp. 116–17.

17 Chartier, *Cultural History*, p. 41.

18 Grondin, 'Hermeneutics and Relativism', p. 52.

19 Livingstone, *Making Sense of Television*, p. 183.

20 Ang, *Desperately Seeking the Audience*, p. 162.

21 Barthes, *S/Z*, p. 76.

22 Fiske, 'Popularity and Ideology', p. 171.

23 Kaplan, *Rocking around the Clock*, p. 28.

24 Allen, *Speaking of Soap Operas*, p. 61.

25 Ibid., p. 76.

26 Buckingham, *Public Secrets*, p. 171.

27 Radway, *Reading the Romance*, p. 205.

28 Schroder, 'The Pleasure of *Dynasty*', p. 68.

29 Ricoeur, 'Hermeneutics and the Critique of Ideology', p. 94.

30 Gadamer, *Truth and Method*, p. 94.

31 Weinsheimer, *Gadamer's Hermeneutics*, p. 103.

32 Gadamer, *Truth and Method*, p. 92.

33 Fiske, *Introduction to Television Studies*, p. 138.

34   C. Brunsdon, 'Television: Aesthetics and Audiences', in Mellencamp, *Logics of Television*, p. 64.
35   Silverstone, 'Let Us Then Return', p. 77.
36   Radway, 'Reception Study', p. 362.
37   Caughie, 'Adorno's Reproach', p. 133.
38   Ang, *Desperately Seeking the Audience*, p. 13.
39   D. Buckingham, 'Lessons from SEFT', *Initiatives*, 11 (1989), p. 3.
40   See Caughie, *Theories of Authorship*, pp. 292–4.
41   Branigan, 'The Spectator and Film Space', pp. 55–6.

1

Television : Familiarity and Phenomenology

Television programmes predominantly intend an experience of recognition for the viewer. Using the concept of 'life-world', this chapter explores the nature of this 'recognition'. I conclude by examining the degree to which (despite a programme's pursuit of familiarity) that recognition is doomed to remain partly unattained by the real viewer. Difference, however suppressed, cannot be eliminated from watching television.

The first section of this chapter introduces the reader to the phenomenological concepts of 'horizon', 'life-world' and 'social role', which will be employed throughout to analyse the 'commonplace' (Silverstone). Some readers will be glad to note that this theoretical intervention has been made as brief as possible. But I include in my account at least some of the 'prejudices, expectations and questions' which govern this research.[1]

Clarification of these ideas will be sought in the second section, by making use of them to give an account of the UK breakfast television programme *TV-am*. I hope that their value in analysing individual responses to television will become apparent. For, as Ang has argued, studies of the audience carried out by media institutions frequently remain very general in their conclusions, perceiving the viewer merely as an instance of a classed, gendered or ethnic type.

The final section discusses the reasons why television's attempts to present its audience with replications of their familiar life-worlds inevitably fail. Such a lack of success has a positive aspect. In the Conclusion I consider how this element of difference (or 'strangeness') allows an audience-centred account of the viewer's distanciation from constructions of his or her life-world in the programme.

1.1 Audience and Life-world

Warning against phenomenology, MacCabe informs his readers that, in this philosophical approach to understanding human existence, the isolated 'subject is seen as the founding source of meanings'.[2] How can a limited description of the lonely 'I' 'in simple evidence to itself', provide a basis of knowledge for justifying claims about the social, the cultural and the historical – let alone film and television ? What does this starting point tell us, for instance, about how an individual relates to others in matters of judgement ? Where a philosophical system seeks to analyse human person-ality as a socially transcending subjectivity – in terms, that is, which exclude any reference to the individual's social context of existence – its frame of reference is clearly restricted (if not impossible).

Nevertheless, I wish to suggest that television studies would find it useful to return to phenomenology and to certain of its concepts, such as 'life-world'. The philosophy of subjectivity found in the early writings of such phenomenologists as Husserl, MacCabe rightly implies, pursued an imposs-ible 'genetic epistemology' in its investigation of how a language-using individual comes to acquire knowledge. As I have indicated, this programme of analysis attempted to account for human experience using descriptions of conscious awareness which referred only to the individual and pre-social. No examination was made of our belief in other minds ; yet this assumption is frequently, if not necessarily, presupposed by processes of correction. 'All actual and possible acts of consciousness were considered acts of *my* consciousness.'[3] The subject's experience of intersubjectivity, of other human beings as conscious agents rather than passive objects, was not submitted to analysis up to this point in Husserl's work.

But subsequent phenomenological investigations assert the existence of 'life-worlds'. For the mature Husserl, they are a 'presuppositionless' presup-position in his theorizing, allowing an account of the community of the *cogitamus* (the 'we think'). By 'thinking through' the intersubjective in terms of a doctrine of the 'life-world', Husserl seeks to establish not simply that we think, but that (to a greater or lesser degree) we think alike. For the 'life-world' is a theory of consciousness and the world. In its terms of analysis we know not only that others think but also, given the familiar life-world of ideas and activities which we share with them, that they think like us – within something like the same framework of concepts. Husserl argues that the individual's experience presupposes the existence and history of intersubjec-tively obtaining categories of thought in a life-world. Such categories are, for example, those of science, a 'sedimented conceptual system which, as taken for granted, serves as the ground' of thinking and perceiving.[4]

In this way Husserl's starting point, the philosophical position to which MacCabe alludes, is inverted. His later phenomenology is 'holistic'. The subject is, at the most basic level of analysis, within an 'articulation', already endowed with the ability to use forms of thought which others can recognize and practise. His or her experience is of a life-world 'pre-given as existing for all in common' :

> it is pregiven to us all quite naturally, as persons within the horizon of
> our fellow men, i.e., in every actual connection with others, as 'the' world

common to us all. Thus it is . . . the constant ground of validity, an ever available source of what is taken for granted, to which we, whether as practical men or as scientists, lay claim as a matter of course.[5]

With the doctrine of the 'life-world' (or life-worlds) as 'human formations' or collective forms of thought supporting action, this phenomenology posits a social subject whose understanding already accords with others at the outset of investigations into the possibility of human knowledge : 'transcendental subjectivity permits and even demands a transcendental community'.[6]

The concept of 'life-world' can be further explained by relating it to the phenomenological idea of 'horizon' : 'to exist in a community is to appropriate and take for granted its experience as a horizon of retention'.[7] Both in Husserl's later phenomenology and in hermeneutics, as I will indicate in Chapter 2, the concept of 'horizon' is used to emphasize the intersubjective basis of cognition. In its focus on the world our cognitive activity both involves relationships with other individuals (for example, in the processes of correcting a mistake) and rests upon shared conceptions of how things are. The word 'horizons', as used in this text, denotes these definitional frameworks : they are emphatically social in origin, existing prior to the particular individual. The term 'horizons' (of understanding) seems to me preferable to, for instance, that of 'problematic'. As I show below, reliance upon the former draws attention to the selectivity and self-effacing familiarity characterizing the presentation and relationship to the world of an ideological typology, a horizon of understanding. Within Australian patriarchy, the horizons of masculinity through which it engages with the world are both limiting and, in their endless repetition, rendered apparently natural. Seeming inevitable, their merely contingent status is made invisible.

Phenomenology explores the 'horizons' of perceptual awareness, the changing categories in terms of which we identify what we see as we see it. On the other hand, more interested in knowledge than in perceptual aspects of experience, the philosophical hermeneutics with which I am also concerned speaks of consciousness as operating within the 'moving horizon' of traditional belief : 'the anticipation of meaning that governs our understanding of a text is not an act of subjectivity, but proceeds from the communality that binds us to the tradition'.[8] But whether perceptual or otherwise, horizons of understanding bear the 'historicity of everyday life' (Lefebvre), drawing upon the individual's cultural memories from which anticipations of meaning can be made.

Husserl's philosophy relies substantially on a concept of 'horizon'. The phenomenological inflection of its meaning associates the term primarily with a cognitive aspect of perception, with the set of general concepts whereby we most fundamentally experience the world.[9] The 'horizons' of experience are those remembered cognitive frameworks, implicit (even if not immediately available to consciousness) within the individual's perceptual processes. They allow the experience of things in the world as familiar instances of known types. Aware that a circle is round, we anticipate that unseen portions will conform to this geometrical pattern, to a cognitive horizon of circularity. Constituting an a priori awareness of the basic 'geography' of the familiar world, horizons generate anticipations that objects have features not yet visible (for example, a rear side) : 'every object stands before us as a familiar object within a horizon of typical familiarity' ; 'the internal horizon [is] the complex of characteristics not yet perceived'.[10]

Cognitive horizons determine our perceptual processes, our looking at the world and its contents. The concept of 'horizon' is important in analysing and explaining the mechanisms whereby the individual's sense of the known and predictable nature of an object (or person) is sustained in place. Husserl is attempting to provide an account of 'familiarity', explaining its presence as a characteristic of everyday experience. Perception is of what is already known, even if only in the most general way. Constantly directed at instances of types of phenomena which (at some level) he or she has already experienced, the subject's look is always at what is in some respect familiar. 'The object is present from the first with a character of familiarity ; it is apprehended as an object of a type already known in some way or other, even if in a vague generality.' For this reason, we 'already "know" more about the thing than is in this cognition alone.'[11] Or as the phenomenologist Schutz later puts it : our awareness is of an object 'as an existent of a particular type ; as a thing of the outer world, as a plant, an animal, a human being, a human product, and so on'.[12]

'Horizons' are the frameworks of cognitive knowledge underlying perceptual experience, allowing aspects of that experience to be recognized and identified as instances of types already encountered. Our concept of circularity, this cognitive horizon, both from and with which we interpret the world, allows us to anticipate that half-experienced circles will turn out to be round and to recognize them as familiar when they do. Our horizons of understanding the people around us permit differences to be perceived between human beings and animals, to anticipate and recognize their distinct activities. These frameworks operate as the fundamental basis of expectations about how things will behave in the future.[13]

It is because the subject's perceptions are constantly of the familiar as it presents itself in the unfolding of experience that what occurs can be anticipated : the object exhibiting a fourth side which has hitherto been hidden, the dog barking at the sound of strangers, the character in the drama behaving as expected. It is the 'horizonal' aspect of familiar day-to-day existence which, as a framework resting on memories and generating expectations connected in time, provides experience with a unity.[14]

Horizons structure and guide subjective perception, functioning as a central aspect of the individual's engaging with the world. As I have indicated, in his later work Husserl argues that a person's experience, at the most basic level of analysis, presupposes a wider culture : 'here it often seems ... that the individual's world of immediate experience, rather than grounding the cultural world, is determined by it'.[15] Horizons of experience are therefore culturally inflected, informed by an intersubjective awareness of the world. 'To live as a person is to live in a social framework, wherein I and we live together in community and have the community as a horizon.'[16] Directed at our surroundings and for the most part supporting our anticipations concerning them, our horizons of understanding generate a sense of the already experienced. As they thus constitute the familiarity of a life-world, horizons allow a cultural knowledge to be used and (apparently) confirmed.

A life-world is formed by horizons woven into action. The subject's experience is, at its most fundamental, of a series of related life-worlds (for example, the life-world of the middle-class family, of Christian religious observance, of academic professional practice). As Husserl states in an important passage in the *Cartesian Meditations*, 'men belonging to one and the same world live in a loose cultural community – or even none at all – and accordingly constitute different surrounding worlds of culture, as concrete life-worlds in which the relatively or absolutely separate communities live their passive and active lives'.[17]

Familiarities provide 'the constant ground of validity'. A life-world is 'pregiven', an everyday pre-reflective and unanalysed world of familiar assumptions and perceptions, 'an ever available source of what is taken for granted'. The experience of a life-world is structured by the awareness of goals for action generated by playing particular roles: 'living towards our ends, which are valid for us habitually, we do of course, live in the horizon of the life-world no matter which ends are "having their turn"'.[18] As a being with goals or 'practical interests', the individual finds him- or herself in life-worlds whose various parts and processes are experienced 'through' their relevance or irrelevance to those interests. A life-world 'is pregiven to us, the waking, always somehow practically interested subjects, not occasionally but always and necessarily as the universal field of all actual and possible praxis, as horizon'.[19] The different interests generated by the roles available in each life-world allow a range of perspectives, producing variations in cognitive purchase on what may be the same physical object. 'Interests constitute special worlds . . . A real estate man, a carpenter, an architect and an antiquarian of course may be perceiving the same house, but the house as perceived by each of them is "incorporated into" each one's specific world and thus presents a different facet to each.'[20]

The natural attitude with which a life-world is encountered is an unreflective awareness of the 'worldly'. In this 'mundane' experience 'nature and culture are merged; the *Lebenswelt* is where physical bodies are transformed into cultural objects, or persons whose physical movements are then meaningful acts, gestures and communication'.[21] A life-world is embodied subjectivity, a structure of behaviour and 'common-sense' assumptions whose unproblematic character is sustained by their familiarity. In the ideal life-world formed around the middle-class or working-class family, for instance, the value and practices of 'caring' go unquestioned. A life-world is a world of routines, of intersubjective horizons of understanding, in which the existence of others is taken for granted. It is 'the horizon of subjective modes of givenness'[22] which, as naturalized assumptions, pass 'mute' and 'concealed', as apparent 'validities'.[23]

The 'engagement of consciousness in the intersubjective community [and] its tacit acceptance of . . . what is "obvious", "taken for granted" [in] that community'[24] produce an implicit agreement in subjective horizons of understanding. The apparent certainty possessed by these 'horizonal' assumptions as constituents of the individual's life-worlds has its source in this intersubjective agreement. It is a certainty which 'naturalizes' the character of any objects which fall within the horizons of understanding concerned. Horizons constitute a life-world for the subject by marking out familiar assumptions as 'obvious'. They provide the basis (and limits) of justifications in verbal discourse which refer to this level of the seemingly unproblematic. These are significant limits, since cognitive horizons of understanding implied by speech, writing and vision are, as I note in Chapter 7, inflected by ideology. Language, I shall suggest, denotes its referents 'perspectivally', organizing them within horizons of understanding whose connotative dimensions deliver ideology to both text and reader.

'From the beginning the phenomenologist lives in the paradox of having to look upon the obvious as questionable, as enigmatic, and of henceforth being unable to have any other scientific theme than that of transforming the universal obviousness of the being of the world.'[25] Husserl argued for a radical doubting of the horizons of experience, the 'suspension' of familiar assumptions through an agnosticism regarding their truth content. This agnosticism was to be directed particularly at the most fundamental conviction of all, that of a mind-independent reality. A 'life world . . . must be rendered "strange" and its mundanity made the subject of a radical *epoché*, suspending the natural attitude and exposing its presuppositions'.[26] Here, Husserl and Brecht appear, momentarily, in harmony. The latter's 'alienation' of the familiar may be reread as an alienation of the apparent obviousness of (bourgeois) life-worlds displayed in the theatre. But Brecht, of course, unlike Husserl, sought to remove this taken for granted knowledge from pre-theoretical awareness to the level of political scrutiny.

For phenomenology, the categories of the pregiven in a familiar life-world operate in opposition to those of a scientific understanding of its content. For 'mundane' thought the experienced world is conceived of through a framework which relates it to human use rather than treating it as a set of objects for abstract analysis. In pre-scientific awareness the familiarities of a life-world are not only easily accessible but experienced as certain, functioning as a basis from which the more exploratory ideas of science may be derived: a life-world is 'presupposed in all scientific endeavour'.[27] Thus (briefly remembering television) the categories of a science documentary may operate to displace the very ideas without whose existence the investigation itself could not have begun. 'The Science of Sexual Attraction' (BBC1, 9.25, 6.3.85), in the UK current affairs series

QED, evoked 'the mechanistic clarity of [the socio-biologist's] approach; his utter repudiation of all things wishy-washy and sentimental'.

The doctrine of a life-world constituted by familiarity, its 'recurrent sameness', is at the centre of a phenomenology of existence associated with Schutz. Here, as for Husserl, objects are experienced within horizons which determine their recognition as instances of types, allowing expectations to be formed as to their further behaviour. The experience of 'typicality' is pregiven and 'prepredicative'. It constitutes, that is, the 'taken for granted' and is the basis on which linguistic description and classification are developed: 'by reference to the stock of knowledge at hand at that particular Now, the actually emerging experience is found to be a "familiar" one'.[28] Schutz specifically relates his phenomenology of social roles in a life-world to Husserl's analyses of experience as an awareness of types. Taking this awareness 'as a point of departure, it can be explained why we interpret the actions of our fellow-men in terms of course-of-action types and of personal types [that is, as instances of role-performance]'.[29]

Familiar practices and assumptions are taken for granted as the 'pre-known', at least until 'rectified . . . by supervening experience'.[30] They form an unchallenged horizon of presuppositions in terms of which the 'unknown' is experienced or questioned. Much of the preknown is inductive in character, consisting of the assumption that 'the world will go on substantially in the same manner as it has so far'.[31]

The concept of a life-world is developed by the critical theorist Habermas as 'a communication concept'. Communication producing factual or evaluative agreement presupposes a common starting point in the pregiven or unchallenged, in a life-world of shared assumptions. In resting on these assumptions, a horizon of common understanding is sustained: 'communicatively structured lifeworlds . . . reproduce themselves via the palpable medium of action oriented to mutual agreement'.[32]

This concept of the life-world is applied in section 1.2 to the relationship between television presenter and viewer. Broadcast communication draws on and maintains a set of cognitive horizons of understanding within life-worlds appropriated by both text and ideal audience. 'Real' individuals inhabit those life-worlds in various ways, reading and extending them in different directions.

The family, or familial life-world, is assumed to be the predominant context of viewing by media organizations. As such its study in respect of television is particularly important. In Wittgenstein's sense, 'family' is a 'family resemblance' concept. There is, that is to say, a set of rule-governed activities at least some of which must be a feature of any group claiming to be a family. Lull gives an indication of what these might be in his article 'The Family and Television in World Cultures': 'families are composed of persons who are related by blood or marriage, but not always. Sharing the same roof, food, dining table, money, material goods, or emotions could define any group as family.'[33] This list of activities would have to take into account ethnic diversity among family relationships (for example, between

nuclear and extended families).[34] In respect of behaviour relating to television it would also, for instance, have to accommodate Lull's distinction
between those families who encourage discussion of television programmes
and those who repress it.[35]

The television viewer, as I noted in the Introduction, 'projects' a meaning
for the text. (I examine this activity further in Chapter 2.) This process is
mirrored in television's own projection of the life-world of its intended
audience. The text 'celebrates' the viewer's horizons of experience, cognitive
horizons both closely associated with the processes of perception and
constitutive of the cultural traditions of the audience. Television replicates
aspects of a viewer's life-world in the text, confirming their status as
elements in lived experience. As broadcasting, however, it must also be
wary of specifying the activities of its assumed audience at a level of detail
which excludes real viewers.

Television gives its intended audiences unending opportunities to recognize the familiar. It constructs its on-screen artefacts as a well-known
presence within the viewer's life-world (a 'horizon of horizons') through
frequent repetition of form, character and content. Programmes, as I
indicate in Chapter 5 on mechanisms of identification, address their viewers
as an extended group of acquaintances, if not old friends. Talk shows engage
their audiences' attention with conspicuous assertions of intimacy (or
conspiracy), the familiar relationship between host and studio audience
intended to mirror that proposed for the programme and audience at home.
Current affairs discussions and the news often rely on the viewer being
aware of knowledge available in previous programmes, creating a sense of
shared participation in events by friends who know both one another and
what there is to know. 'When a story carries over from one day to the next,
it is assumed that the audience will be familiar enough with the topic to
allow its background to be largely taken for granted.'[36]

The discourses of a presenter or interviewer frequently attempt to
construct the life-world of the audience. 'The questions that a lot of viewers
may be asked themselves ...' asserts Dimbleby in the BBC's Sunday
lunchtime politics programme *On the Record* (BBC1, 1.00, 18.3.90), establishing the practices of textual understanding associated with the role of
viewer. Here (implied) audience and interviewer identify in a rule-governed
questioning. Roles (like horizons) are constituted by 'a network of typifications', characteristic activities which are appropriated in the processes of
identification. They are 'typifications of human individuals, of their course-
of-action patterns, of their motives and goals'.[37]

The concept of 'social role' with its constituent rules (discussed in Chapter
2) is central for the phenomenological study of the life-world. Likewise, in
the empirical examination of the living arrangements adopted by a television
audience, understanding its activity as formed around roles and rule-
governed practices is important. Differences in viewing 'are the effects of
the particular social roles that these men and women occupy within the
home'.[38] Similarly, for Lull, 'many characteristic patterns of audience

involvement with television can be regarded as *rituals* that are manifestations of microsocial (family) and macrosocial (cultural) *rules*'.[39]

To argue that an audience is always and everywhere an audience-within-a-life-world of familiarities which television attempts to reproduce is not to regard the familiar as unchanging. For individuals who endow their environment with intelligibility, the perceptions of usefulness by which an audience conducts the practice of its life-world will not remain unmodified. When economic circumstances change, for instance, television itself may be understood in terms of its usefulness to viewers with an interest in comprehending their new situation. The popularity of genres concerned with violence, horror and terror may be related to 'the structural insecurity and sense of acute vulnerability among the working class at a time of economic recession'.[40]

Television re-presents to its intended viewers their horizons of experience, their role-based needs, desires and their perception of what is rational. To this degree television does resist innovation. But the real audience is defined by the inevitable difference between its horizons of experience and those attributed to it by the text. Audience assumptions about the world are inflected by individual biographies of experience; no text can accommodate these within its construction of an ideal viewer, articulated across broad categories of gender, race, class or age. While similarities between intended and real audiences are often such as to allow the latter's recognition of something like itself in the text, the complete closure of the epistemic 'gap' between text and 'empirical' reader is logically impossible. Reading is always appropriation of meaning from a position of greater or lesser semiotic difference. In the Conclusion I show how an awareness of this difference can motivate a distanciated reading of the text. As Habermas notes, a 'controlled distanciation [*Verfremdung*] can raise understanding from a prescientific experience to the rank of a reflective procedure'.[41]

Television's direct address appears to engage with its implied viewers as individual members of the audience. The response of reading is an appropriation of sense and reference articulated by subjects in the programme. But reading is always and everywhere a 'fusion of horizons' drawing upon, and producing, difference. It cannot be considered as attaining 'the' meaning of the text, anchored for all time and for all readers as the intended communication of its author. Appropriation 'does not imply any direct congeniality of one soul with another'.[42] Assigning the 'authorship' of a television text (let alone speculating on his or her intentions) would be irresolvably controversial: producer, director or media institution would all emerge as systematically disputed sources of meaning.

1.2   Beginning the Analysis: The Breakfast-time Viewer

Well, there you are. You can see what it's like. The camera's hot probing eye, these monstrous machines and their attendants, a kind of twentieth-

century torture chamber, that's what it is. But I must try and forget all this
paraphernalia and imagine that you are sitting here in the room with me.

Harold Macmillan, *Television and Number 10*

Television is, in a particular respect, the communication of the familiar, of
'the horizon of the life-world in which life goes on unquestioningly'.[43]
Many programmes take as their audience the family, characterizing their
implied viewers in particular ways. Both within and between its texts, such
television seeks to construct a life-world which, in its icons, images and
values, a family audience can recognize as its own, as familiar : 'broadcast
TV, its institutions and many of its practitioners alike assume that its
domestic audience takes the form of families'.[44] Often the assumption
appears to be of a life-world which is middle class in its experienced needs
and rationalities.

'Television condemns us to the Family, whose household utensil it has
become.'[45] Here, television modifies its 'what' in terms of 'how' it is
communicated, where the 'how' of communication attends to the assumed
nature of the audience.[46] The text addresses the preformed familarities of
the familial, sometimes verging on the construction of boredom : 'because
we have it on all the time it's like second nature'.[47] In the life-world of
television's 'family' a primary segmentation (at least in the UK) occurs
around time and the child : 'up to 9.00 p.m., ITV and Channel Four seek to
provide programmes suitable for viewing by all the family' (*TV Times*). In
Australia analogous divisions of the familial audience are programme
specific ; an 'AO' certification excludes the young from the intended viewers
(and guarantees an audience among the voyeuristic).

Recent television research has also assumed the audience to be constituted
by the family : in this context, reading is a social process. For Morley, at
least, this has become central to the paradigm which guides his empirical
investigations : the 'unit of consumption [is] more properly the family/
household rather than the individual viewer'.[48] In a family, for instance, the
temporal familiarity of 'their favourite series' (the known channel and time
of transmission) often functions for women as the basis on which plans for
watching television are formulated : 'it is the men, on the whole, who speak
of checking through the paper (or the teletext) to plan their evening's
viewing'.[49]

Commercial television in the UK (ITV) screens a daily breakfast 'magazine' programme *Good Morning Britain*, operating a particularly noticeable
mediation of its subject matter using concepts, practices and values associated with 'family' and 'nation'. In this it resembles *Good Morning, America*,
whose 'mode of address is embedded in a mutually reinforcing ideological
problematic of national and family unity'.[50] Likewise, *Good Morning
Australia* (Channel Ten), unlike the more 'serious' *Today* (Channel Nine)
programme, addresses its early morning Australian viewers within a framework of familial and leisure-time references.

To illustrate the phenomenological theory initiated by section 1.1, I shall offer an analysis of *Good Morning Britain* and its intended and actual audience.[51] The programmes I have chosen belong to the 'classic' phase of ITV's breakfast show, with Anne Diamond and Mike Morris as presenters. At the time of writing, although the hosts have changed, programme content appears not to have altered significantly.

Good Morning Britain (7.00 a.m.–8.50 a.m.) and a preceding offering, *The Morning Programme* (6.00 a.m.–7.00 a.m.), constitute ITV's morning breakfast show *TV-am*. Here I shall discuss only *Good Morning Britain* and its day-to-day presentation from a studio domesticity of lounge, settees, orange juice and coffee pots. Images of 'birthday children' appear regularly and on time. Mediation in these terms establishes a consensual domain of familiar recognition and shared belief between broadcasters and (intended) viewers, a national audience of families both inside and outside the studio. Only the news studio, appearing at half-hour intervals, is clearly non-domestic.

In *Good Morning Britain* mode of address and programme ideology converge. Its texts are hierarchically organized around the 'parental' voice of the presenter. Permitted to engage the viewer in familiar direct address, they are the source of authoritative meanings in the text. It is the presenters who bear a privileged reference, even pre-textually in the *TV Times* : 'Mike Morris and Anne Diamond interview the people making the news and headlines.' In the hierarchy of familiarity constructed by *Good Morning Britain* the 'truth', meaning and familiarity of the 'interviewers' mediate the unfamiliar in a defusion of difference. Information is 'shot through with explanation', intended as immediately intelligible. The world is discursively encountered, often contextualized within a 'horizon of suspicion'. In the studio the regular hosts identify with the familial roles and horizons of understanding found in the life-world of their (implied) audience. That audience in its turn identifies with the programme's presenters, occupying in an effortless 'fusion of horizons' the roles of the knowledgeable and caring. For this audience a critical scrutiny of the text is unlikely. *Good Morning Britain* routinely produces epistemological security for its viewers, providing both the experience and guarantee of an intelligible world, 'from our family to yours'.[52]

In constructing a familial life-world, *Good Morning Britain* respects the time and place of the audience. Its on-screen clock can be read as asserting that programme time and audience time coincide in a communication of meaning which is 'live', spontaneous and, therefore, honest. A repeated and segmented content of news inside a magazine format of 'story' and discussion allows the programme to address viewers with different breakfast schedules and different definitions of pleasurable watching. It anticipates their needs, needs associated with both leisure and preparation for work, providing a basis and focus for 'audience talk'.

Frank Bough, writing about the former BBC evening magazine pro-gramme *Nationwide* (in many ways very similar to *Good Morning Britain*), indicated how the temporal dimensions of the life-world to which it believed it was broadcasting were inscribed in the text itself. This produced a segmented organization of the programme's topics which did not demand the viewer's prolonged attention: 'the format of *Nationwide* is such that you can pause for a minute or two to watch an item that interests you or catches the attention, and then return to what you are doing'.[53]

Good Morning Britain, of course, contains a distinctive account of the family. Indeed, the specificities of its construction around a particular *mise en scène* (of middle-class comfort and conspicuous ease) may distance viewers who find it difficult to recognize this life-world as their own. Equally, to share a life-world need not also be to share a space and time: but *Good Morning Britain*'s spatio-temporal references can interfere with its construction of a life-world which the intended viewer is able to 'inhabit'. Marking out space in a weather forecast as 'here in the south-east' for many viewers also marks out difference.

But the times of the life-world in the text may become the times of a life-world outside *Good Morning Britain*, whereby the unfolding of the viewer's day is indicated not by the clock but by the measure of the televisual. Morley and Silverstone refer to a family in which the mother hurried the children off to school with the reminder, 'you know that the second commercial means it's time to go'. They conclude: 'in this family, media schedules seemed to have taken over from clock times as the standard of time measurement against which other activities were defined'.[54] Television schedules define the passing of time, producing a 'regulation of simultaneous experience'.[55]

The 'subject interpellated by television has been always already familial'.[56] To analyse television as an address to a life-world of shared and intersubjective activity and thought draws attention to viewing as a social process. Unlike cinema, it is not an activity of individual subjects within a darkened auditorium.[57] In the life-world of the family each individual relates to others in this group of viewers and non-viewers within a complex rule-governed interaction, 'a preconstituted system of typifications, relevances, roles, positions, statuses not of his own making, but handed down to him as a social heritage'.[58]

Collett's empirical research on the television viewer has emphasized 'the essentially social nature of a good deal of television-watching'.[59] Variations in level of attention to the screen, for instance, may be due not to qualities of the text, or to an absence of pleasurable engagement with the programme, but to interaction within the social context of the audience's 'looking'; 'it is not uncommon for one person to initiate an activity which disturbs the other person's concentration'.[60]

The 'empirical' audience's appropriation of a familiar life-world within the text (as in *Good Morning Britain*) sustains 'a cultural tradition that they at once use and renew'.[61] For Habermas, 'the reproduction of the lifeworld' in communication forms a context of the familiar and agreed in which discursive investigation can take place.[62] This is 'an intuitively known, unproblematic, and unanalyzable, holistic background',[63] 'intuitively pres-

ent', 'transparent', a 'vast and incalculable web of presuppositions' underlying and supporting the processes of successful communication and
judgement.[64] An individual's attention is usually directed not at the web of
presuppositions but at that which in the terms of the life-world is 'unusual' :
'the unusual appears within an horizon of the taken-for-granted ordinariness
typical of the "natural attitude". We are not motivated to question the
meaningful structures of this life-world.'[65]

Within the unquestioned and 'taken-for-granted ordinariness' of *Good
Morning Britain*, presenters Mike Morris and Anne Diamond exchanged
complaints about the unpredictable weather (5.9.88.), speculating on its
cause in 'strange things . . . up there' beyond the settled familial life-world
of *Good Morning Britain* and its intended audience :

> *Mike Morris* :   Strange things happening up there in that ionosphere, I
>   tell you.
> *Anne Diamond* : Yes.
> *Mike Morris* :   Strange things.
> *Anne Diamond* : Yes. Can't blame it on the Russians any more though,
>   can you, now we're talking to them.

In its day-to-day investigation of the 'strange', *Good Morning Britain*'s
address to the viewer conforms to 'universal validity claims' (Habermas)
implied by the speech-acts of communication which has the goal of reaching
an 'accord' with another individual. These claims are to be engaging in a
discourse marked by truth, sincerity and intelligibility, and to have imparted
information whose acceptance draws on shared assumptions, implicitly
reasserting them as correct : 'speaker and hearer can agree with one another
in the utterance with respect to a recognized normative background'.[66]

The presence of the familial and recognizable acts for the intended viewer
as a guarantee of the text's operations being contained by a horizon of the
ordinary, a 'recognized normative background'. In our time and space,
recognized by viewer and presenter alike, the experience will be of our
ideas, our familiarities, our friends. The construction of the viewer's sense
of the 'ordinary' is the construction of a life-world. Even the weather
forecast can be used as a moment in the programme in which to assert that
the difference of *Good Morning Britain* presenters consists in being more
ordinary than many viewers : 'the rain will increase in the south-west, but
with a bit of luck that middle bit's going to stay reasonably bright for your
posh hats and frocks and everything at the races, those of you who are
going, not us underprivileged folks, of course' (18.6.87).

Like *Nationwide*, *Good Morning Britain* mediates an often complex and
unpleasant world in terms and values associated with the family ; those of
individual romance, entertainment, leisure, caring and a concern with
children. In the 'true life' stories of *Good Morning Britain* what is often
important is that these values can be seen to be triumphantly illustrated.

Appeals to the familial sustain the address to the viewer: 'now it is always sad, isn't it, when children announce their intention to leave home and go it alone' (5.9.88).

Outside the news space of the text, identification with the roles enunciated in *Good Morning Britain* presumes the familial: 'we can all associate ourselves with it [the sitcom *Bread*], though [speech unclear], 'cos it's about the family' (5.9.88). Within the limiting horizons of understanding associated with *Good Morning Britain*'s construction of the family, analysis involving the politics of race, class, age or gender looms small to the point of invisibility. Precisely because issues are deliberated upon in the familial sphere of individual action and attainment, they are easily described in what appear to be appropriate terms of leisure, morality and entertainment: 'keeping it in the family, we're going to be chatting to Roger Moore's son and Paul Newman's daughter' (18.6.87). So, for instance, a 'Help the Old and Needy' campaign marginalized the politics of age to concentrate on the metaphysic of morals implicit in the personal charity of Christmas gifts. *Good Morning Britain*, as with the reduction from the social and economic to the individual in television's popular fiction, exhibits a 'need to explain factors which in reality are "outside" in terms of the "inside"' of the family.[67]

It is in so far as members of the audience occupy familial roles, and can identify with presenters who appear to fulfil analogous positions, that *Good Morning Britain*'s analysis of worldly events within the moral horizons of individualistic caring will seem recognizable, unproblematic and without reasonable alternative. The 'otherness' of both what it sets out to explain to the viewers and the cultural differences of the real audience is likely to recede from view. These are positions beyond its horizons of understanding, alternatives from which critique is possible but (here) denied. The programme has little in common with the ethnographer who 'must render the foreign familiar and preserve its very foreignness at one and the same time'.[59]

Good Morning Britain interprets the world on behalf of its potential viewers, mediating the horizons of experience of interviewees and others through discourses familiar to the studio 'family' and to the intended family audience. This is a project of cognitive assimilation: 'to interpret is to render near what is far (temporally, geographically, culturally, spiritually)'; 'interpretation brings together, equalises, renders contemporary and similar'. *Good Morning Britain*'s semiotic operations 'appropriate' meaning not to preserve distance but to '"make its own" what was initially "alien"'.[69] In semantic terms, *Good Morning Britain* possesses the world for the viewer, marginalising its difference.

The programme's address to leisure establishes a set of discourses informed by an interest in 'play'. 'Play, determines content (for example, the physical exercise routines) and a constantly euphoric address to the audience. But with 'its incessant flattery of the audience by the medium', *Good Morning Britain*'s 'game' is both limited and limiting.[70] The cognitive play of identification is restricted, with little space, time or encouragement for the intended viewer to appropriate horizons of understanding outside the familial. In this narcissistic consumption of meaning while viewing, the text holds back the audience from a playful appropriating of new 'modes of being' made fleetingly available in the programme. 'Appropriation is the process by which the revelation of new modes of being – or, if you prefer Wittgenstein to Heidegger, new "forms of life" – gives the subject new capacities for knowing himself.'[71] Instead, *Good Morning Britain*'s conservative address to its audience offers to the *subject en famille* a range of self-congratulatory images of him- or herself.

Like *Nationwide* before it, *Good Morning Britain* familiarizes the world in a domestication of events for the watching family. Industrial action in the Post Office is interfering with a couple's marriage arrangements : 'a rather poignant story from the press office of the Post Office here in Manchester. There's a lady there getting married *this* weekend and guess where her wedding ring is !' (5.9.88) A report on the Gibraltar inquest into the SAS shooting of members of the IRA concludes with a mention of the husband and wife who disagree on their evidence. This domestication of the world informs *Good Morning Britain*'s understanding of values as well as events. Anne Diamond's association of 'moderate' politics with the familial and heterosexual leads to her instant rejection of 'lesbian and gay rights' as a likely topic for party political broadcasts by the Labour Party : 'but Mr Kinnock doesn't seem to want to allow [sexual politics] at all, he doesn't *want* that, does he ? . . . He wanted to paint the Labour Party as being a *moderate* Labour party' (12.6.87). *Good Morning Britain* not only understands the events it describes using the frameworks associated with a familial life-world but can reduce complex public occurrences to the domestic activity of individuals. On breakfast television 'the public possesses the private, the private encompasses the public'.[72] As descriptions of the world, references to household events display an innocent validity which inevitably attaches itself to other reports from *Good Morning Britain*. In the programme's analysis of the British general election of 1987 frequent visits and revisits were made to the doorsteps of sleeping politicians : 'the papers have just been delivered, there's been a bunch of flowers taken in . . . I think there's a faint sound of snoring coming from upstairs here, we can't hear an awful lot, but, I mean, we're told that she is fast asleep and getting some well-earned rest' (12.6.87).

Domesticity is constituted both as form and content of understanding. With this the text discloses its similarity to the continuous serial. Wilson's comments on (an early version of) the BBC's programme *Breakfast Time* also provide a pertinent insight into *Good Morning Britain* : 'all in all, *Breakfast Time* attempts – and succeeds in – the heroic enterprise of creating a cosy sense of family normality out of the least amenable material : world news and current affairs are miraculously transformed into a family soap opera'.[73]

The domestic life-world is characterized in patriarchal thought as ordinary and routine. *Good Morning Britain* reproduces this ordinariness within the text where a daily repetition of programme structure mediates and relays the extra-textual and the extraordinary to the viewer. Television's times and places are generally a part of, rather than apart from, those of the everyday. Unlike cinema, the act of watching television is generally not a special event. It is contained in the uneventful, bringing to bear on the text the horizons of understanding associated with the commonplace. Television's pleasures are frequently those of the affirmation of the ordinary rather than distraction by the new.

The importance of recognizing television to be the continual reproduction of the ordinary is acknowledged in the political process. Former British prime minister Harold Wilson saw television as an ally. Its regime of the everyday was one in which his Tory adversary at election time, the aristocratic Lord Home, who 'looked as if he'd spent all his life on the grouse moors', could not compete: 'at last you were able to get into people's homes and to do that you *had* to be like someone they would know, you couldn't be some stiff, remote figure, you had to be a relaxed, identifiable figure' (Lady Falkender, *Television and Number 10*, BBC2, 5.40, 24.9.88).

The ordinariness claimed by *Good Morning Britain*'s address to its audience is an attempt to display its commitment to what its presenters perceive as an egalitarian and rational communication. But in the programme's understanding of television (and its address to an audience) profound asymmetries of power in respect of the circulation of ideas are ignored. These deficiencies can be highlighted by comparing the relationship between this text and its audience to the open and unconstrained discussion between equals in an 'ideal speech situation' (Habermas).

The conditions of ideal speech include an equal (or 'symmetrical') opportunity to participate in the speech-acts of discussion. Broadcast television's communication with its audience clearly does not allow the viewer to intercede directly in the text. Nevertheless, *Good Morning Britain* does engage in *vox populi* interviews (for example, getting 'plenty of reaction' at Victoria Coach Station to the 1987 general election). It responds to viewers phoning in and asks questions on their behalf: 'the reaction to the cod liver oil talk, business, we're talking about today has been incredible. I don't know if ever [sic] had so many phone calls about one particular subject. So Dale Alexander [the expert] is staying with us and we ought to ask him a few more questions' (5.9.88).

An 'ideal speech situation' is characterized by the operation of rational discussion between the equal: 'no force except that of the better argument is exercised . . . as a result, all motives except that of the cooperative search for truth are excluded'.[74] Interviewing in *Good Morning Britain* implies that it is the production of knowledge through reasoned discusssion between interviewee(s) and interviewer, in which the latter represents the audience. The implicit, if rarely emerging, product of such apparently cooperative debate is to be consensual agreement on the truth. For an interviewee to enter the discussion is for him or her, whether trade unionist or Conservative politician, to acknowledge the demands in respect of his or her contribution of ostensibly fully rational argument. These demands suggest an egalitarian openness to questioning which is rarely exploited. Nevertheless, the illusion of rational commitment maintains the appearance of placing the interviewee on an equal footing with all other actual and possible interviewees: 'the simple right to ask questions and the expectation that they will be answered truthfully . . . is the mark of equality in social relations in private and in public life'.[75]

Good Morning Britain's address to its audience is collaborative, suggesting a 'co-operative search for the truth' which, as in ideal speech, is unfettered by psychological or political constraint. The programme scrupulously avoids examining the possibility that the cultural distances and constraints of social class produce an unequal relationship between presenter and audience. It devotes considerable time and space to sustaining an illusory equality of social standing between textual subjects and viewer: 'We're going to go terribly up-market now [sounds of studio laughter and mock protest] . . . All the punters and the toffs have been descending on Royal Ascot to watch some of the racing . . . joining the *crème de la crème* of high society, both the horsy and the human variety . . . *don't* they look posh ?' (19.6.87)

The discussion of horse-racing at Ascot operates from the point of view of the everyday, in terms of the horizons of understanding generated by the ordinary, 'our' everyday and 'our' 'ordinary'. By retaining a critical distance from aspects of the social ritual of racing ('yes, there were some horror jobs') it is clear that this discursive exchange seeks to establish a consensual agreement on the values of the 'normal', of day-to-day culture and ways of dressing in which 'we' all share. Here a mythical unity and equality are created by the programme around its viewers and presenters. Sustaining this 'normality' in existence is its difference from the 'horror job' of Royal Ascot, where even 'smartness' relies on a cultural capital belonging to others, 'the *crème de la crème* of high society'.

The visit to Royal Ascot is used to allow presenters and (implied) audience to unite in terms of a prolonged expression of commitment to a familial reading of the ordinary (in the 'skint members' enclosure' ?). This familial and unifying 'ordinary' is even briefly extended to include the 'Queen Mum' with 'the hardest job in the world'. In short, with the exception of those in 'posh gear', the 'sights' and 'horror jobs', in this spurious celebration of the apparently egalitarian 'we've all got our shoes to show, all muddy'.

But the relationship between *Good Morning Britain* and its audience differs further from Habermas's ideal speech situation, in the text's evident awareness of a plurality of concerns among those who watch. The domestic ordinariness of the programme's address recognizes that viewers in their varying familial roles have different needs and consequently make use of the text in different ways. In this it is unlike communication in 'ideal speech', where the only personal interests which should influence the discussion are 'generalizable' or shared by all the participants.[76]

Good Morning Britain's intended audience utilizes the programme to satisfy a variety of needs. This functional treatment of a text can be examined by referring to recent television research. For academic inquiry has exhibited a new concern with a 'uses and gratifications' model of the relationship between television and its audiences. Unlike the older version of the model, however, its current resurrection as a guiding paradigm for research relates the use of a text to its interpretation : 'questions of interpretation and questions of use have not previously been investigated in relation to each other'.[77]

In presupposing a shared interpretation of a text prior to (and independent from) audience utilization, gratifications theory subscribed to a positivistic fiction of textual content as an unproblematic fact. But the horizons of viewing, the typifying categories in terms of which spectatorship allows meaning to emerge from a programme, are not 'read off' from the screen. Rather, these frameworks of watching television are, in part, the result of using it to satisfy a range of interests and needs related to goal-directed action upon the world. As with other categories of understanding, they are a 'conceptual – perceptual scheme rooted in deep-seated structures of human action'.[78]

An audience's reliance on a text presupposes and produces particular interpretations of its content. 'The same text is different in different contexts' of use.[79] This is the 'applicative' (Gadamer) aspect of understanding : consumption generates its own epistemology. Within the experience and life-world of the domestic the text functions in terms of its relevance to the viewer's interests, which are in turn generated by the social roles which define the private domain of the familial. Like the roles themselves, these role-related needs are understood and managed by a particular reader in distinct ways.

At a fundamental level the familial life-world operates through conversation, a need for speech which, when the television is on, is often 'related to what is happening on the screen'.[80] This conversation constructs the text as a resource, an interest-relevant source of information and prompting. Some of this talk around television allows it to function educationally as a basis for parent – child discussions about its understanding and interpretation.[81] The processes whereby these and other uses of television operate are governed by rules, constituting norm-governed activities in the sphere of domesticity.

To argue that the uses of television are related to interests associated with roles, often in the space and time of the family, is not to assert a determination by social role. For as I argue in Chapter 2, the viewer can 'read' the roles which he or she inhabits in particular ways, inflecting them through an individual experience and understanding of the world. The concept of 'role' allows a theorizing of the relationship between subject and society which suggests neither a determination of behaviour by social structure nor a reducing of the societal to the individual. It is the starting point for an analysis of the 'cultural dimension' of an individual's life without, 'on the one hand implying a mechanistic and deterministic relationship to the deep structures [of the social], and on the other sliding into methodological individualism'.[82]

Good Morning Britain is used by its (intended) audience in the satisfaction of role-related interests, often to do with leisure and entertainment. ('Stay with us', promises Anne Diamond, 'for a glittering week on *TV-am*, the brightest way to start your day.') The exercise of almost all interests involves, in one way or another, the acquisition of information. Readers make a distinction between what they treat as problematic, as demanding inquiry, and what they (at least temporarily) take for granted as the 'preknown'. 'Interests' map out the viewers' horizon of relevant and useful information, 'what has to be known and with what degree of clarity and precision it has to be known in order to solve the emergent problem'.[83]

Different interests are 'at hand' at any moment. There is 'no such thing as an isolated interest' since each is always present in a context of others, a 'plan'.[84] The taken for granted knowledge of a life-world includes a 'knowledge of trustworthy recipes'.[85] These are prescriptions for rational behaviour, 'logics-in-use' (Hall) whereby interests can be satisfied. This rationality is ideologically informed. The logic of a life-world is inflected, for instance, by class and interpretation of gender relations. 'Recipes', Schutz tells us, guide both practices of interpreting the social world and action, 'handling things and men' 'to obtain the best results'.

A viewer's interests are hierarchically ordered in terms of his or her understanding of their importance. Corresponding to this hierarchy of different interests, he or she is likely to perceive a hierarchy of texts, organized in respect of their anticipated ability to satisfy experienced needs. Programmes such as the news or soap operas may be described in terms of their capacity to fulfil these wishes (for example, to be kept well informed). A text can issue an ironic address to the viewers, attributing to them needs they are unlikely to possess. In the Sunday night documentary series *Everyman*, 'The Mighty Quinn' (BBC1, 10.30, 4.2.86) introduced its content to an intended audience of those interested in religion with the words : 'to dry out in Detroit you go to the Sacred Heart Rehabilitation Centre, one of the biggest treatment centres for alcoholics in the United States'.

The Morning Programme (preceding *Good Morning Britain*), according to presenter Richard Keys, meets in a variety of ways its audience's role-related needs for 'the top story' (5.9.88) :

> the top story this morning . . . and the top financial story . . . right, now the top five. Each morning during the week we like to keep you up to date with what's at the top in the world of entertainment. We take a look

at the top five books, the films, the television shows and the videos and this morning it's the top five pop records.

A subject's interests produce a 'reading' of a life-world through cognitive horizons of understanding which foreground the varying relevance of its items to experienced need. The result is an interpretation of the world as a domain of relevance, a 'relevance structure' of people, objects and television programmes perceived to be useful and classified in terms of their relationship to particular concerns.

A relevance structure is also to be found embedded in the 'natural' or 'common-sense' language of a life-world which refers to its items in terms of their purpose. Exploring the semantics of 'tools' or 'food' immediately shows the meaning of these terms to be related to a human interest or need. Objects referred to in this way constitute a domain of the useful: 'it is always the system of relevance that chooses from the vocabulary of my vernacular'.[86]

Considered as members of a life-world, individuals exist as subjects-with-interests, generating particular cognitions of the relevant. The 'empirical' or actual domain of relevance which television inhabits is formed (in part) around interests related to social roles mapping out domestic responsibility and its absence. Here television is 'read' in accordance with needs defined by a rule-informed practice. It is for reasons of this kind that Morley's recent research on family television argues that many women prefer local to national news, news about children to news about the stock market: 'the programme material has a practical value to them in terms of their domestic responsibilities'.[87]

Both programmes and advertisements, then, are understood within frameworks of meaning generated by their relevance to the role-related interests of a life-world occupied by the audience. Reading a text occurs against a horizon of categories produced by the needs and interests of a 'real' viewer in using the programme in particular ways. As Morley writes in *Family Television*, 'we need to deal more directly with the relevance/irrelevance and comprehension/incomprehension dimensions of interpretation and decoding'.[88]

Particular requirements allow particular identifications. The use of *Good Morning Britain* as a source of national news will permit identifications which are scarcely those made possible for a child whose pleasure rests upon adopting Popeye's understanding of the world. The mirror of identification may operate in complex ways. An individual can inhabit several roles simultaneously, generating interests and identifications which are contradictory or incompatible.

Whether or not the empirical audience acknowledges that it inhabits the ideal life-world proposed for it by the text, producing patterns of identification, depends on the 'fit' between their spatio-temporal world of interest and values and that constructed in the programme. A discursive analysis of 'audience talk' along the dimensions of space, time, interest and evaluation will produce a qualitative measure of the degree of convergence between real and intended viewer achieved by the programme. As I indicate in section 1.3, this cognitive 'fit' is never perfect.

Good Morning Britain perceives its audience to be a nation of individuals who, despite their different role-related interests, share certain values in the life-world of the familial. A basic assumption underlying the text, guiding its agendas and focusing its concerns, is that families, whether as viewers or as viewed, care about caring. In the bourgeois family the individual is, or should be, 'at home'. The family audiences implied by *Good Morning Britain* care not only about their own members but about individuals in other families. 'Care' is used to mobilize audience consensus around the ethical, often functioning to displace an inevitably divisive political analysis (cf. 'Caring in Belfast', an item on gifts for old-age pensioners at Christmas time in Northen Ireland). Like the continuous serial (and the Bible), *Good Morning Britain* contains 'parables', moral prescriptions, telling us how we ought to care. It presents little narratives, 'positive or negative apprentice-ships', 'positive or negative models'[89] in caring and morality ('Richard Branston, incidentally, was a real star') Our 'family of the nation' is held together and united by relationships of individual caring, disturbed only by such events as natural catastrophe, industrial action or terrorism.

But here the identification of presenter and viewer in a celebration of caring becomes a problem. The ideal and real life-worlds addressed by the text begin to part company. In a return within the text of its political repressed *Good Morning Britain* was forced, for instance, in 1987 to report a political outcome in the British general election which clearly indicated a Britain of many divisions, not the least of which appeared to centre on differences about the importance of caring. A prime minister had been elected whose image was that of someone 'not sufficiently caring'. Labour Party leader Neil Kinnock confidently distinguished his people of Wales from voters elsewhere in Britain: 'I feel great. Real people here [speech unclear] who care. People who care.'

The 'real' life-worlds of 'real' viewers may be inflected away from *Good Morning Britain*'s attempts to construct their life-world by the recognition of other aspects of experience as familiar. These will be the cultural familiarities, perhaps, of being black rather than white, Scottish rather than English. Real life-worlds involve 'the saturation of communicative action by tradition and established ways of doing things', which *Good Morning Britain* may not recognize.[90]

1.3 Television's Familiarity and 'Personal Sense'

Television presenters construct the life-world of their intended viewers. Their address is user-friendly, with a privileging of the spoken and familiar which asserts itself in a distrust of writing. Discourses often draw upon the speech genres of familiar conversation (for instance, anecdote). The individualistic style of the 'authored' (such as Chris in Grassic Gibbon's *Scots Quair*, discussed in a later chapter) is unusual. But despite this there is always a distance between the life-worlds of implied and real viewers, between the 'familiarities' of text and audience.

Television encounters the written within a horizon of suspicion in which writing is understood not only as a more formal means of communication but as conveying the 'unfamiliar' and difficult. Writing is the medium of the personal letter and the 'personalized' tabloid press. But it is more frequently the medium of the formal communication of information, the legal and scientific report and the 'classical' work. It is likely to be used for the communication of the impersonal and complicated. Speech, on the other hand, unless it has an association with the written (in the lecture or the sermon) is not a medium in which the difficult or complex is anticipated.

In this opposition between (informal) speech and (formal) writing television marginalizes its association with the latter. Like radio, 'it suppresses these literary origins'.[91] Significantly, newscasters rarely read continuously from a script; continuity announcers do not acknowledge their use of a standardized and carefully prepared set of works. In this 'scripted spontaneity' the 'newscaster's art consists of evoking the cool authority and faultless articulation of the written or memorized text while simultaneously "naturalizing" the written word to restore the appearance of spontaneous communication'.[92]

Television recasts in familiar terms those genres of speech which have an association with the formality and complexity of written discourse. Sermons have a basis in writing, yet these 'lectures' by their very nature represent the mediation of the theologically abstract and difficult by the parable of the everyday. The television sermon can heighten this assertion of the familiar by translating a religious message into the form of a personal visit to the viewer (cf. the title of Scottish Television's brief religious programme *Late Call*).

As Mancini points out, television's address to its viewer simulates a conversational situation through the inclusion of 'verbal elements such as the use of subjects "I", "we", "you", "the listener" etc. or through direct discourse "now you will see the reporting of", "now we will show you" etc.'[93] But television's construction of a conversational discourse may (perhaps unavoidably) signal its origins in writing. For this communication, particularly in voiceovers, is often 'well formed' and integrated, lacking the gaps, hesitations and repetitions characteristic of everyday speech. Such a perfected discourse betrays its source in the prepared and written. Following each other in an uninterrupted flow of speech, the opening words of one *Late Call* (ITV, 1.00 a.m. 19.8.88) signalled their origin in a script. This familiar, friendly address approached the viewer in terms of recent shared experiences, but its integrated structures of speech appeared constructed and artificial: 'Can you remember back to June when we had week after week of glorious sunshine? The mornings were fresh and dewy, holding promises of long hours of warmth. I remember the evenings in particular when it was possible to sit outside after work. The sunsets *too* were pretty spectacular.'

Television's audio-visual communication generally effaces that ability which it shares with writing, the capacity to transmit meaning over spatio-temporal distance. Its speech relies upon close-up, engaging the viewer in a direct verbal and visual address which, in the reality-effect of television's 'liveness', appears to reject the possibility of a more distanced, voyeuristic relationship with the text. The electronic immediacy of the image asserts a closure between the spatio-temporal moment of a programme's discourse and the world of the viewer: 'one of the main features of modern technologies of communication is that they no longer allow distance in space to govern temporal distance in mediated interaction'.[94] This electron-ically produced 'presence' of textual content is a denial of mediation, functioning in consequence to assert that the viewer has access to an undistorted truth.

Writing has the capacity to 'cross distance', to draw on a remote language system whose concepts are cognitively unfamiliar to the reader. Such unfamiliar linguistic practices will be produced by those temporal or spatial distances in which, for instance, different class or ethnic cultures have emerged. In this sense of the term 'distanciation' 'is constitutive of the phenomenon of the text as writing': writing is characterized by 'the otherness that transforms all spatial and temporal distance into cultural estrangement'.[95] Like writing, speech inscribed on videotape can surmount distance, bearing to the viewer forms of understanding which are 'difficult'. But television hides this potential 'otherness' of its content through discur-sive filtering by familiar speech, denying the different, the source of political and other oppositions. Television abhors a distance, whether physical or cognitive, seeking almost always to fill it with meaning.

The scripted voiceover in television documentaries and news reporting constructs itself as 'spoken discourse' with its assumption of a space and time shared by presenter and viewer (cf. Chapter 5 on identification). As the phenomenologist Ricoeur indicates, it is a characteristic of 'spoken discourse' (unlike writing) that source and recipient share a spatio-temporal location. In spoken discourse, if 'we cannot point to the thing about which we speak, at least we can situate it in relation to the unique spatio-temporal network which is shared by the interlocutors. It is the "here" and "now", determined by the situation of discourse.'[96]

Television's references in continuity announcements to proximity and distance often bear no relationship to the 'real' spatio-temporal origins of textual content. Instead, they are used to construct a space and time for familiar address 'here' and 'now', an address which eventually allows a parting between 'friends' until 'tomorrow': '(a) Over on BBC2 now there's a second chance to see (programme title), while here on 1 we continue with part six of (programme title); (b) And we hope to see you again tomorrow.'[97]

Television separates itself from the 'written' in other ways. While some television texts, such as the single play, assert their distinctiveness by emphasizing their association with an author and hence with writing, most television genres do not. Allen argues for the 'unauthored' in the case of the continuous serial. Soap operas, by virtue of their presentation of a continuous diegesis, cannot allow themselves to be inflected by a particular aesthetic vision. 'In order to "work" on us most effectively the soap opera world must appear to be autochthonous – an unauthored, autonomous, self-generating realm existing alongside the world of the viewer.'[98]

Much of television's direct address to the viewer in current affairs and news programmes is a written discourse presenting itself as spoken in a further sense. Here, the experience of viewing is of an address in the singular, of apparent eye contact as an individual member of the audience with particular media personnel. But the television text, while appearing to speak to 'me', the specific and actual viewer, 'potentializes' (Ricoeur) its audience. The experience of a direct and appropriate address is, on any given occasion, available to a large number of viewers. Television's addressee is not the individual but a social role (within a life-world) which is open to being filled by the 'unknown reader'. This is akin to a relationship not between speaker and listener in a conversation but between the written discourses of a text and its readers. It is 'the "potentialisation" of the audience, which is no longer the partner in dialogue but the unknown reader that the text procures'.[99]

Ricoeur's concept of 'distance' is at the heart of a reader-centred aesthetics of the written, in which readers rather than the author of a text attribute, and are the final arbiters of, its meaning. In attaining the place of its consumption, the written text has severed the relationship both with the space and time of its creation and with the intentions of the author as definitive of its sense: 'thanks to distanciation by writing, appropriation no longer has any trace of affective affinity with the intention of an author. Appropriation is quite the contrary of contemporaneousness and congeniality: it is understanding at and through distance.'[100]

The meaning of the television text, on the other hand, like that of spoken discourse, is established through negotiation between recipient and source of the meanings involved, often in the context of other discursive information (Bennett's 'textual shifters'). These interchanges occur in broadcasting journals and particular viewer response programmes like Channel Four's *Right to Reply* in the UK, and *Hotline* on the Special Broadcasting Service in Australia.

If television addresses its audience with a spoken discourse emphasizing the individual and familiar, the reaction of the viewer could be considered similarly conversational. As I argue in Chapter 2, on the hermeneutics of reading television, the programme – audience relationship is such that the reader attempts to gain an understanding of what he or she hears and sees by directing questions at a text whose subsequent provision of information is read as a response. There are moments of high intensity in the relationship between text and viewer which also possess the immediacy of conversational speech, signifying considerable involvement in the programme. When Bobby Ewing (Patrick Duffy) of *Dallas* was hit by a car, one woman viewer 'clutched her throat shouting "No! . . . Noooooo!" As she watched Pam (Victoria Principal) cradling the dying Bobby in her arms, she screamed at the TV: "Get an ambulance, you stupid woman!"'[101]

Television, then, assumes an opposition between writing and speech, attempting to detach itself from the former in favour of the apparently unproblematic communication in the latter. But as Ricoeur and other Marxist linguists have indicated, the assumption that there is a fundamental opposition between writing and speech is mistaken. The written may be the medium privileged by those with the power to define proficient communication: 'adequacy of language is now judged by conformity to the forms of the written language'.[102] But as I noted in the previous section, the spoken too can function hegemonically in its distribution or denial of equality or power.

Ricoeur argues, referring to Hegel for support, that the distance characterizing written discourse is also a feature of speech. For the act of saying fades into past time, growing gradually distant from what is said, which remains in the mind of speaker or hearer: 'the *saying* vanishes, but the *said* persists'.[103] Distance is a potentiality of spoken discourse which is always realized.

Marxist linguists (as well as those interested in the relationship between gender, race and language) have likewise disputed whether there is a distinction between speech and writing in terms of ease and immediacy of understanding. Spoken communication between individuals from different class backgrounds is likely to provide evidence of its own complexity, displaying systematic ambiguities generated by differing class interests (for example, competing conceptions of 'fairness' in industrial disputes). The semantic frameworks of what is said are likely to be contested: 'class does not coincide with sign community, i.e., with the community which is the totality of users of the same set of signs for ideological communication. Thus differently oriented accents intersect in every ideological sign. Sign becomes an arena of class struggle.'[104]

Even where the 'users of the same set of signs' belong to the same class, gender or race, television's attempt to efface the distance between the cognitive horizons of speaker and listener in a 'perfect' discourse of familiarity cannot in principle attain its goal. In the relationship between text and (actual) audience there is always a distance: this is the distance in understanding of signification which is produced by the gap between the needs of the text and those of the viewer. On the one hand, the text needs to construct generalities of meaning for an intended audience unknown in 'concrete' detail. These are, in the terms used by the Soviet psychologist Leont'ev, 'objective', 'indifferent' meanings. On the other hand, the particular viewer reads these meanings in relation 'to his life, to his needs and motives' to produce a differing 'personal sense'. Viewers may be said to 'enrich' concepts 'by means of individual contributions'. In this way, 'meanings are individualized and "subjectivized"', beginning 'to live as if in someone else's garments'.

In the Conclusion I consider readings of television programmes where the viewer rejects the text's familiar advances in favour of a distanciated criticism of the way of life depicted. In Leont'ev's words one might put this point by saying that where television is submitted to a distanciated reading, 'the lack of correspondence of [personal] sense and [objective] meaning in individual consciousness may take on the character of a real alienation between them, even their opposition'. 'Externally "ready" meanings' which have no basis in the individual's 'practical life experience' are perceived to be stereotypical.[105]

Good Morning Britain's understanding of the 'family' to which it broadcasts across the nation cannot be identical with the understanding of the term possessed by each individual viewer. In 'the real duality of existence of meanings for the subject' the subject's interpretation of any concept is sufficiently shared with other ('indifferent') members of society to allow communication. But it is also inflected to produce 'personal sense' by the specificities of that individual's experience, the difference of 'an interest, a desire, or a passion'.[106] More specifically, 'the "knowledge" gained from a news story may not even have to do with the "world out there" but may instead be of relevance as internal, private meaning'.[107] This is to argue for the constant presence of difference across the readings made by individual viewers, while retaining the relative openness of each interpretation to another's understanding. 'However individual may be the meaning realised in each case, the act of composing it will always have intersubjectively verifiable characteristics.'[108]

More generally, in this play of meaning centred on the subject an account of reading which suggests an identity of understanding between viewer and text can only be established by ignoring the distance between their respective 'detours' through semantic difference. 'Every concept is necessarily and essentially inscribed in a chain or a system, within which it refers to another and to other concepts, by the systematic play of differences.'[109]

Television's spoken discourse is inevitably implicated in 'difficulty', however 'easy' it may appear prior to a conscious hermeneutic reflection upon its horizons of understanding. Reading the popular, as Radway has argued, involves only the *prima facie* unproblematic circulation of apparently familiar meaning. 'Because the prose is so familiar, individual words or signs appear to make their meanings immediately available to any reader operating according to certain procedures and assumptions.'[110]

In the Conclusion I suggest that when more closely examined the text's construction of the familiar life-world of the ideal viewer will be seen as always being at some distance from the real viewer's interest-related interpretation of the rules, roles and regularities of the life-worlds in which he or she actually exists. Here analysis can foreground the unfamiliar. A recovery of this distance in a defamiliarized reading which takes 'real' viewers' experiences seriously reveals that television's stereotypical construction of the life-worlds of its intended audience has a claim to be really only 'the *atopon* (the strange), that which does not "fit" into the customary order of our expectation based on experience'.[111]

Notes

1   Grondin, 'Hermeneutics and Relativism', p. 54.
2   MacCabe, 'Realism and the Cinema', p. 226.
3   Carr, *Interpreting Husserl*, p. 79.
4   Husserl, *Crisis*, p. 71.
5   Ibid., pp. 121–2.
6   Gadamer, *Philosophical Hermeneutics*, p. 191.
7   Carr, *Interpreting Husserl*, p. 102.
8   Gadamer, *Truth and Method*, pp. 272, 261.
9   Husserl makes a distinction between the 'internal' and 'external' horizons of an object. Its internal horizon is constituted by those aspects of it which are not seen on some occasion of looking at it but which are known to be there because it is an object of a certain type. For Husserl, our knowledge of the internal horizon generates the experience of an object rather than a two-dimensional surface. The external horizon of an object is the context in which it occurs, the background against which it forms a foreground. How an object's external horizon is perceived may contribute to an understanding of its identity, its internal horizon of existence. Generally, however, television's 'naturalistic' *mise en scène* adds little to the meaning of its objects. The following are useful commentaries on the concept of a 'horizon' in Husserl's work: Bruzina, *Logos and Eidos*, pp. 68–75; Gurwitsch, *Studies in Phenomenology and Psychology*, in which the doctrines of both 'horizon' (pp. 332–49) and 'life-world' (pp. 418–26) are discussed; H. Kuhn, 'The Phenomenological Concept of "Horizon"'; Pietersma, 'The Concept of Horizon', pp. 278–82.
10 Husserl, *Experience and Judgement*, pp. 42, 35.
11 Ibid., pp. 105, 32.
12 Schutz, 'Type and Eidos in Husserl's Late Philosophy', p. 95.
13 Individual instances of phenomena, of course, have characteristics over and above the typical: 'every concrete real thing still has its *individual attributes*, though, at the same time they have their *typical form*' (Husserl, *Experience and Judgement*, p. 331). Nevertheless, individuating characteristics can themselves be regarded as instances of general types.
14 Husserl refers to this as the 'protentional' aspect of experience.
15 Husserl, Introduction to *Crisis*, p. xli.
16 Husserl, *Phenomenology*, p. 150.
17 Husserl, *Cartesian Meditations*, p. 133. In allowing the individual to occupy several different (if related) life-worlds, I am following the Husserl

of the *Meditations*. Elsewhere (e.g. in *Crisis*) he may be read as asserting the uniqueness of the life-world (cf. Carr, *Interpreting Husserl*, pp. 213–14). In these contexts 'life-world' could be taken to consist of the set of a priori conditions which all social life must satisfy (e.g. the presentation of meaning within space and time). Gadamer's discussion of the 'life-world' as referring to both a varying plurality and a unique a priori set of conditions of knowledge brings these two interpretations together. He writes of 'the great variety of subjective – relative world-horizons, involved in the a priori of the life-world' (Gadamer, 'The Science of the Life-World', p. 182). Using the term in the former sense, I intend life-worlds to occupy an intermediate level of generality. They do not, for instance, consist of the lifestyle of a particular family, nor of that of families in general. Rather, there is the life-world of the middle-class or working-class family, with its distinct needs, rules and rationalities, made concrete to form communities within society.

18 Husserl, *Crisis*, p. 138.
19 Ibid., p. 142. If phenomenology argues that the horizons of experience are constructed pre-socially by the individual, it must resolve the question of how the subjective awareness of a life-world is at the same time shared and intersubjective. This is 'the problem of monadological production of the intersubjectivity of the lifeworld ... the problem of how different subjects can share the same lifeworld' (Habermas, *Theory of Communicative Action*, p. 129). For this reason a phenomenological basis for television studies must rest on intersubjective descriptions of a life-world.
20 Mohanty, ' "Life-world" and "a priori" in Husserl's Later Thought', pp. 111–12.
21 Gier, *Wittgenstein and Phenomenology*, p. 124.
22 Warnke, *Gadamer*, p. 35.
23 Husserl, *Crisis*, p. 149.
25 Ibid., p. 180.
26 Benson and Hughes, *The Perspective of Ethnomethodology*, p. 50. Here, an 'epochal' suspension of the natural attitude of the television viewer would be directed at his or her assumption of a text as unproblematically presenting reality.
27 Ibid., p. 50.
28 Schutz, *On Phenomenology and Social Relations*, p. 75. Cf. also Schutz and Luckmann, *The Structures of the Life-world*, for an extensive theorizing of the philosophy of existence upon which this volume is based.
29 A. Schutz, *Collected Papers*, vol. 1, edited by M. Natanson (The Hague, Nijhoff, 1962), p. 148.
30 Schutz, *On Phenomenology and Social Relations*, p. 117.
31 Ibid., p. 80.
32 Habermas, *The Philosophical Discourse of Modernity*, p. 295.
33 Lull, 'The Family and Television in World Cultures', p. 10.
34 Kumar, 'Indian Families Watching Television', p. 6.
35 Lull, 'How Families Select Television Programs', pp. 802, 803.
36 Scannell, 'Radio Times', p. 23.
37 Schutz, *On Phenomenology and Social Relations*, p. 119.

38 Morley, 'Domestic Relations', p. 34.
39 Lull, 'Constructing Rituals of Extension', p.238.
40 Tulloch, *Television Drama*, p. 197.
41 Habermas, 'A Review of Gadamer's *Truth and Method*', p. 355.
42 Ricoeur, 'Appropriation', *Hermeneutics and the Human Sciences*, p. 191.
43 Gadamer, *Philosophical Hermeneutics*, p. 189.
44 Ellis, *Visible Fictions*, p. 113.
45 R. Barthes, 'Upon Leaving the Movie Theater', in *Apparatus*, edited by T. H. Kyung Cha (London, Tanam, 1961), p. 2, quoted in Flitterman-Lewis, 'Psychoanalysis, Film and Television', p. 188. Television's conformity to the domestic is presupposed by the successful incorporating of the machine as well as its contents. 'Television's inclusion in the home was dependent upon its ability to rid itself of what *House Beautiful* called its "unfamiliar aspect"' (L. Spigel, 'Television in the Family Circle', in Mellencamp, *Logics of Television*, p. 80).
46 Scannell, 'The Communicative Ethos of Broadcasting', *passim*.
47 Female viewer quoted in Morley, 'Family Television', p. 18.
48 Morley, 'Family Television', p. 4. This conference paper and his subsequent *Family Television* investigate, as Morley acknowledges, a fairly restricted sample of 'viewing patterns within white working class/lower middle class nuclear families in a stable inner city environment' ('Family Television', p. 15).
49 Morley, 'Family Television', p. 20.
50 Feuer, 'The Concept of Live Television', p. 18.
51 Note also my discussion of this programme in T. Wilson, '*TV-am* and the politics of Caring', pp. 125–37.
52 Feuer, 'Narrative Form in American Network Television', p. 103.
53 F. Bough, *Cue Frank!* (London, Queen Anne, 1980), quoted in Root, *Open the Box*, p. 28. The television research on *Nationwide* by C. Brunsdon and D. Morley is to be found in Brunsdon and Morley, *Everyday Television*, Morley, *The 'Nationwide' Audience*, and Morley, 'The *Nationwide* Audience', pp. 3–14. A useful discussion of Morley's methodology, arguing that more attention should be paid to the group processes often involved in decoding a text, is in Jordin and Brunt, 'Constituting the Television Audience', pp. 231–49.
54 D. Morley and R. Silverstone, 'Domestic Communication : Technologies and Meanings' (paper presented at the British Film Institute/University of London International Television Studies Conference, 1988), p. 20. (A 'substantially edited' version of this paper appears under the same name in *Media, Culture and Society*, 12 (1990), pp. 31–55.)
55 Ibid., p. 22.
56 Feuer, 'Narrative Form in American Network Television', p. 102.
57 It is worth, however, comparing this model of the individual cinema-goer, devoid of social interaction, with some of the audience behaviour revealed in Richards and Sheridan, *Mass-observation at the Movies*.
58 Schutz, *On Phenomenology and Social Relations*, p. 83.
59 Collett, 'The Viewer Viewed', p. 9.
60 Collett, 'Watching the TV Audience', p. 6.

61   Habermas, *Theory of Communicative Action*, p. 137.
62   Habermas, *The Philosophical Discourse of Modernity*, p. 342.
63   Ibid., p. 298.
64   Habermas, *Theory of Communicative Action*, p. 131.
65   Benson and Hughes, *The Perspective of Ethnomethodology*, p. 49.
66   Habermas, 'What Is Universal Pragmatics ?', p. 3.
67   Feuer, 'Narrative Form in American Network Television', p. 106.
68   V. Crapanzano, 'Hermes' Dilemma: The Masking of Subversion in Ethnographic Description', in Clifford and Marcus, *Writing Culture*, p. 52.
69   Ricoeur, 'Phenomenology and Hermeneutics' and 'Appropriation', *Hermeneutics and the Human Sciences*, pp. 111, 185.
70   Berman, *How Television Sees its Audience*, p. 105.
71   Ricoeur, 'Appropriation', p. 192.
72   Connor, *Postmodernist Culture*, p. 169.
73   E. Wilson, 'All in the Family', pp. 7–9.
74   Habermas, *Legitimation Crisis*, pp. 107–8.
75   Scannell, 'The Communicative Ethos of Broadcasting', p. 26.
76   Dallmayr argues for a tension within Habermas's work between the demands of ideal speech and 'teleological' interest. 'Habermas is unable to isolate the communicative category from purposive intent' (*Critical Encounters and Understanding*, p. 88).
77   Morley, 'Family Television', p. 3.
78   Habermas, *Knowledge and Human Interests*, p. 35.
79   Grossberg, 'The In-difference of Television', p. 29.
80   Collett, 'Watching the TV Audience', p. 9.
81   Ibid., p. 10.
82   Gray, 'Reading the Readings', p. 5.
83   Schutz, *On Phenomenology and Social Relations*, p. 74.
84   Ibid., pp. 112–13.
85   Ibid., p. 81.
86   Ibid., p. 118.
87   Morley, 'Family Television', p. 24.
88   Morley, *Family Television*, p. 45.
89   Lyotard, *The Postmodern Condition*, p. 20.
90   Giddens, 'Reason without Revolution', p. 101.
91   Crisell, *Understanding Radio*, p. 62.
92   Stam, 'Television News and Its Spectator', p. 28. For a wider discussion of written and spoken communication in relation to the media see Kress, 'Language in the Media', pp. 395–419.
93   Mancini, 'Strategies of TV News Dramatization', p. 5.
94   Giddens, *Central Problems in Social Theory* (London, Hutchinson, 1979), p. 204, quoted in Morley and Silverstone, 'Domestic Communication', p. 41.
95   Ricoeur. 'The Hermeneutical Function of Distanciation', *Hermeneutics and the Human Sciences*, p. 139, and *Interpretation Theory*, p. 43.
96   Ricoeur, 'The Hermeneutical Function of Distanciation', p. 141.
97   Morey, *The Space between Programmes*, p. 15.

98 Allen, *Speaking of Soap Operas*, p. 56.
99 Ricoeur, 'Appropriation', p. 182.
100 Ricoeur, 'The Hermeneutical Function of Distanciation', p. 143.
101 Collett, 'The Viewer Viewed', p. 10.
102 Kress, 'Language in the Media', p. 407.
103 Ricoeur, 'Hermeneutics and the Critique of Ideology', *Hermeneutics and the Human Sciences*, p. 92.
104 Volosinov, *Marxism and the Philosophy of Language*, p. 23.
105 Leont'ev, *Activity, Consciousness, and Personality*, pp. 87–94. I am indebted to C. Collins for drawing my attention to Leont'ev's work.
106 Ibid., pp. 89, 91.
107 Dahlgren, 'The Modes of Reception', p. 238. Note also his discussion of the 'dispersion of subjectivity' in 'What's the Meaning of This?', pp. 285–301.
108 Iser, *The Act of Reading*, p. 22.
109 Derrida, *Speech and Phenomena*, p. 140. In making use in this chapter of the work of both Husserl and Derrida, my assumption is clearly that my reading of the former can avoid the latter's critique (e.g. of 'solitary discourse').
110 Radway, *Reading the Romance*, p. 197.
111 Gadamer, *Philosophical Hermeneutics*, p. 25.

2

Television : Hermeneutics and Horizons

I now turn to examining the relationship between viewer and television programme, an account of which can be formulated with the help of hermeneutic philosophy. This methodological perspective on the text – audience relationship regards it as important to acknowledge that the reader brings the distinctive features of his or her experience to bear on viewing the programme. Identification between subject and viewer is, therefore, constantly shifting, a process limited by the awareness of difference.

In the first section I discuss a hermeneutic of understanding as an activity in which the distance between interpretations of the world contained in the text and those held by viewers is overcome. Understanding results in a setting into place of textual perspectives within those of an audience, a 'fusion of horizons'.

The second and third sections bring together the phenomenological analysis of Chapter 1 with hermeneutics to produce an account of identification. Empirical evidence indicates that the focus of identification is inherently general rather than specific. Philosophically, I wish to say, identification is primarily with a social role or role-dependent. It involves, that is, a viewer appropriating a role occupied by a character, and experiencing subsequent similarities and differences between self and textual subject in fulfilling that position (for instance, in modes of detective work). Inhabiting a role generates interests which in turn are responsible for interpretations of the world, interest-related horizons of understanding events and situations. I examine these in the third section. In the role of viewer each member of an audience has an interest in assembling a coherent narrative. This then generates an understanding of the text as, at different moments, aiding or resisting this process. Hermeneutics provides an account of this activity, theorizing the role of reader in a life-world.

The phenomenology of Chapter 1 explored television's familiar address to its audiences. Within this philosophy, I suggest, one can find the tools for refining the concepts used in current ethnomethodological research into the behaviour of viewers. As Lindlof and Meyer indicate, in their very useful introduction to *Natural Audiences*, ethnomethodology 'appropriated the aims of phenomenology in its studies of the logics-in-use of situated everyday behaviour.'[1]

A programme like *Good Morning Britain* (or *Good Morning Australia*) was seen to locate at least some of its subjects in a life-world familiar to the intended viewer, allowing conditions which enabled identification to emerge. Television, I indicate below, further constructs the world as a structure of relevance to a viewer whose interest is in producing a coherent narrative. This interest in interpreting events is likely to be shared with a subject in the text, and to function therefore as a basis for identification.

Identification, then, is with a role in a given programme and as such involves assuming an interest-related way of making sense of a life-world. Since characters (or presenters) already exist in those roles, it is possible to speak also of identification with these individuals, and with how they make the world around them intelligible. This means, it is worth pointing out, that 'identification' can occur with dogs or other animals, or with a camera's narrative presentation of reality, to a qualified extent. Animals (unless constructed by a text as quasi-human) are capable of establishing coherent meaning in only a limited way, and cameras require observers for what they show to acquire significance. Identification is also possible in a restricted sense with other aspects of textual content. In one's imagination one might identify with a landscape counterfactually, locating oneself in the role of someone who might live there (but does not).

Morley and Silverstone hold that 'identification implies not just a one-to-one correspondence between a viewer and some favoured character, but a more general identification at a number of different levels, between what appears on the screen and the lives, understandings or emotions of those who attend to it'.[2] My argument below is that identification involves assuming a subject's social role(s), together with role-related perceptions of life within the text. I have attempted to indicate the 'different levels' at which identification has implications for the lives of viewers.

2.1   Understanding as a 'Fusion of Horizons'

A text is 'like an orchestration that strikes ever new resonances among its readers'.[3] From a hermeneutic perspective, the viewer's production of meaning in the text occurs within a 'fusion of horizons' – 'the fusion of the horizons of understanding which is what mediates between the text and its interpreter'.[4] This phrase refers to a relationship between audience and programme, an interpretative process informed by the reader's awareness of the text as both similar to and different from those experienced previously. A viewer's participation in the processes of understanding is defined as active presence, a condition of the generation of meaning, rather than as passive and textually determined : 'in the process of understanding, there takes place a real fusing of horizons'.[5]

Structuralist theorizing of the reader's fundamental relationship to the text as one of recognition misrepresented the processes in which the meaning of a programme is appropriated. For the central feature of these processes is interpretative understanding, the *overcoming* of a semiotic distance between programme and viewer. But 'overcoming' semantic difference never reaches fruition in a final act of perfect understanding. As I argued in the last chapter, there will always remain at least the distance between communication and recipient attributable to 'personal sense', the autobiographical inflection of meaning in which viewers develop their own particular understanding of what is seen or heard. Nevertheless, clearly a certain comprehension of textual significance must occur if meaning, involvement and identification are to be attained and a text rendered intelligible ; 'the learning of our position in the cinema is also the learning of . . . social reality'.[6]

Within the structuralist paradigm, as I indicated in the Introduction, the relationship between text and audience was such that the viewer who found the text intelligible was simply engaged in reproducing the ideological positions already occupied by agents in the space and time of the programme. For a hermeneutic television theory, however, as Gadamer puts it, understanding is 'not merely reproductive, but also productive'.[7] Reading always generates a new meaning from a text. In this sense understanding is always interpretative, 'both bound and free' : 'interpretation is probably, in a certain sense, re-creation'.[8]

Gadamer's account of a reader coming to understand a text involves mediation between non-identical frameworks of interpreting the world in which, as in conversation, 'something different has come to be'. Such contrasting horizons of programme and viewer may consist of opposing interpretations related to class, race, age or gender, of a range of concepts setting out the 'nature' of things. Audience and text can attach very varied meanings to 'justice', 'pleasure' or 'beauty'.

On the one hand, it is differences such as these between character and audience readings of terms which generate the cognitive distance that understanding a text must (with inevitable imperfection) overcome. On the other hand, however thorough those processes of understanding, there must remain differences in how the world is made intelligible. These are differences between the interpretative horizons of viewer and textual subject, producing varied readings of that to which they are applied, emphasizing a range of aspects of events in a text. The cognitive play of audience perspectives upon the linguistic evidence of a programme generates a host of readings. Where they occur in a text, ideas about 'moderate politics' or 'family relationships' require not only understanding by the audience but an understanding which is necessarily innovative.

The readings produced by a viewer are, then, articulated through conceptual frameworks characterized by both similarity to and difference from those available in the text. The reader can be co-opted into producing meanings for a television programme which maintain his or her ideological oppression. But equally, I noted in the last chapter, it is from those semantic resources which the reader has brought to the text in producing its meaning that an ideological critique can be mounted, distanciating its terms of 'familiar' address in the process of criticism. Understanding representations of ageism, racism and sexism is compatible with rejecting them. To theorize the relationship of programme and viewer as a 'fusion of horizons' allows both for different audience readings of the text's cognitive perspectives and for different positions of distanciation from its definition of the 'real'. Reading permits resistance, never finally producing a loss of subjective autonomy for the reader.

The relationship between text and viewer can be formulated as one of appropriation or a mediation of meaning which (imperfectly) overcomes the cognitive distance between text and reader. Hermeneutics perceives this as a distance which allows the two poles of meaning creation to coexist : unlike structuralism, it does not accede to the 'absence' of the real audience as a cost of producing meaning. But if the text's operations are remembered, identified and anticipated through a range of pre-textual horizons which the audience brings to its viewing, this implies that constraints are inevitable on the readings which any particular audience can achieve.

In viewing a programme, the concepts in and through which the text is expressed are 'replayed' or 'reworked' in terms of the concepts belonging to the reader, so that even identification involves interpretation. Reading is theorized by hermeneutics as rereading, the construction of the new, its result never merely the effect of the text. As Gadamer puts it, 'one understands otherwise if one understands at all'; 'understanding ... is always the fusion of these horizons which we imagine to exist by themselves'.[9] The extent to which audiences merely 'glance' (rather than 'gaze') at a television programme, with the implication of an only half-sustained attention, would appear to allow a particular space for awareness of self and the world to be retained during viewing.

Ricoeur argues for a concept of interaction with the text in which to understand is to 'receive a self enlarged by the appropriation of the proposed worlds which interpretation unfolds'.[10] Reading is always from a pre-existing point of view. Understanding cannot disengage itself from the presuppositions of the reader or investigator, somehow adopting in their place those of the subject within the text. In reading we are always in prior possession of a horizon : 'to adopt the other's point of view while forgetting one's own, is that not objectivity ? Yet nothing is more disastrous than this fallacious assimilation.'[11]

Empirical research on television repeatedly reveals that horizons of understanding associated with different generations, genders, ethnic backgrounds and classes produce different readings of a television text. As Dyer points out, one cannot conclude 'from a person's class, gender, race, sexual orientation and so on, how she or he will read a given text'.[12] Nevertheless, the usefulness of these groupings is as predictors of which horizons of understanding are likely to be drawn upon in reading. These, as I indicated in the last chapter, are assumptions (pre-judgements) which are likely to be considered unproblematic by the individual and therefore used in making sense of a programme.

So diverse are these interpretations in the case of a continuous serial like *Dallas* that the presence of a preferred reading in the programme seems questionable, allowing the possiblity that it is, within limits, an ideologically 'open text'. Continuous serials, argues Buckingham, lack a 'single "pre-ferred" perspective', a 'single authoritative voice'; their large number of characters allows a proliferation of points of view, each of which is allowed to function as a possible focus of identification for the viewer.[13]

Readings of *Dallas* vary quite fundamentally in the allocation of blame and responsibility and, indeed, in the very perception of an issue as 'ethical' or 'political'. Different age groups perceive Sue Ellen (Linda Gray) as 'ruined by her husband' or as 'her own problem': 'J.R. does not stand for the threats of business as an institution as has been surmised from an American point of view. German viewers see in him an individual scoundrel of excessive dimension, responsible for problems that can happen in every family.'[14]

Some of the recent work on postmodernist film and television is also a source of evidence for the wide range of readings produced when audiences of a dissimilar age and generation 'gain purchase' on a text through horizons drawing on varying cultural competences. Successful intertextual reference (allowing a discourse to be recognized as 'pastiche') is a function of the knowledge underlying audience responses to a programme. The same text can be read both as 'allusive' in respect of its predecessors and, in the absence of appropriate cultural knowledge among its readers, as 'straight', as lacking in intertextual reference. Films like *Star Wars*, according to Jameson, 'functioned as nostalgia films for parents familiar with the cinema serials of the '30s and '40s but could be taken "straight" by children'.[15]

Gadamer writes of 'the tension and release that structure all understanding and understandability'.[16] Understanding is an overcoming of, a 'release' from, the cognitive distance (the 'tension') between the terms of intelligibil-ity associated with subjects located in the text (however popular) and those operated by the audience. The result, if successful, is a 'mapping' or translation of one conceptual framework, the programme's, on to the terms of another, the viewer's. A text 'enters into its history of meaning, in which new meanings emerge in accordance with the horizon of transmitted presuppositions in which it is read'.[17] In understanding we are 'placing the other meaning [of the text] in a relation with the whole of our own meanings'.[18]

But understanding or appropriating the meaning of a programme cannot be solely and undialectically described in terms of 'distance' or 'difference'. The viewer also needs to recognize points of semiotic familiarity, similarities between a new text and others previously experienced, on the basis of which his or her understanding of a programme can begin. 'Recognition' of various kinds characterizes the text–viewer relationship where understanding has commenced : recognition of frequently recurring personnel, recognition of the genre or type to which the programme belongs as well as recognition of the conceptually known and familiar in language, shot and action. Understanding can therefore be regarded as a fusion of horizons in which the experience of similarity engages with that of difference : 'we must always already have a horizon in order to be able to place ourselves within a situation'.[19]

The 'fusion of the horizons of understanding ... is what mediates between the text and its interpreter'.[20] But to understand a belief is not simultaneously to accept or 'rehabilitate' it (Habermas), 'just as in a conversation, when we have discovered the standpoint and horizon of the other person, his ideas become intelligible, without our necessarily having to agree with him'.[21] Agreement in horizons of understanding is implicit, not within understanding, but in identification.

For viewers to identify with a character is for them to appropriate one or more of that individual's social roles, with its rules and rationalities of behaviour. It is, moreover, necessarily to adopt the interests, needs and horizons of understanding the world appropriate to those roles, perceiving programme content as a structure of 'relevances' (Schutz) to those interests. Here, 'understanding is primarily agreement or harmony with another person' in respect of cognitive truth rather than merely the meaning of a proposition.[22]

Like understanding, identification consists of a mediation of difference through the experience of similarity. The audience which identifies can be described, at least temporarily, in new ways : to conform to a necessary condition of managing a character's social role (for example, by asking questions) is already to occupy it. Television has its own mechanisms and textual strategies for producing this experience in the intended viewer, and I shall discuss these in Chapter 5.

2.2 Identification and Social Roles

A viewer identifying with someone in 'factual' or 'fictional' television, I suggest, appropriates one, or more, of the social roles occupied by that individual. This is to begin following a set of rules and criteria of rational performance associated with that role, and to perceive aspects of textual content as 'relevancies', as meeting needs or interests associated with the role in question. It is to move within a life-world articulated by the programme.

The experience of identification is, one might say, to be analysed 'ontologically', in terms of taking up a mode of being in the text, such as 'inquiring' or one of the more particular social roles which embody this practice (for example, detective, journalist). Identification generates the experience of similarity to, and difference from, a textual subject in the 'management' of social roles. Where viewers find that a character's 'playing' of roles in a programme becomes different to the point of being wholly inappropriate or incorrect, they are likely to begin reading the text as text, as a constructed and unfamiliar artefact. Just as in 'real' life, breaking rules draws attention to their existence. In section 7.2 I discuss distanciation as the conspicuous production of the 'incorrect', rendering the performance of social roles opaque rather than transparent.

Roles consist of networks of rules, sometimes not precisely definable. Expectations directed at the incumbent of a social role exhibiting conformity to its rules can be ethical in nature. Managing behaviour in a role is producing activity appropriate to it, conforming to expectations: 'a role relation in a social situation has some notion of conduct as appropriate or inappropriate built into its description'.[22] Expectations may concern motives and goals as well as behaviour. As the phenomenologist Schutz indicated, 'whoever (I included) acts in the socially approved typical way is supposed to be motivated by the pertinent typical motives and to aim at bringing about the pertinent typical state of affairs'.[24] In the text the articulation of social roles is inflected through the aesthetic needs and requirements of its construction of meaning.

The social roles occupied by members of an audience will clearly differ, varying at the very least as a function of whether the audience is watching film or television. Managing the roles of domestic television viewer or cinema-goer involves following different rules of behaviour (for example, 'glancing' at a screen rather than 'gazing') and permits the exercise of different powers (in controlling the flow of the image and the relationship of others to that image). The social definition of roles assigns powers to their incumbents both 'automatically' and as a consequence of successful performance in the role in question.

The social roles of television viewer and cinema-goer are associated with finding different items in the visual text of 'relevance' to needs and interests. For instance, the television viewer has a need for information relatively absent in the role-conforming cinema-goer. The varying social roles of film and television audience membership offer a range of relationships to other roles (such as those associated with the domestic, discussed in section 1.2).

The hermeneutic philosophy with which I am presently concerned can be read as a theory of what it is to occupy the role of reader (viewer or spectator). It asserts the rules for, rational activities within and relevant aspects of textual content in regard to producing coherent meaning. To perceive elements of the text as relevant to constructing sense is to perform a cognitive interpretation of those elements in respect of a selective and practical interest in producing an intelligible narrative.

Both the roles of television viewer and cinema-goer are structured around a similar rationality whose goal is assembling a coherent meaning for the text being read. In the fusion of horizons of text and reader there occurs a projection of sense in which understanding is slowly made 'complete'. 'Understanding must be conceived of as part of the process of the coming into being of meaning, in which the significance of all statements ... is formed and made complete.'[25] Or, as Berry argues, using language suggestive of the hermeneutic assumptions implicit in television investigation as currently practised, 'experimental research suggests that the message registered depends largely on a person's background knowledge, which guides a construction of a received message from fragmentary points picked up'.[26]

Hermeneutic theory holds that, in the face of uncertainties of meaning in the text, the viewers 'investigate' the sense of a programme through processes of 'checking out' their informed speculation as to its likely outcome. They 'project', that is, a hypothetical space, time and content, a projection of sense informed by their knowledge of television form and genre. Ideas as to what constitutes, for instance, a 'completed' detective narrative are strongly influenced by a knowledge of what is appropriate for the genre.

'A person who is trying to understand a text is always performing an act of projecting. He projects before himself a meaning for the text as a whole as soon as some initial meaning emerges in the text ... The working out of this fore-project, which is constantly revised in terms of what emerges as he penetrates into the meaning, is understanding what is there.'[27] The subsequent relationship of text and audience, in other words, is determined by a concern for the truth of projections of meaning which, if correct, are likely to assist the viewer in assembling a coherent sense for the programme. To 'anticipate is to adopt a questioning attitude to the text' in which speculations find support, are revised or are rejected.

So, for instance, a group of hermeneutically self-aware viewers of *Dallas* revealed to their interviewers Liebes and Katz 'the built-in compulsion to find out what will happen next week or, better, to spend the week inventing possible solutions to last week's problems or to next week's continuation'.[28] Projections of possible programme content and the viewer's concern with their truth produce the to and fro movement, the play of meaning across the processes of a text. This is the 'hermeneutic circle' of understanding a programme by relating part to whole in a fundamentally rational speculation about meaning. In this 'game' of understanding, the text 'responds to [the viewer's] move with a counter-move', the confirming or falsifying of a projection of sense with information provided at a later point in time (in the next episode, and so on).[29] Narrative continuity can be understood as the provision of information which may or may not validate earlier audience work on the experience of finding information absent from a text. It is in this way that we can 'theorize how we may both grasp the *continuousness* of television and integrate the *experience* of viewing into analysis'.[30]

The pleasures of viewing are frequently those of the 'detection' of meaning, the achievement of a gestalt of satisfying intelligibility centred on understanding the programme's description and narration of events. Description of character or environment (with which I deal in section 4.3), while sometimes rich in detail, can also be read, I would suggest, as an aid to the viewer who is producing a coherent narrative. Watching television is a process in which the audience engages in cognitive 'play' with the semiotic resources of a programme : 'the reader actively produces meaning from the indications provided by the text, and has a significant degree of power to determine it'.[31]

This is a projection and confirmation of meaning which can be playful not only in the viewer's temporary abstraction from public work to private entertainment but, as I indicate below, in the audience's loss of 'reality' and involvement in the text itself. Establishing an intelligible text brings with it 'the characteristic lightness and sense of relief which we find in the attitude of play'.[32] For Barthes as well as for Gadamer, reading is 'play', a rule-governed construction of meaning where the text's flexibility permits an active production of sense : ' "playing" must be understood here in all its polysemy : the text itself *plays* (like a door, like a machine with "play") and the reader plays twice over, playing the Text as one plays a game, looking for a practice which re-produces it'.[33]

But many texts themselves are structured around the 'detection' of a coherent sense for events, with its achievement the responsibility of a subject (detective, investigator) in an appropriate social role within the space and time of the programme. In these circumstances both audience and subject are engaging with the significance of textual events in ways which foreground the production of unified meaning. Between the projects of investigator as audience and investigator as textual subject there will be the similarity of a concern to establish coherent sense and the difference that for the audience (alone) this will be the coherent sense of a text.

If this conjectural rationality informs the reading practices inscribed in the role of viewer, it may induce its incumbents to identify with those in analogous investigative roles belonging to the television programme itself. Here the practices of reading are near to fulfilling some of the necessary requirements of occupying particular role(s) in the text, aligning as they do the extra-textual audience with an intra-textual subject. For this character, as I have noted, will, like the audience, be 'placed' in terms of a task associated with the hermeneutic assembling of coherent meaning.

A character's construction of meaning is a 'response-inviting structure' (Iser) in respect of the reader : in this way the text can be read as making 'offers-of-identification' (Jauss). According to Fiske, where there are uncertainties in a subject's activity, the viewer resolves those indeterminacies to establish a coherent sense. This adds to the apparent reality of the individual in the text with whom identification is taking place. 'The real-seemingness of the character results from the viewer's projection of her/his own "real" self into the character in the process of identification.'[34]

In identification the viewer moves from the role of reader to a role in the life-world(s) of the programme. Identifications centred on 'investigation' presuppose roles involving similar projections of meaning around unity and intelligibility. For a member of a television audience to take up an investigative social role within a programme is for him or her to appropriate the rules and forms of rational behaviour implicit in that role. It is to adopt the horizons of understanding the world associated with the needs and interests generated by that position. As a necessary condition of 'playing' this role the viewer will pose at least some of the questions asked by the subject in the text, will respond cognitively to events in not wholly dissimilar ways.

Here the conditions of reading a text (the social role of reader) are temporarily effaced ('forgotten') in favour of the conditions of occupying a social role enunciated in the programme. The object of readerly concern is no longer the 'problem' of the text but, for example, the problem of a crime; the text *qua* text is, for the time being, transparent, 'lost' to consciousness. Involved here is an audience's 'closing off the here and now and sinking into another world', the 'inclusion of *elsewheres* and *elsewhens* in the here and now'.[35] This movement out of the role of reader and into the space and time of the text might be termed the *ekstasis* of viewing.

Set within the context of understanding, the real readers can both dispense with and appropriate particular social roles. In identifying they can become investigator, detective, journalist. Perceiving a difference between the performance of self and textual subject in a role, they may continue to identify with the role but not the subject (by, for instance, asking different but apparently reasonable questions). Alternatively, they can return to the role of reader. This is the play of similarity and difference which constitutes identification, a moving from (and to) the role of viewer, into (and out of) the roles delineated in the text.

As Morley notes, audience conversation while watching television sustains the movement back and forth between involvement and detachment. Talk about television 'is comment on and about something we do not in any simple way "confuse" with reality – and at the same time sustains involvement and identification (in varying degrees of intensity) with what is on the screen'.[36]

'Play fulfils its purpose only if the player loses himself in his play.'[37] This movement between the roles of extra-textual viewer and textual subject constitutes a changing self. As Ricoeur puts it, 'in reading I "unrealise myself". Reading introduces me to imaginative variations of the *ego*. The metamorphosis of the world in play is also the playful metamorphosis of the *ego*.'[38]

Taking part in the play of identifications excludes involvement at one and the same time in a more distanced reflexive scrutiny of the changes in rules of investigation brought about by the movement between roles. In identification I may become concerned with a crime (rather than with understanding a text about a crime). But I cannot at the same time reflect upon the differences which have occurred (for example in the sorts of questions I ask) in moving between the roles of reader and detective. Gadamer writes that 'the mode of being of play does not allow the player to behave towards play as if it were an object'.[39]

Similarly, the play of identification may become ironic. Here I move from identification as a 'transparent' awareness of similarity and difference between myself and a character in the text to a 'superior' awareness (morally, politically, intellectually), to monitoring my engagement in the play of identification. But achieving this form of ironical onlooking constitutes a process in time. I cannot simultaneously identify *simpliciter* as well as entertain a conscious awareness of my patterns of identification as I move in and out of roles within a programme.

For Ricoeur, the playful relationship of text and reader involves the displacement of the pre-textual self. It generates the acquisition of a 'new' self which is both similar to and different from the old, concerned perhaps with investigation but no longer of a text: 'it is always a question of entering into an alien work, or divesting oneself of the earlier "me" in order to receive, as in play, the self conferred by the work itself'.[40]

The role of investigator or detective is fulfilled in different ways throughout film and television. One variation occurs in *Coma* (directed by Crighton, 1977). A spectator attempting to make sense of this text will ask many questions similar to those whose answer is pursued by Susan Wheeler (Geneviève Bujold) in the film. This is already to go some way towards taking up her social role of 'investigator'. But, according to O'Brien, Susan Wheeler fails to satisfy the demands of this role because she 'does not operate from a hypothesis, nor does she anticipate what she might discover from her investigations'.[41] Whether an investigator occurs extra-diegetically (as audience) or diegetically (as character), he or she projects a sense for events in an attempt to construct a coherent interpretation.

The role of investigator is particularly significant in terms of patterns of audience identification. For, depending on the manner in which the role is played out in the text, so it is possible for the audience to recognize itself in a consequent structure of similarities and differences. Alignment with the character can, for instance, pass through a phase of being closely placed in terms of the possession of knowledge, a positioning which shifts to one of distance when the audience knows more than the 'investigator'. At the beginning of *Coma* Susan 'knows nothing and she never has more knowledge than the viewer and on occasion, the viewer actually knows more than Susan'.[42]

As with the film spectator, so a television viewer has a role-dependent interest, for example, in formulating a coherent meaning for a weekly episode in a series. He or she would ask, with a certain degree of difference, the questions 'private eye' James Hazell (Nicholas Ball) sets out to answer in an episode of that now classical instance of the British television detective genre, *Hazell Meets the First Eleven* (ITV, 9.00, 13.2.78). Here, he attempts to understand the social relationships of the rich. Both viewer and Hazell seek to enjoy the social role of the knowledgeable investigator, to possess a coherent body of information, the hermeneutic role *par excellence*. But the viewer's cognitive interest, unlike Hazell's, is directed at the text as text. The processes constituting identification would consist of moving beyond this concern with a text, of attempting to satisfy the interrogative demands of the role of 'private eye' itself.

In *Hazell Meets the First Eleven* Hazell and the intended audience (at least) identify, they engage together with the 'semantic economy' or meaning of the text from within, from an epistemic location defined by the role of detective. Hazell's knowledge of events is, like the viewer's, retarded in the text. Like the viewer, his projections of sense may require redirecting; 'I thought detectives were supposed to have lightning fast, computer-like brains,' he is told at one point. In identification with Hazell the viewer is 'playing' at being a detective, asserting similarities to Hazell in his or her counterfactual management of this role rather than the differences of occupying an actual role of reader.

It is to this process of 'forgetting' the role of viewer in identification that an interviewee refers in Schroder's account of the Danish experience of *Dynasty*: 'when I sit down in front of the t.v. . . . during that hour one could say that I immerse myself in that world, in those fine dinners and fine drinks and fine clothes. And when it's over, well then I'm just myself again.'[43] Schroder describes this involvement as an experience 'of being transported to a state of "not-myself", i.e. a ludic putting on of another identity or other identities'. It is a 'subjunctive involvement' in which 'the conditions of everyday life have temporarily been suspended for the benefit of a daydream about what might be'.[44]

The viewer's relationship to a role already inhabited by a textual subject is mediated, then, through a varying 'play' of similarities and differences: the reader may occupy that role or realize his or her differences as reader (the source of distanciated criticism). Only the viewer *qua* viewer, for instance, reads a subject's behaviour within the social role in terms of a framework of understanding determined by a knowledge of genre. A structure of identification between reader and textual subject may be organized around the role, rules and rationality of the 'investigator'. But, as I discuss in the next chapter, many other grounds of identification can be found (for example, the role of 'carer', which is inscribed in an entirely different network of rules, rational activity and perceptions of what is appropriate to the satisfaction of interest and need). To identify with a character is always to identify with him or her under a certain description, the description of a textually articulated social role: detective, father, adventurer and so on. Textual subjects frequently occupy several roles simultaneously, each available as a point of identification for the viewer.

In respect of the textual incorporation of the reader Gadamer argues that reading 'puts the spectator in the place of the player'.[45] Both spectator and player are charged with the production of a meaningful artefact; the spectator 'is the person for and in whom the play takes place'. But here Gadamer must be read with care. The viewer identifies not with a 'player' if by this is signified 'actor', but with a 'player' in the sense of a 'subject occupying a role' within the television programme being watched. From there meaning is produced without reference to the text as text. To analyse identification as an appropriation of social role is to emphasize the temporal aspect of identifying. Identification is a process, for the viewing subject cannot appropriate a social role other than by inhabiting it in rule-governed activity and discourse through time.

Identification, I am suggesting, involves sharing a way of being in the text as well as a cognitive apprehension of its content. This is to redefine the conception of 'subject position' with its reference to 'the stability and unity of the construction of the self', a conception which originated with the structuralist paradigm.[46] For in hermeneutics a 'subject position' becomes a complex of aesthetically influenced but nevertheless social roles and interest-related horizons of understanding through which some aspect of a text is conceived and judged. To assert that these roles are 'social' allows the content of the text as social organization to be acknowledged. The viewer is not 'held' within textual roles, but passes into and out of them in the process of identification.

The concept of 'social role' is also of use in understanding the relationship between individual and dominant ideology. A role often embodies and inflects an ideological interpretation of reality in its associated horizons of understanding and social activities (cf. the 'male role' under patriarchy and its definition of male need and female object). Social roles can, on the other hand, enable cultural action for freedom. As articulations of ideology into practice, roles are to be characterized in terms of a necessary coherence and contradictoriness. Without a certain consistency between many of the rules which constitute them, social roles cannot guide action. But, considered as an insertion within a capitalist social reality of ideological perspectives on behaviour, a Marxist understanding of roles will be that they embody principles displaying fundamental contradictions in their construction of human personality and appropriate activity.

Ethnomethodology locates the individual in a complex of social roles, thereby avoiding the 'dualism of agency-and-structure'.[47] 'Roles', or the complexes of rules and conceptions of rationality and relevance in which they consist, enable action to occur but do not cause it to take place. They provide a cultural framework for activity which underwrites and informs its rationality. Without this framework the action cannot occur; a society which has no concept of, for instance, religious roles, rules and relationships cannot contain religious practices.

A spectator's management of a role inscribed in the text is mediated by his or her interpretation of that textual position. Within a 'playful' sharing of a social role which allows reader and textual subject to identify there will be, therefore, differences of style and role management. In a current affairs programme a concern to elicit particular information may relate viewer and interviewer in the performance of a role. This will be the social role of the critical inquirer, a position clearly central to this type of media text. The role is elaborated around obtaining information which has relevance to at least the interviewer's concerns. Where the viewer cannot share those concerns, where difference becomes too apparent, he or she will disengage

from the relationship of identification. Indeed, the interviewer may foreground the audience's status as audience (for instance, by addressing it as
such), reminding it of its distinctiveness.

An individual, that is, 'inhabits' a role in one of a variety of ways,
'playing' it with a particular style and competence, and in so doing
constitutes his or her freedom with respect to the role and its various
expressions. Here there can be a politics of 'style'. The discourses of role
are not to be understood as structuralist determinations of activity. Rather
they are inflected through the individual's understanding and experience,
experience which generally precedes the point at which the role is assumed
(just as the role, as abstract social concept, exists prior to the individual).
Like gaining a purchase on conceptual meaning, to adopt a role is simultaneously to interpret it, to read it through difference: 'language always
already offers a position to the speaker and yet, at the same time, the act of
speaking may itself displace those positions'.[48]

As I have noted, a subject's interpretation or 'management' of a role may
distance viewers who have previously found it possible to locate themselves
within it. In the Channel Four documentary series on Scandinavia, *Fat Man
Goes Norse* (C4, 7.15, 9.8.87–30.8.87), the (pre)dominant social role with
which the text seeks to align the viewer is that occupied by the traveller and
inquirer Tom Vernon. The popular television magazine *TV Times* described
the programme in the first week of transmission: 'Tom Vernon pedals his
bicycle to the Russian border across Norway, Sweden and Finland:
exploring the countryside and discovering the people.'

The programme offers the pleasures of an easy acquisition of his roles,
displayed in a flow of images which centre on Vernon both as spectacle and
as source of point-of-view shots. As he cycles through the Scandinavian
countryside, these images clearly define for the intended audience a subject
with which they can identify. For it is his role of inquiring tourist,
constituted as it is in the aesthetic terms and limits of the programme, which
is allowed the ideal viewer. This is a role which, finding it echoed in his or
her lived experience, that viewer can 'playfully' occupy. Aligned with Tom,
the audience is positioned in terms of distinctions between the interests and
horizons of leisure, on the one hand, and work on the other, and the clear
realization that what is at hand is the self-fulfilment associated with the
former.

But identification with Vernon's position is also the discovery of unfamiliarity. For his point of view is articulated through linguistic specificity, his
distinctively formulated understanding of what he finds around him. The
viewers' pleasure in appropriating the social role of inquisitive tourist is
inherently unstable since they experience that position as being already
occupied by the particular differences of Vernon. The audience competes
with him in a definition of role. It may identify with the role (in its
construction through camera work which permits the looking suitable for a
tourist and a *mise en scène* rewarding to that look) rather than with the
particular subject, Tom.

1   Tom Vernon in *Fat Man Goes Norse*

As the description of the programme in the *TV Times* makes clear, Tom the character in the role of traveller is fulfilled by difference to the point of excess, managing to encounter a remarkable collection of phenomena by apparently casual chance. The empirical viewer's identification is, necessarily, disturbed through the programme's disclosure of Tom Vernon's 'differences', his 'otherness'. For this (over)playing of a role draws attention to its existence in a text of which the viewer is but a reader. Here the real viewer is likely to 'commute' (Schroder) back and forth from identification to a distanciated awareness of textuality : 'Today Tom Vernon cycles across Finland to the Russian border, encountering: stars of the Finnish stage, screen and radio; a close shave with a sauna; a sea shanty; a hum for Sibelius; a gypsy matriarch with a remarkable skirt; a railway junction and an accordian factory; a cavalry on bicycles; and the sense of loss of Lost Karelia.'

More generally, the experiences of both difference and similarity are a necessary condition of a programme's producing an audience-in-identification as it moves back and forth from identification with a role to identifying with a subject. The textually defined social role with which identification occurs is recognized as familiar, the character inhabiting that role often experienced as a source of difference. Particular characters manage social roles in particular ways, generating a variety of comprehensions of the rules and powers, the rationalities and horizons of understanding through which those roles are articulated. A text places bounds on identification for its viewer by the mere fact of representing in a social role a finite subject of identification whose activity necessarily will be regarded at certain points as unlike the viewer's. To experience the limits of identification is to perceive another's conception of subjecthood. Sometimes, as with this Australian viewer of *Carson's Law*, identification can be terminated not by what a character does but by what he or she suffers : 'part of me is inside Linda – it feels rude when she takes off her stockings – it feels lovely when they kiss – but when she gets slapped I'm right back in our living room'.[49]

If individuals act in accordance with their reading of a social role, their activity can be analysed as 'self-directed rule-following'.[50] This is to study the 'rules, meanings and so on which are responsible for the structure' of behaviour or its 'generative mechanisms'.[51] Such mechanisms will produce both verbal and non-verbal behaviour in the text and be referred to in the speech of its subjects (cf. the rule-related 'ethical' discourse of the continuous serial). For the television theorist, an awareness of the concept of 'role' (with its associated terms) will therefore permit analysis of this activity and serve to elucidate often verbally complex structures of identification (discussed in Chapter 5). Analysis of roles and their construction in speech is particularly suited to television, for programmes frequently present characters, through a verbal statement of their identity, as incumbents of one or more social roles.

Language can function both descriptively and performatively in respect of 'roles', articulating their characteristics and maintaining them in play. Roles are accompanied by prescriptions governing their rational performance. A text may accede to these prescriptions, subvert them or revalue them as a form of knowledge. (For example, in ITV's game show *The Price Is Right* the knowledge underlying a successful performance in the role of consumer is constructed as worthwhile.)

Accounts of behaviour locate subjects within the complexes of action-guiding social rules which form a role in a life-world. As I indicated above, individuals and viewers inhabit their social roles with a variety of 'styles', playing the rules in different ways. Rule following may be implicit rather than explicit, occurring without an ability to formally state the rules in question. However, since all actions are rule governed, it is likely that any action conforms to one or more of a set of rules constituting a role: 'all behaviour which is meaningful (therefore all specifically human behaviour) is ipso facto rule-governed'.[52] Most actions, therefore, exemplify the management of at least one social role.

Identification can, then, be conceptualized as the viewer's appropriation of a social role elaborated in the text. That role may often be experienced as familiar, producing an easy conformity to its rules and horizons of experience. But in the course of a television programme the spectator may move not only to a recovery of the position of viewer but to a critical observing of the role as a generative mechanism sustaining rules and associated behaviour being played out within the text. In this way the familiarity of the role, naturalizing it to the point of a seemingly inevitable flow of action and thought, is alienated in a distanciated reading of the programme. Here, 'the bouncing of complicity and distance defines forms of identification and subjectivity'.[53]

2.3   Identification and New Perspectives

Branigan in his book *Point of View in the Cinema* refers to a 'popular usage' of the term 'identification'. This appears to involve the recognition of similarity to and difference from a given subject. Identification is 'a process of forming and reforming one's identity in comparison with or against something else'.[54] In this chapter I mark out an instance of this 'popular' concept of identification as it applies to television by specifying the process of 'forming and reforming' an image of self in relation to a subject's display of roles in a programme.

'Identification' is partly to be described in terms of appropriating a character's (or presenter's) social role(s). However, as I noted in the first chapter, roles bear with them a set of related interests and needs, in turn responsible for generating a certain perception of the world. Occupying a social role *necessarily* implies adopting particular horizons of understanding experience. The interests and needs associated with a role produce generalities of interpretation in which the details of daily living are encountered: investigators perceive events as problem or solution. For a female Australian viewer of *Carson's Law*, identification is (in part) a matter of adopting an ethical position, the role of a person with principles, Godfrey. The 'strength' with which this role is articulated in the text is a feature not only of Godfrey's behaviour but of his tenacity in understanding the world in a particular fashion. 'I identify most with Godfrey, because I like his strength; I feel strength in myself, I admire his strength plus I like all the things he stands for.'[55]

Identification is therefore to be further analysed as appropriating a subject's role-related perspective on events, a horizon of understanding effected by the needs and interests of the role in question. In this way identification is constituted by a 'fusion of horizons', the sense of a similarity of outlook in which difference remains 'at the edge'.

Here the reader's interpretation of his or her role-related horizons of understanding the world is affirmed. His or her particular inflections of their generalities of meaning are given support. For both investigative subject and reader, there is agreement in the rightness of conceiving of some aspect of the world as problematic, and those difficulties appear to be under consideration in much the same way. As with the audience's mediated reading of a social role, so a subject's horizons of understanding experience are identified with by a viewer in terms of detailed readings of their sense.

But, as I stated in section 2.2, identification must be thought of as constituted dialectically by the experience of difference. On the one hand, the reading subject is a subject with a horizon of expectations and assumptions in which the world is experienced. A similar discursive articulation of horizons in the text permits the viewer's identifications to be constituted through recognition. Discourses define a subject position which may be occupied with ease, generating for the audience both pleasure and a promise of intelligibility.

On the other hand, the viewer's understanding of his or her perspectives may be changed and developed by readings available and appropriated from within the text. An audience's identification with a particular character position is normally motivated by recognition. It can develop further, not with the continuing experience of similarity, but by disagreeing with the individual concerned in interpreting cognitive horizons of understanding. In a UK Channel Four television series, also shown on the Special Broadcasting Service in Australia, *To the End of the Rhine* (C4, 6.30, 17.10.87–21.11.87), Bernard Levin's understanding of the Rhineland may be in part, acquired by the viewers but partly also resisted as more than tinged with cultural elitism. They can share the role of tourist, reading their surroundings as appropriately interesting, but realizing significant differences in their political or aesthetic responses. The experience of identification evolves through its dialectical tensions.

In the movement between similarity and difference the time and space are opened for a 'playful' learning of a subject's horizons of understanding and projections of meaning within the programme. This play involves the pleasures of reaffirmation where the viewer's assumptions and 'knowledges' are apparently restated before him or her in the text, as well as the pleasures consequent upon a successful projection of meaning. The continuous serial offers members of its audience the rewards both of recognizing themselves in others and of reassurance in making their knowledge work successfully in attaining understanding. (The pleasures of the television serial will be discussed further in the next chapter.)

Such rewards may of course be either progressive or regressive, depending upon the possibilities of meaning available for appropriation and upon which spectatorial horizons are celebrated through their presence in the programme. ITV's *Good Morning Britain*, for instance, will be familiar to its implied audience in precise ways. Its images of the family in a life-world of well-defined horizons of understanding are constructed to allow recognition and identification by the intended viewers (the family) while simultaneously upholding a reactionary ideology (as I indicated in Chapter 1).

The limits of identification are circumscribed by the experience of difference. A text can itself undermine the very possibility of identifying. It may construct for the viewer a position from which to make an ironical reading of what might otherwise have appeared to be a preferred position of identification. In *To the End of the Rhine* Levin is both 'our guide' and at times shown to be slightly ridiculous. For those who choose to occupy the role of tourist less prejudicially than Levin, this difference of a 'superior knowledge' is available in the look of the camera, revealing him as the idiosyncratic traveller.[56]

Yet an audience, bearing its *own* experience within the activity of reading, may come to realize that a subject's horizons of understanding are being articulated in ways it would resist. An experience of cognitive difference replaces one of familiarity and identification. The audience may continue to identify with the role but not the subject, articulating its horizons of understanding the world in other ways. Or it may return to the role of viewer, exercising a distanciated criticism of the text (cf. the audience's discussion of television's ageism which is analysed in the Conclusion). Previous differences which have passed unnoticed may become apparent. In this way the temporality of reading provides a basis for a growing awareness of the text's perspectives as being other than the reader's, for a distanciated critique of its social roles and horizons of understanding.

As a phrase descriptive of understanding, 'fusion of horizons' refers to the inevitable mediation between perspectives associated with text and reader. But as an account of identification, 'fusion of horizons' is a dialectical phrase denoting a cognitive 'play' in which horizonal readings move into and out of a relationship in which one appropriates and the other is appropriated. This is a process and movement based on the experience of similarity and difference in fleshing out interpretative horizons of understanding the world : 'by restoring the dialectic of points of view and the tension between the other and the self, we arrive at the culminating concept of the *fusion of horizons*'.[57]

It is in realizing that there is a distance between his or her own (readings of) horizons and those enunciated in the text that the viewer contributes to a developing conception of his or her identity. In dialectical terms, discovery of the other is the discovery of self ; 'only insofar as I place myself in the other's point of view do I confront myself with my present horizon, with my prejudices'.[58]

The idea that discovering cultural distance from the other is discovering one's identity is firmly expressed in 'Parallel Lines', a BBC 'audience access' television programme in the *Open Space* series on the two religious communities in Northern Ireland (BBC2, 7.35, 23.11.87). Two young people, Mark Adair and Nuala Nic Sheain, discuss their cultural and religious differences, with Adair observing that 'one's awareness of one's identity is based largely upon a recognition of what you are not'.

2.4   Post-structuralist Hermeneutics

A central distinction between the structuralist paradigm and subsequent understanding of film and television studies is their differing accounts of 'identification' between viewers or spectators and individuals in the text. For the structuralist, as I have noted, as part of a more general theory of society, audience subjectivity is an effect of the text: 'the activity of the individual (or, for that matter, collective) "subject" is held to be a function of its structural conditions'.[59]

For later media theory, concerned to distinguish between 'actual' and 'intended' spectator, it is important not to make the mistake of 'assuming that audiences are *always* bound to programming in a transparent relationship'.[60] Identification can never be perfect, for the viewer is always in some respect different from a character in the text. Empirical research, often emphasized in current media analysis, must examine the discourses and context of audience decoding. 'Identification' involves mediation, an interpretation of the ideology articulated by textual subjects through the categories of understanding constituting the ideological position of the extra-textual viewer.

A hermeneutics of the text–reader relationship can align itself with these post-structuralist developments, arguing that the real spectator never coincides with the ideal addressee of a textual enunciation. Similarly, 'there is always a discrepancy . . . between the author as historical subject and the image of the author as inscribed subject' implied within the text.[61] The spectator in history is constrained to produce an interpretative reading of the text's address.

Identification always involves mediation, an appropriation of difference. Past experiences of character and viewer do not coincide. The life-worlds of audience and subject are unavoidably distinct; their horizons of understanding are shaped by assumptions about the self-evident and structures of familiarity generating different perceptions of the 'real'. Viewers are viewers-in-excess, with 'no necessary link between the intended reading of the text . . . and any particular viewer's attitude at the moment of viewing'.[62] The social subject exceeds that implied by the text. There is always a gap, a distance between the ideal viewer and readings which draw on the specificities and complexity of experience possessed by the real audience. In the terms of the phenomenological account of reading provided by Iser, the position of implied viewer 'must be able to accommodate all kinds of different readers'. He argues for the variety of 'experiences that we are constantly bringing into play as we read – experiences which are responsible for the many different ways in which people fulfill the reader's role set out by the text . . . Each actualisation therefore represents a selective realisation of the implied reader.'[63]

Johnston writes in *The Cinema Book* that according to film structuralism 'the effect of [textual] operations is to "place" the *subject* in a fixed position of knowledge towards the text'.[64] But after structuralism, audiences occupying specific social and historical locations are seen to take up a 'position of knowledge' in terms necessarily mediated through diverging horizons of gender, class, racial and generational experience. For as Morley has noted, where audiences do not all belong to the same group, they are likely to have access to different cultural resources with which to interpret a text. The appropriative dimension of viewing covers a variety of socially related interpretations and understanding. In 'The *Nationwide* Audience' Morley's concern was with the 'way a person's position in these structures [of age, sex, race and class] may be seen to determine that person's access to various discourses in play in the social formation', and how those discourses subsequently influenced readings of the BBC's *Nationwide*.[65]

The range of cultural competences among a film's audience generates a plurality of ways in which to occupy positions defined by the text : 'we could say that the whole thrust of so-called "post-structuralist semiotics" has been to question and replace the notion of any single fixed relation between a fully constituted reader at once held in place and "moved" by the narrative and a finished text'.[66]

To assert variety as a characteristic of reading is not to propose an unconstrained diversity of interpretation. Readings may be more or less 'reasonable', which is to say that there are limits beyond which the identity of an interpretation as a reading of a particular text becomes implausible : 'the text itself imposes definite limits on their [individuals'] room to manoeuvre'.[67]

Identification is the awareness of a similarity between aspects of textual and extra-textual subjects, perceived, for instance (as I have previously argued), in their construction of meaning in comparable ways because of the roles they occupy. Press, for example, in her paper 'Class and Gender in the Hegemonic Process' defines 'identification' as taking place where 'women saw a part or parts of themselves in a particular television character'.[68] Implicit in 'identification' here, I would suggest, is the recognition that events are being understood and reacted to in similar ways within similar social roles.

From a hermeneutic perspective members of an audience themselves share a status and role as readers of a text. In attempting to understand a programme, they exercise this common position in active and rule-governed 'projections' of meaning : 'the meaning of a literary text is not a definable entity, but if anything, a dynamic happening'.[69] Buckingham's book on the BBC's *EastEnders* draws attention to the subjective processes by which the audience overcomes indeterminacies of meaning in the text. Using their generic knowledge of soap opera, they ' "fill the gaps" between scenes' and assemble coherent stories 'out of the series of fragments they are shown'.[70] These processes bear a resemblance to a character's assembling of meaning within a text.

For a hermeneutics of television the television viewer is an 'active' viewer whose identifications are a function of reading the differences as well as the similarities between his or her own experiences and those available in the text.[71] Spectators may identify in a range of ways, ways united despite their variety as mediations of one position. But at the heart of a viewer's or spectator's identification with a subject it is also necessary to theorize a difference from that subject. In Chapter 1 I tried to suggest phenomenological grounds for the importance of establishing this distinctiveness.

Structuralist theory claimed for the audience an ideological identity of outlook in the face of a wholly determining filmic ideology. The antithesis signalled by what came after claimed, if not a total liberation for interpretations of the text, at least a variety and difference of audience readings. A theory grounded in phenomenological hermeneutics asserts, in an attempt at a dialectical synthesis of these previous positions, both similarity and difference of understanding between audience and subject of identification.

In engaging with a text, a viewer 'commutes' between a series of positions. Sometimes he or she will identify in a subjective reading of textual meaning characterized by an experience of similarity to the individual concerned. At this point, the textuality of the text is forgotten in a 'transparent' awareness of its contents. Camera work and editing will be unproblematically invisible.

At other points in viewing, however, differences from the behaviour of that textual subject will be experienced. These may range from alternative interpretations of a social role (and its implicit horizons of understanding the world) to the point where a subject's managing of a role resists comprehension by the viewer. Here the audience is likely to be returned by the awareness of increasing difference to 'reality', to the context of viewing and the role of viewer. As if disengaging from a distracted consciousness akin to that of 'play', the audience's involvement with events will be displaced by an awareness of the text as text. A television detective's investigations, for instance, may at particular moments assert an individuality and 'otherness' from the viewer's expectations of appropriate behaviour. To be prompted by this increasing oddity to remember its context in a television programme is for readers to recover an awareness of their status as members of a television audience. Such viewers may subsequently enlarge their differences with the text in a distanciated criticism of its terms and perspectives: the relationship between self and subject becomes 'negative-contradictory' rather than 'positive-reinforcing'.[72]

This discovery of difference or distance at the heart of involvement and identification with the subjectivities of the text is an important dimension of viewing. It is referred to in viewers' reports on their experience of at least some kinds of television and can be a feature of their providing the report itself. As Buckingham indicates in his account of interviews with the audiences of *EastEnders*, a 'process of shifting into and out of the fictional world of the programme was very frequent in these discussions'.[73] In the Conclusion I discuss the ways in which distanciated readings of a text arise from the discovery of difference between self and subject.

The frequency of 'commuting' will vary among viewers and depend on the type of television being watched. Some viewers' involvement in soap opera is less constant than others, while the intended audience (at least) at the resolution of an investigative serial is likely to be wholly involved. It is this differing level of cognitive commitment which is to be found in most viewers' attention to television, rather than the constantly superficial concern asserted by Barwise and Ehrenberg, the 'little physical, emotional, intellectual, or financial effort or investment'. 'Television is relaxing', they assert, 'because it takes our minds off other things without giving us too much else to think about.'[74]

Ellis refers to television viewing in *Visible Fictions* as being more akin to the 'glance' than the fixed 'gaze' of the film spectator.[75] If television watching is intermittent, characterized by an often distracted audience which is frequently 'absent' from the programme, it is also to be defined by an audience more 'present' in its own (often) domestic conditions of viewing. I attempt to show in the Conclusion that these are conditions not simply of spectatorship but of a critical spectatorship in which the audience's experience is more likely to be used to assess the life-worlds articulated before it in a programme. (This is not, of course, given my arguments above, to regard the conditions of cinematic viewing as a site for the unquestioning absorption of ideology.)

The structuralist paradigm established a coherent spectatorial conscious-ness by marginalizing difference in the spectator's experience of the text. These differences, in structuralist terms, were merely aberrations or remnants of a pre-ideological individuality, a consciousness prior to the 'free' accept-ing of 'subjection'.[76] But differences are for later theory rarely 'autono-mous'.[77] They are marks of the audience's location within other ideologies, forms of knowledge and experience from which a critique of the text may be pursued. The concept of structuralist 'positioning' is here seen to involve a 'loss' for the spectator in which, conceived of as passively produced by the text, he or she is thought of as 'absent' from a 'self' whose experiences, differences and contradictions are in fact a potential source of progressive readings. Willemen, writing of the 'suggestion that texts *construct* spec-tators', vigorously asserts that this carried 'implications of subjugation, unilateral determination, not to say terrorism'.[78]

Both the programme's account of the world and those implicit among the audience inevitably involve references to the tensions and clashes of gender, class, generation and, perhaps, race. Neither the discourses of subjectivity associated with a text nor those of the viewer can be regarded as enjoying an autonomy from social contradiction. The programme itself functions as a discursive process through and in which the tensions and oppositions of society and history are mediated and written. Its articulations of ideological unity are inevitably fractured in a 'leaky system' where 'contradictory ideologies do in fact appear : it reproduces the existing field of the political class struggle in its contradictory state'.[79] Superimposed on these contradictions will be others generated by a programme's need to subscribe to the conditions of pleasurable recognition for the intended viewer. A text whose values are those of the socially dominant may yet be found to contain evidence that it celebrates the 'unassimilable' outlook of an audience whose self-understanding is in part formed around a subordinate order of sense-making.[80] The film *Mildred Pierce* (directed by Michael Curtiz, 1945) both respects the independence of the heroine and tries to contain it, offering to feminine and masculine readings respectively the contradictory pleasures of liberation and those of patriarchal containment.[81]

It is, as I noted, also the case that contradictions in the spectator's understanding of 'self' and the text are a witness to the source of that understanding in more progressive forms of knowledge as well as in the dominant hegemonies of class, culture, race and age. As MacCabe puts it in a renunciation of formalism, 'we have to consider the relation between reader and text in its historical specificity . . . It is a question of analysing a film within a determinate social moment.'[82] The reader inscribed in the text of bourgeois ideology signified for structuralism an ideological unity. Subsequent work, in its theorizing of ideological critique, argues for the audience's conscious experience of a disunity among the discourses constituting its position, that of 'real' spectator.

This is the hermeneutic paradox underlying the processes of contemporary reading, in which far from unified subjects attempt to construct a story, a unified reading of a text. But '*Dallas* is as contradictory, unstable, and fluid a concatenation of discourses as any person'.[83] The empirical individual engages, progressively or otherwise, with a far from coherent text through the conflicting discourses which he or she brings to its reading. Just 'as it is important to recognize the dialectic of ideology and utopia in the very forces of the everyday life-world, it is even more important to acknowledge the same contradictory forces within the mass media'.[84] In the language of technical analysis, the text is the 'articulation of different, contradictory subject positions or interpellations, to which the . . . individual worker [a contradictory subject, traversed by different discursive practices] is "hailed" '.[85]

In post-structuralist theory, in general, and in hermeneutics in particular, the discourses of speech and writing are an important area from which to determine the ideological operations of the text. Gadamer writes of the 'linguistic nature of the human experience of the world'.[86] Habermas, attempting to politicize linguistics, argues for the need to study language as a medium of 'domination and social power; it serves to legitimate relations of organised force'.[87] In television studies the hegemonic force discernible in both spoken and written discourse, within as well as without the text, becomes centrally important. My argument in the chapters which follow is that the cognitive ('horizons') and ontological aspects ('roles') of identification are to be foregrounded as an arena of largely verbally stated 'difference' and 'similarity' between subject and audience. It is in language that the hegemonizing operations of the television text and their rejection (or otherwise) by the viewer can be scrutinized.

As a mediation between cognitive perspectives, identification is part of a more general 'process of meaning production' between the text and an audience which is already established within discourse and society prior to its reading : identification is part of 'a production of and by subjects already in social practices'.[88] It is by taking the disunities within the processes of meaning production as the terrain for ideological struggle, contradictions imbricated within the experience of class, gender, race and age as it confronts and is engaged with by the media, that the study of film and television has asserted its progressive moment. 'Both the contradictions sustained by the lived relations of class position in a confrontation with the meanings of film and the strategies of film to contain those contradictions should and could be analysed.'[89] As with film so with television.

Notes

1   Lindlof and Meyer, 'Mediated Communication', p. 5.
2   Morley and Silverstone, 'Domestic Communication', p. 47.
3   Jauss, *Toward an Aesthetic of Reception*, p. 21.
4   Gadamer, *Truth and Method*, p. 340.
5   Ibid., p. 273.
6   MacCabe, 'Theory and Film', p. 25.
7   H.G. Gadamer, *Wahrheit und Methode* (Tübingen, 1965), p. 280, quoted in McCarthy, *Critical Theory of Jürgen Habermas*, p. 175.
8   Gadamer, *Truth and Method*, p. 107.
9   Ibid., p. 272. With literary reception theory there are a range of concepts analogous to the 'horizons' of an audience. Freund gives an account of some of these in her book *The Return of the Reader*: they include I.A. Richard's concept of the reader's 'stock responses' (p. 35) and J. Culler's idea of the reader's 'system of conventions' (p. 80). Culler's concept of 'naturalization' ('integrating the read into the known') bears some resemblance to the hermeneutic understanding of a 'fusion of horizons'. Freund also considers S. Fish's idea of an 'interpretative community', the system of strategies or norms of interpretation to which both text and reader belong.
10   P.Ricoeur, 'Hermeneutics and the Critique of Ideology', *Hermeneutics and the Human Sciences*, p. 94.
11   Ibid., pp. 74–5.
12   Dyer, 'Victim', p. 19.
13   Buckingham, *Public Secrets*, pp. 80, 36.
14   Massing, 'Decoding *Dallas*', p. 97.
15   Hayward and Kerr, Introduction to *Screen*, p. 7. The paper referred to is Jameson, 'Postmodernism and Consumer Society'.
16   Gadamer, *Philosophical Hermeneutics*, p. 19.
17   Kisiel, 'Repetition in Gadamer's Hermeneutics', p. 199.
18   Gadamer, *Truth and Method*, p. 238.
19   Ibid., p. 271.
20   Ibid., p. 340.
21   Ibid., p. 269.
22   Ibid., p. 158. Gadamer is sometimes indeterminate in respect of whether he

intends 'understanding' to signify agreement on truth, or on meaning *simpliciter*.

23 Emmet, *Rules, Roles and Relations*, p. 15.
24 Schutz, *Collected Papers*, vol. 2, p. 237.
25 Gadamer, *Truth and Method*, p. 146.
26 Berry, 'Meanings, Misunderstandings and Mental Models', p. 6.
27 Gadamer, *Truth and Method*, p. 236.
28 Liebes and Katz, 'On the Critical Abilities of Television Viewers', p. 217.
29 Gadamer, *Truth and Method*, p. 95.
30 C. Brunsdon, 'Television: Aesthetics and Audiences', in Mellencamp, *Logics of Television*, p. 62.
31 Buckingham, 'Television Literacy', p. 31.
32 Gadamer, *Truth and Method*, p. 97.
33 Barthes, *Image, Music, Text*, p. 162.
34 Fiske, *Television Culture*, p. 174.
35 M. Morse, 'An Ontology of Everyday Distraction', in Mellencamp, *Logics of Television*, pp. 193, 195.
36 Morley, *Family Television*, p. 9.
37 Gadamer, *Truth and Method*, p. 92.
38 Ricoeur, 'Hermeneutics and the Critique of Ideology', p. 94. A concept of 'identification' similar to that of a process constituted by movement between the role of audience and a role marked out in the text is discussed by Metz. For Metz, spectators assume that individuals in a film share their own criteria of rational thought and action. It is on this basis that they make sense of the action, using 'all the schemata of intelligibility' that they have within them. But it is by acknowledging difference, not 'taking myself for him', 'that the fiction can be established as such' and the audience 'returns to the real' *(Psychoanalysis and Cinema*, p. 57). The account of 'identification' given by Poulet is not unlike Metz's analysis. This is discussed by Freund in her *Return of the Reader*. The 'I' with which I identify 'is not myself'. In reading 'there has to be a thinking subject with whom, at least for the time being, I identify, forgetting myself, alienated from myself'; implied here is the eventual return to the role of a member of the audience (p. 138).
39 Gadamer, *Truth and Method*, p. 92.
40 Ricoeur, 'Appropriation', *Hermeneutics and the Human Sciences*, p. 190.
41 O'Brien, p. 8.
42 Ibid.
43 Schroder, 'The Pleasure of *Dynasty*', p. 73.
44 Ibid., p. 15.
45 Gadamer, *Truth and Method*, p. 99.
46 Bordwell, *Narration in the Fiction Film*, p. 25.
47 Sharrock and Watson, 'Autonomy among Social Theories', *passim*.
48 MacCabe, 'Theory and Film', p. 12.
49 Davies, 'The Television Audience Revisited', pp. 90, 91.
50 Harré and Secord, *The Explanation of Social Behaviour*, pp. 5–6, 70. Harré's work is of particular use here because of its detailed philosophical account of 'role', 'rule' and so on, concepts central to my argument. He

provides an analytical treatment of ideas whose source is the phenomenological philosophy of Husserl and Schutz.

51   Ibid, p. 208.
52   Winch, *The Idea of a Social Science*, p. 52.
53   Houston, 'Viewing Television', p. 151.
54   Branigan, *Point of View in the Cinema*, p. 9.
55   Davies, 'The Television Audience Revisited', p. 91.
56   Caughie, 'Rhetoric, Pleasure and "Art Television"', p. 20.
57   Ricoeur, 'Hermeneutics and the Critique of Ideology', p. 75.
58   Ibid., pp. 75–6.
59   Benton, *Rise and Fall of Structural Marxism*, p. 44.
60   Hall et al., 'The "Unity" of Current Affairs Television', p. 89.
61   Willemen, 'Notes on Subjectivity', p. 59.
62   Paterson, 'Restyling Masculinity', p. 219.
63   Iser, *The Act of Reading*, pp. 35, 37.
64   S. Johnston, 'Film Narrative and the Structuralist Controversy', p. 245.
65   Morley, 'The *Nationwide* Audience', p. 3.
66   Hebdige and Hurd, 'Reading and Realism', p. 75.
67   S. Johnston, 'Film Narrative and the Structuralist Controversy', p. 245.
68   Press, 'Class and Gender in the Hegemonic Process', p. 27.
69   Iser, *The Act of Reading*, p. 22.
70   Buckingham, *Public Secrets*, p. 60.
71   This use of 'active' in respect of the reader of dominant film or television
     undermines the opposition which structuralism posed between the passive
     spectator of the classic realist text and the active audience of an anti-realist
     cinema. This opposition, for instance, is implied in the analysis of Straub-
     Huillet's *History Lessons* to the effect that 'the reader has to construct the
     text instead of vice-versa' (Hebdige and Hurd, 'Reading and Realism',
     p. 73).
72   Morley, *The 'Nationwide' Audience*, pp. 143–4.
73   Buckingham, *Public Secrets*, p. 169.
74   Barwise and Ehrenberg, 'Television as a Medium', p. 2. See also their
     Television and Its Audience.
75   Ellis, *Visible Fictions*, p. 163.
76   Althusser, *Essays on Ideology*, p. 56.
77   Chambers et al., 'Marxism and Culture', p. 116.
78   Willemen, 'Notes on Subjectivity', p. 45.
79   Hall et al., 'The "Unity" of Current Affairs Television', p. 116.
80   Lovell, 'Ideology and *Coronation Street*', p. 49.
81   L. Williams, 'Feminist Film Theory', p. 29.
82   MacCabe, 'Theory and Film', pp. 24–5.
83   Fiske, *'Critical Response'*, p. 240.
84   Silverstone, 'Let Us Then Return', p. 85.
85   Morley, 'Texts, Readers, Subjects', p. 165.
86   Gadamer, *Truth and Method*, p. 414.
87   Habermas, 'A Review of Gadamer's *Truth and Method*', p. 360.
88   Willemen, 'Notes on Subjectivity', p. 47.
89   Brewster et al., 'Reply', p. 115.

3

Audiences : Constructions of Sense

The viewer's identification, I have been arguing, is with a character playing out a social role in a programme. Central to this process is a certain conformity by the viewer to rules, to rational forms of thought and action, and to understanding the world in a way which discloses its relevance to interests and needs generated by the role in question. As Eco indicates, every 'reception of a work of art is both an *interpretation* and a *performance* of it'.[1]

Identification involves, although is not reducible to, understanding the world in particular ways. Identification with the presenter of a travel documentary, for instance, can bring with it the pleasures of looking at a changing environment. But it is also (necessarily) associated with understanding those surroundings in ways appropriate to someone in the role of 'tourist' or 'explorer'. In this chapter I would like to examine the relationship between 'identification' and the forms of 'understanding' which it presupposes and generates.

In earlier chapters I indicated that the viewer's attempts to understand a programme provided a basis for identification with presenters or characters similarly pursuing a search for intelligibility. Section 3.1 examines the nature of viewing activity further, and section 3.2 suggests examples of this 'intellectualist' pattern of identification.

'Identification' however, is associated with the construction of meaning in more complex ways. Viewers have experiences other than watching television and trying to make sense of programmes. Section 3.3 discusses the possibilities of identification and interpretation which rely on dimensions of living beyond viewing television.

3.1 Watching Television

The segmented, interrupted text of television belongs to the everyday, to a daily routine where programmes are accommodated in a context of intermittent audience attention. The unfinished nature of a soap opera episode, characteristic of television's aesthetic practices, is frequently referred to as a text's construction of enigma. But such a description leaves open the question of the 'real' viewer's response to this feature of television programmes.

An enigma operates as an invitation to the reader to engage in a hermeneutic activity of sense construction analogous to that occurring in the programme. But it does not determine such a response (for the reader may always refuse to engage in delivering meaning to the text). Nor does the experience of indeterminacy created by the unfinished nature of an episode exclude the reader's experience of the text at other moments as indeterminate in meaning in other ways (for example, because he or she has missed part of the programme). To fail to note this is to repeat the essentialist mistakes associated with structuralism. 'The suspicion of essentialism arises whenever the study of the production or of the structure of literary texts is pursued at the expense of their reception'.[2]

The theory of textual meaning which I have been considering needs to be developed in the direction of the audience. This further theorizing will consist of a more extended examination of how a reader assembles a coherent and unified meaning for a programme. The viewer not only constructs a particular sense out of available textual evidence, arranging events as a series of causes and effects, but also 'maps out' a diegetic (or mimetic) space and time in which those events take place. Like the anthropological translator, the reader is likely to operate a principle of interpretative charity and assume he or she is confronting a coherent whole, the programme.[3] But under conditions of a dominant hegemony of thinking which can never be reconciled with how things are, the everyday reader is also likely to be prepared for uneasy pleasures, pleasures suffused by the awareness of emerging contradiction between television's images and worldly experience.

In this section I shall develop further a hermeneutic theory of the audience, providing an account which, while a priori, applies to all but the reader determined not to make sense of a text. In articulating this theory I refer to the work of the philosophers Gadamer and Ricoeur and the response theorists Iser and Jauss. Later in the chapter this hermeneutic account of the viewer is developed from the point of view of the 'real' reader's response to the text, his or her reading of the enigmas encountered by its subjects. The hermeneutic circle is a description of how people read, rather than how they ought to read.

The hermeneutic theory of the television viewer is prefigured by Elsaesser's account of the cinema spectator in his article 'Narrative Cinema and Audience-oriented Aesthetics'. Elsaesser argues for film spectating as an active process of generating meaning, often on the basis of generically inspired expectations as to what will occur in the text and how it will be represented: 'no film ... encounters a "neutral" audience, but a tissue of expectations and potential stimuli-responses'.[4]

For Elsaesser, the reader's activity is one of establishing a coherent text or, at a more specific level, a consistent account of a sequence of actions occupying a limited space and time (for example, a journey, a meal, a conversation). Expectations of consistency may even concern the relationship between image and music, or assume a non-contradictory relationship will obtain between image and commentary: 'it is the endeavour towards "consistent readings" within the fictional framework (an endeavour heavily relying on recognition) that provides the basis for stimulating active participation'.[5]

According to Elsaesser, the spectator anticipates likely events in the film (as well as how they are represented) after recognizing the presence within it of structures and patterns of textual activity which he or she has encountered previously. 'Recognition in the cinema . . . can take a variety of forms . . . all of which in their different ways and on different levels of intellectual sophistication create a matrix of expectations and anticipatory projections coexisting and fusing with the more primary matrix of the viewing situation itself.'[6] These anticipations may of course be disappointed or their fulfilment continuously postponed.

A similar, if much fuller, account of the spectator's active generation of filmic meaning is provided by Bordwell. For Bordwell, in the process of viewing a narrative film the audience produces the *fabula* or story from a series of 'cues' within the text itself. These cues constitute the film's *syuzhet*, their mode of presentation in the *mise en scène* resulting in the film's 'style'. Narration 'is the process whereby the film's syuzhet and style interact in the course of cueing and channelling the spectator's construction of fabula'.[7]

For Bordwell, therefore, the film's story exists in the mind of the spectator, constructed from 'cues, patterns and gaps' in the text. The audience brings its knowledge and experience to the film in an active viewing process involving 'the testing of hypotheses'. This is a cognitive strategy which can be described as 'hypothetico-deductive', the imaginative construction and subsequent evaluation of hypotheses in an attempt to ascertain the development of the story. (The strategy is not, as Bordwell asserts, 'plainly inductive', for this term refers to the derivation of universal laws from particular instances.)[8]

Bordwell's argument is that in developing the meaning of the film the audience draws on a wide range of past knowledge, both of a filmic and non-filmic character, which allows it to generate assumptions about how the story will develop. (Filmic knowledge includes an awareness of 'prototype schemata' or genre.) Reading the text is, *inter alia*, the activity of checking these assumptions, confirming, refining or rejecting them in the process of building a unified and sequential account of the contents of the film, the *fabula*. Spectatorship consists, that is, in the active construction of a textual unity often through the speculative addition of information to a film, information whose truth is later confirmed in the narrative process itself. As with perceptual experience in general, the more films seen, the more sophisticated these anticipations: 'one's perceptual and conceptual abilities become . . . supple and nuanced'.[9]

When analysing the varieties of coherence within a text, Bordwell refers to the idea of an 'action sequence' which appears to function for him as a unit of meaning in terms of which gestures, words and deeds can be related and further defined. Constructing a meaningful text

> involves an effort toward unity . . . the viewer must test the narrative information for consistency: does it hang together in a way we can identify? For instance, does a series of gestures, words, and manipulations of objects add up to the action sequence we know as 'buying a loaf of bread'? The viewer also finds unity by looking for relevance, testing each event for its pertinence to the action which the film (or scene, or character action) seems to be basically setting forth.[10]

The structures of perceiving a film are a particular instance of perceiving generally. Identifying objects within or outside a filmic text presupposes the non-conscious application to perception of cognitive frameworks which allow recognition to occur. Objects in the audience's life-world are generally defined and understood in terms of their use: likewise in a film, objects are 'read' by the spectator or subject in terms of their relevance to the project of constructing coherent sense. 'The spectator shares in the characters' battle for a solution to the mystery.'

Bordwell's analysis is of the narrative film, yet his account could be extended to the non-narrative or, as I describe it in Chapter 4, 'mimetic' film, which foregrounds description rather than narration. In the mimetic text (such as documentary), its genre and title set up a range of expectations concerning the detail which will be communicated to the spectator in an accomplished and completed reading.

The Elsaesser and Bordwell analysis of film spectatorship is of an active looking, a discussion of what they consider to be the 'real' audience who brings knowledge to the text. It is not an account of an ideal spectator implied by the processes of narration (or description). If this thesis of an active reader is appropriate for the cinema, then it is an even more likely account of a television audience. For its modes of viewing, as I have indicated, are much less fixed by the text than the cinematic spectator's gaze at the screen.

Texts, argues Bennett, 'exist only as variable pieces of play within the processes through which the struggle for their meaning is socially enacted'.[11] A thesis of textuality with its construction in reading as a species of 'play' is to be found in phenomenologically oriented literary theory. De Man writes of 'understanding as a complex interplay between knowing and not-knowing'.[12] Similarly, Jauss refers approvingly to Rifaterre's account of 'the reception of a poem as the play of anticipation and correction' and regards it as more properly applicable to narrative texts.[13]

Likewise, a hermeneutic theory of the television audience can draw on Gadamer's analysis of theatrical spectatorship as 'play' to develop an account of the relationship between text and viewer in which the latter is active in the resolution of enigma. Faced with uncertainties of plot development, the reader 'plays' with the television programme, anticipating a coherent construction of meaning and fulfilling its production in a range of different reading strategies. The processes of play involved here are such that

> every revision of the fore-project is capable of projecting before itself a new project of meaning, that rival projects can emerge side by side until it becomes clearer what the unity of meaning is, that interpretation begins with fore-conceptions that are replaced by more suitable ones. This constant process of new projection is the movement of understanding and interpretation . . .
>
> The working-out of appropriate projects, anticipatory in nature, to be confirmed 'by the things' themselves, is the constant task of understanding.[14]

In this playful anticipation and checking of developments in the text the audience completes its meaning. For both television programme and dramatic artefact, 'openness towards the spectator is part of the closedness of the play . . . the play itself is the whole, comprising players and spectators . . . [In the spectator] the game is raised, as it were, to its perfection'.[15] The television viewer is a rule-governed player moving back and forth across a programme, attempting to relate the sense of individual parts to an overall meaning for the whole: 'the movement of understanding is constantly from the whole to the part and back to the whole. Our task is to extend in concentric circles the unity of the understood meaning.'[16] The playful engagement of audience with televisual or dramatic text both passively conforms to and constructively interprets this hermeneutic circle of understanding in ways which will vary from reading to reading. To play is to be limited and to limit. On the one hand, play exerts a 'primacy' 'over the consciousness of the player'.[17] But on the other, in establishing a meaning for the text, the player exerts a 'freedom of decision, which at the same time is endangered and irrevocably limited'.[18] Here the audience 'represents' itself (Gadamer): for this freedom of aesthetic choice means that 'the game presents itself, plays itself; but it also means that we present ourselves in it'.[19] The cognitive processes associated with the hermeneutic circle of understanding may relate an indeterminacy of sense to its resolution in a segment of text, or that segment to the wider programme or story itself. This hermeneutic structure sets goals and motives for those in the particular game of understanding meaning: 'play has its own essence independent of the consciousness of those who play'.[20] 'The harmony of all the details with the whole is the criterion of correct understanding.'[21] Where the text does not conform to this 'presupposition of completion', it may be that 'understanding has failed' or that we should 'start to doubt the transmitted text'.[22]

Like the festival, television has 'its being only in becoming and in return'.[23] Forms of television can be distinguished hermeneutically. The viewer of a weekly series with a narrative which 'closes' at the end of each episode simultaneously completes the sense of an episode, text and story. But in the serial, attempts to assemble sense for the weekly text are likely to be complicated by its episodic status, requiring a certain attention to be paid to other instalments. As a *Coronation Street* viewer puts it, 'I've got to watch again to find out, you know, what is going to happen, what's she gonna do, is Brian gonna go back, and I hate it when you read in the paper, if they put it in before it happens.'[24] While a meaning can be established for each episode of a serial, an absence of indeterminacies in its reading may only be established retrospectively with the conclusion of the story.

The account of viewing proposed here relies on the idea of the audience's perceiving 'indeterminacies' (Iser) of meaning. An (empirical) viewer finds an indeterminacy of meaning in a text when she or he finds it marked by an absence of information, a semiotic process in some way incomplete. This awareness may bear with it a kind of aesthetic or moral judgement, a belief that given the genre to which the programme belongs, providing such information would have been appropriate.

The presence of enigma and attempts at its solution in the text may constitute an opportunity for the television viewer to identify with a particular subject. But, as I noted earlier in this chapter, a 'real' member of a television audience, with his or her 'wandering viewpoint' (Iser), may find other aspects of the text difficult to comprehend, other absences of meaning. (For instance, someone who begins watching a programme after it has started.) This experience of indeterminate sense will have no echo in the experience of subjects in the text and hence it cannot function as the basis for identification. The enigma-resolving knowledge provided by an 'omniscient' textual subject will not remove these uncertainties. The viewer's experience of such absences of desired information or 'blanks' (Iser) is his or her experience of 'indeterminacies' of meaning.

I shall use the term 'enigma' as a tool of analysis to refer to an absence of information at a point in a text where this contributes to its preferred reading by an ideal reader. 'Indeterminacies' of meaning, however, are experienced by 'real' readers puzzled by a lack of information in the text, whether or not that 'puzzlement' is part of its preferred reading. The distinction between 'enigma' and 'indeterminacy' marks a distinction between the theoretical concept of the 'ideal' reader of a text and the 'real' reader of experience. Only the real reader can produce and experience indeterminacies of meaning, mediated readings of the text's enigmas and uncertainties. Indeterminacy is an absence of meaning in the audience's understanding of the programme.

The viewer's projection of meaning over the indeterminacies in the text is his or her construction or concretization of a story.[25] This is an actualizing of meaning which may begin with the continuity announcements preceding the programme. Underlying the process of interaction with the text is 'an indeterminate, constitutive blank . . . which is continually bombarded with projections' so that it is 'the very lack of ascertainability and defined intention that brings about the text–reader interaction'.[26] In anticipating solutions to 'blanks', understanding is (so to speak) always ahead of itself. It brings to bear on the text retentions of general awareness from past viewing experience, projecting in turn a 'protensive' anticipation of the future. Viewing a particular segment or element of text occurs within a holistic experience of television, 'a *Gestalt*, a whole which is prior to these elements, and determines their sense as they determine each other reciprocally'.[27] Projections of sense depend for their very possibility upon a textual content which prompts a minimal recognition on the part of the audience.

The viewer's relationship with a programme is characterized not only by the work of overcoming the gaps in its meaning, but by a reading practice which is itself responsible for assigning indeterminacies of sense to the text in the first place. Strictly speaking, indeterminacies, the preoccupation of the real audience, exist not in the text but in the text as it is read by the viewer. Indeterminacies are the product of particular audience strategies. An implicit and unexamined consensus on these strategies among readers will produce an agreement on indeterminacies whose existence in the text may for this reason appear self-evident.

Indeterminacies in televisual discourse are functions of an audience's readings of individuals' speeches, of segments and episodes, where a perceived absence of information can exert a profound influence on how the viewer establishes a text's economy of meaning. The relation of viewer to programme may be regarded as analogous to an individual's relationship to everyday conversation. The discourses of both television text and familiar speech are experienced as 'gappy'. The work of a reader or participant in conversation who attempts to understand these discourses is constituted in substantial ways by the task of removing these gaps through further questioning and interpretation of the 'response'. As Gadamer indicates, 'the dialectic of question and answer . . . makes understanding appear as a reciprocal relationship of the same kind as conversation'.[28] Both contain a set of questions formulated to guide the projection of a coherent meaning.

Like conversation, the process of coming to understand a programme has both passive and active aspects. 'The process of becoming mastered by the conversation is the process of understanding through which interpretation and application unfold as the conversation progresses.'[29] But unlike the conversational situation, the television text must be read by the viewer *as if* it were producing a response to his or her questions rather than (for the most part) engaging in an actual response to a known empirical audience.

The dialectic of question and 'answer' supporting the construction of a determinate meaning for a text is centred on the reading situation of the viewer. As I observed above, the circumstances of watching films and television are generally different; television's transmission of texts is such that, unlike film, some viewers may not have seen earlier episodes of a serial. They may as a result note indeterminacies and puzzles in the text which are not an aspect of its preferred reading. The 'story so far', the information normally provided at the beginning of the second and consecutive episodes of a serial, can be read as an attempt at preventing the experience of indeterminacy other than that articulated as enigma in the text's preferred reading.

Nevertheless, the experience of indeterminacies of sense which would be difficult to accommodate in a preferred reading does occur. For this reason at least it is often not the case that 'segments each make sense by themselves'.[30] In a useful collection of articles on 'factual' television, *Documentary and the Mass Media*, Corner and Richardson examine audience reactions to *A Fair Day's Fiddle*, a documentary about social security recipients broadcast on BBC2 in March 1984. Many viewers, apparently, were puzzled by a large pile of toys wrapped and stacked up in one little boy's bedroom: 'this speculation suggests a need to *make* sense of something which lacks a *given* sense . . . The possible "explanations" are all underdetermined textually – including the nonrealist explanation that the arrangement of the toys was at the request of the production team.'[31]

Here the television text contained indeterminacies into which the viewers attempted to read meaning. But as Corner and Richardson indicate, the truth of each of these projections of meaning remained unconfirmed by evidence in the programme. It is difficult to read this experience of indeterminacy as one of 'enigma' belonging to the preferred reading of the text, for the viewers' reaction to it only distracted their attention from the questions the text was raising. It disturbed rather than produced the experience of identification, of the apparently unmediated involvement with the events of a programme which the presence of enigma is designed to encourage. The effect of the indeterminacies in *A Fair Day's Fiddle* was rather to produce 'nonrealist' speculation among the audience, speculation which presupposed an awareness of the text as text. This conjecture consisted of explaining 'the arrangement of the toys' in terms which relied on regarding the programme as a televisual construction, an artefact manufactured by producer and director.

With such conjecture the play of 'the reader's continual oscillation between involvement and observation' is suspended. On occasions such as these, a programme has resisted its audience's narratival projections of meaning, producing in the process a detached consideration of its discourse. Under these circumstances, even where involvement occurs, it is likely to be ironically aware of itself as relying on the artifice of television: 'the observer finds himself in a strange, halfway position: he is involved, and he watches himself being involved'.[32]

Projections of meaning need not be future oriented. They can equally function retrodictively, as rereadings of parts of the text already viewed. Corner and Richardson note audience reactions to a remark about advertising made by someone in the programme : 'it doesn't ask me to purchase the product, it dares me not to purchase the product'. This remark leads the audience to reread a sequence of the text already viewed, a sequence involving the individual in question : 'the argument about advertising can be read back into the circumstances of the previous participants'.[33]

As already noted, a frequent mode of attention in television viewing is that of the 'glance' rather than the 'gaze'. Consequently, it is unsurprising that aspects or even whole segments of a television text are never seen by the viewer, creating a series of uncertainties and indeterminacies which are not part of its preferred reading. The concept of 'indeterminacy', marking as it does a distinction between intended and real viewers, allows the theorizing of a more active role for the audience in establishing the meaning of a television programme. The experience of frequent and wide-ranging indeterminacies produces the reader as co-author of a text which is 'open' to new meaning, rather than a text which engages in 'pulling the reader along a predetermined path'.[34]

Television analysis, argues Fiske, has to move away from regarding a text as the expression of a dominant ideology exerting 'considerable' control over its reading. Rather, the audience contributes substantially to the meaning of a programme in ways which draw on the experience of everyday living : 'analysis has to pay less attention to the textual strategies of preference or closure and more to the gaps and spaces that open television up to meanings not preferred by the textual structure, but that result from the social experience of the reader'.[35]

A hermeneutic theory of the audience asserts that while viewers are watching television they are actively engaged in a range of subjective processes which in general terms can be described as follows :

1 the production of a determinate and unified meaning for the programme being viewed, where what is to count as 'determinate' rests on, among other factors, the viewer's understanding of the programme's genre and form ;
2 when indeterminacies of meaning are experienced, viewers construct a hypothetical occurrence or state of affairs, usually within the time and space of the programme, to overcome ('negate') the lack of information ;
3 the subsequent relationship with the programme – or in the case of the serial, with future programmes – is inflected by the viewer's cognitive interest in the accuracy of the hypothetical meanings and processes he or she has projected within the text. This interest is capable of producing involvement and identification with subjects.

Clearly these are abstract principles of sense construction, established through a wide range of reading practices displaying different degrees of thoroughness and attention to detail. Television is used in a variety of ways 'according to who we are and how we feel at a particular time. In one night, an individual may experience both the "joys of slumping" *and* the pleasures of closely following a personal favourite.'[36] The hermeneutic circle of meaning construction, the construction of readings which are coherent, finds detailed embodiment in a variety of viewing practices among an audience: 'recollecting past events which they have seen; imagining ones which they have not; hypothesising about future events; testing and adapting these hypotheses in the light of new information; drawing inferences, particularly about the characters' unstated emotions and desires.'[37]

In this theorizing of a 'television audience' which is active in its everyday viewing, I am drawing on the work of the phenomenologist and literary theorist Iser. Whatever Iser's concern with 'high culture',[38] in a passage which might have applied to everyday television he writes that what 'is missing from the apparently trivial scenes, the gaps arising out of the dialogue – this is what stimulates the reader into filling the blanks with projections ... Whenever the reader bridges the gaps, communication begins.'[39] The spectator's hermeneutic or interpretative activity is not fundamentally initiated by what is present in his or her field of vision. Rather, it is directed by 'indeterminacies', 'absences', 'blanks', by what that spectator does not find in the text. 'A powerful myth of coherence compels us to make sense of gaps and indeterminacies.'[40] An aspect of television's specificity is that it allows these gaps to appear both in and between segments and episodes, as well as in breaks for advertising.

Reading is directed at accomplishing a meaningful unity of sense for the text. The processes of interpretation which constitute and develop this coherence of meaning may be performed either by the individual or through discussion in a group (perhaps a family). Establishing a sense for the text both inflects and is inflected by the reader's understanding of its relevance. Any use to which a text is put by its viewers, any satisfaction of their need to be entertained, distracted or informed, presupposes that they have produced a meaning within its limits and organization. Equally, the construction of meaning cannot but be shaped by the use-value which an audience discerns the programme as possessing.

The need to ascertain the validity of his or her projections of meaning ranks alongside the processes of identification with characters as a fundamental aspect of the relationship between viewer and programme. Projections represent the audience's operations upon what it considers the empty times and spaces, the absences, in the text. This work draws the viewer into the life-worlds of the serial or series. It is a process of active response to the text which positions viewers cognitively in respect of its events, often aligning them as I have noted, with a textual subject.

Here, philosophical theory can be integrated with empirical analysis. *Watching You Watching Us* (ITV, 7.00, 6.4.87) was a UK programme of discussions and video extracts showing audience behaviour which set out to establish viewers' experiences while watching soap opera. At one point a viewer admits to a compulsive concern with the events of a continuous serial: 'I think it's 'cos it finishes and you've gotta think, well what's going to happen next, you've gotta watch it next time.' A viewer of the Australian soap opera *Sons and Daughters* refers to the same hermeneutic process of projecting a possible content for a programme, with her interest in the accuracy of this speculation allowing her to perceive the subsequent episode as a source of verification: 'I wouldn't miss *Sons and Daughters* if I could help it, because the story holds me. It always ends on a note that you are wondering where the next programme's going ... That makes a person want to switch it on.'[41]

Viewing, as I indicated above, is 'play', an active employment of rules and evidence. For Ricoeur, in the 'to and fro' movement of play 'whoever plays is also played: the rules of the game impose themselves upon the player, prescribing the to and fro and delimiting the field where everything "is played"'.[42] On the one hand, the 'rules of the game' of viewing a television programme prescribe for the audience the manner of its engaging in the cognitive movements of projecting a sense for the text, an anticipating and checking of possible readings which is guided by pre-textual knowledge. On the other hand, readers are active players: 'we play with a project', assembling an account of programme content.

The anticipation of building a generically appropriate completeness of narrative is a fundamental cognitive framework through which the viewer experiences a programme: 'people like to know in advance something is going to happen, but what they want to do is to turn the set on and see actually how it's going to happen. That's the excitement of it' (Laurie Taylor in *Watching You Watching Us*, ITV, 7.00, 6.4.87). A soap opera's hold on viewers may weaken after they have produced what they regard as a unified and final reading of a story.

The content a reader anticipates assembling in the case of a particular television programme depends on his or her knowledge of the genre or programme type to which he or she believes the text belongs. Sometimes television offers an easy hermeneutics. Barwise and Ehrenberg point out that the viewer with a thorough experience of programme types may be able accurately to predict the conclusion of a particular text without viewing it: in this context 'we seldom ask afterwards what happened'.[43]

Viewing occurs upon a 'substrate of habitualities' (Husserl). The distinction between serial and series can be understood as a difference not only between texts but between expectations on the part of the audience based on past experience. Weekly episodes of series, unlike serials, can be reliably anticipated to allow the viewer to 'realize' completeness, an ending. The projection of meaning in a text draws on acquired horizons of expectation: 'in each experience, [understanding] functions simultaneously as implicit pro-ject and as retro-spect'.[44]

The audience's expectation of finding determinate, intelligible stories in a serial or series imposes, if it is to be rewarded, a formal constraint on the programme. To be read with pleasure a soap opera, for instance, must provide information which allows the viewer to exercise his or her capacity to assemble recognizably determinate stories. In Channel Four's 'progressive' soap opera *Brookside*, these are the stories of the death of Harry Cross's wife, the collapse of the relationship between Heather Haversham (Amanda Burton) and her husband or (subsequently) a lover, the death of Sheila Grant's son and so on.

A documentary series may use the opening voiceover in each episode both to construct the central enigma with which it is concerned and to issue the promise of information which will allow the audience to resolve that enigma and produce a unified programme: 'exposition usually makes a tacit proposal to the viewer as part of its contract negotiations: the invocation of, and promise to gratify a desire to know. Its beginning proposes an ending; inauguration signifies closure.'[45]

Much television drama allows formally determinate stories to be assembled. Teleology precedes causality in the provision of meaning; the text is constructed to allow the intended audience to establish a narrative. As Silverstone points out, production processes are substantially determined by the perceived needs of the 'completed and final text' (a completion thought of as attained without the contribution of the viewer): 'the completed and final text is a major element in the constraints on production before a frame has been shot or a sound recorded'.[46]

But there are exceptions, and not only in US television's experimentally inclined *Hill Street Blues*. *Intimate Contact* (ITV, 9.00, 9.3.87.–30.3.87) is about a business executive, Clive Gregory (Daniel Massey), who, in the words of the *TV Times*, 'returns home from a lengthy trip abroad – when he is taken ill, the results of the hospital tests bring shattering news'. In the fourth and final episode, Gregory 'bravely faces death', finally succumbing to AIDS. His funeral provides a vantage point from which his life-story can be 'read' by his wife, Ruth (Claire Bloom), and the viewer as a finally terminated process of melancholy events and family melodrama.

But the programme continues after Gregory's death, ending only when Ruth, along with her 'new friends', confronts public opinion, 'helping to stop another wave of cruelty and ignorance from destroying another victim of the same disease'. In a school hall she argues against a large group of parents who demand that Fraser (Scott Funnell), a small boy who contracted the AIDS virus as a result of a blood transfusion, is banished from classes; 'Look, we're not hard, we're not monsters, but it's our own kids we're talking about.'

In the closing moments of the serial Ruth Gregory and her friends, having briefly left the hall to allow the parents to discuss the issue by themselves, go back to find out what they have decided. Her words bring this short serial to an end: 'Everyone look optimistic as though we're expecting to win.' In this new 'story', a barely commenced tale of a young child with the AIDS virus, the audience learns only the beginning. The enigma of Ruth's campaign and its success or failure is left unresolved. That 'story' will remain uncompleted by the viewer.

3.2 Viewers and Varieties of Meaning

The viewer's identification is with a subject occupying a textual position, a discursively elaborated matrix of roles, rules and horizons of understanding. This section examines the way television texts articulate characters, presenters and social roles with which an audience can identify. For texts frequently place their subjects in roles associated with a foregrounding of the hermeneutic activities of sense construction referred to in the last section. These roles permit the viewer, engaged in a similar construction of meaning, to identify with the textual subject concerned. However, as I explain below, identification may draw on other experience as well as that of reading. It may involve the audience in re-viewing its life-worlds through new narratives.

Television rarely offers to its viewers an experience of the unmediated 'difficult'. In drama, for example, at least one of the central characters often has a role of sense-building, of understanding and presenting events to form an intelligible and coherent whole. Here the viewers can acknowledge similarity, recognizing that both they and a subject in the text are engaged upon the hermeneutic task of 'completing a meaning', solving an enigma or removing an absence of information. *Thin Air* (BBC1, 9.30, 8.4.88–6.5.88), for instance, was a short serial about corruption in London's dockland developments. The role of news reporter 'played' by Rachel Hamilton (Kate Hardie) allowed the viewers to identify with a hermeneutic quest for sense. She is 'drawn', like the reader, into attempting to 'read' a complex 'web' of political intrigue, 'a web of drug dealers, corrupt financiers and local activists spawned by the riverside development boom' (*Radio Times*, 15.4.88). Both her role and that of the viewers are constituted by a process of coming to understand the political tensions of the area. The inevitable difference between them is that the viewers' insights are constrained from time to time by realizing that, unlike Rachel Hamilton, they are dealing with a text. But otherwise, as far as the intended audience is concerned, it is offered 'a moving viewpoint which travels *inside* that which it has to apprehend'.[47]

More generally, television reporters and newsreaders both interpret the 'difficult' in terms of the familiar and occupy the position of the professionally knowledgeable. This is a social expression of the hermeneutic role of the successfully inquisitive, a social role which allows for reader identification.

Television's representation of human activity may be regarded as an audio-visual discourse whereby goal-directed behaviour, whose rules are recognized by the viewer, can be inscribed in the text, providing the basis for identification. Here, activity which solves problems, issuing in the solution of an enigma, is seen by the viewer to follow the same logic to that required for his or her construction of a meaningful text. In *To the End of the Rhine* (C4, 6.30, 17.10.87–21.11.87, and later on SBS) Bernard Levin's

2   Bernard Levin in *To the End of the Rhine*

search for a coherent sense and understanding of the cultural environment of the river 'mirrors' the reader's pursuit of a coherent text and is governed by similar rules of problem solving.

The viewer who identifies with Levin can subsequently move back and forth from the role of 'inquiring tourist' to that of 'reader of a text'. Levin's frequent use of deictics universalizes the subjective experience of his 'authored' documentary, assuming identification. 'We would simply drown' in a 'concentrated treatment' of Wagner, he informs us in the first episode. Schubert's music is 'unrivalled' 'for the truths it tells us about the human condition'. But while the text must remain an object for those in the role of its reader to understand, the Rhine's identity for Levin is ultimately revealed as a fellow subject, a 'friend'. Drawing the past into a present shared by himself and the viewer, Levin concludes his investigations : 'When I started this journey, as the first trickle came down the Swiss mountainside, the Rhine was my hero. He is still my hero [pause] but now he's my friend as well.'[48]

For an audience to identify with Levin is for it to appropriate his role of cultural inquirer. This is to 'commute' from reading the culture of a text to investigating the culture of a river. But, as I noted in the last chapter, appropriation of a role is the discovery of difference as well as similarity. Even the ideal viewer must recognize this difference, for otherwise he or she would be identical with an aspect of the text, losing that separation which is the fundamental condition of being an audience. The 'playing' of a subject's role by an extra-textual subject, the reader, must be unstable, continually subject to 'interference' and challenge.

Levin 'manages' the role of inquisitive tourist differently. His discursive occupancy of this role draws on both sides of the opposition between private celebration of interests and public realization of duty and work. It is a role elaborated here in a self-fulfilling mission to display the standards belonging to a particular, if widely shared, definition of 'civilization'. Levin visits the art galleries and attacks popular culture. He has distinctive 'insights'; for instance, 'the vain yearning for things not achieved, for these I find solace in Franz Schubert's music' (21.11.87).

In general terms, the problems and speculations involved in fulfilling the role of reading a text and finding it meaningful provide an experiential basis for identifying with similar problem-solving roles in the text itself. The viewers' pleasures of 'escapism' are consequent, paradoxically, upon recognition of a textual role as similar to that they already inhabit as members of an audience, a recognition through which they align themselves with a textual subject. To reread a remark in the *TV Times* by Redmond, the executive producer of Channel Four's *Brookside*: 'they do say that escapism is watching someone else do your job'. Where the audience takes up the position of a character, this 'kind of being present is a self-forgetfulness, and it is the nature of the spectator to give himself in self-forgetfulness to what he is watching'.[49]

Processes of identification in viewing a text are always articulated around (although not reducible to) the activity of sense-making. Arriving at an understanding of the text provides the reader with an experience fundamental to his or her ability to identify with intra-textual subjects. For their varied activity equally presupposes an attempt to understand the situations in which they find themselves. Projecting an interpretation of a situation and having it confirmed (or falsified) are not only implicit in the subject's understanding of an intra-textual world but present also in the reader's understanding of the text. In this way identification between viewer and subject is always premissed upon the shared experience of managing a hermeneutic role. In its most abstract form identification is not with a transcendentally conceived process of perceiving by the self (Metz's 'pure act of perception') but with a hermeneutic inquiring by another.

Here, identification can be described by using a set of distinctions suggested by the philosopher and linguist J. L. Austin.[50] When (textual) subjects engage in 'locutionary acts' (speak), in so doing they are also performing further 'illocutionary' actions. For they are providing information about their sense-making activity, their success or failure in the processes of coming to understand their surroundings. But this linguistic activity additionally has an effect on the (real) audience and as such is to be regarded as 'perlocutionary' action. It allows viewers to recognize the cognitive processes implied by these 'locutionary acts' as being similar to the cognitive processes employed in coming to understand the text, thereby enabling them to identify with the subjects concerned.

The desire and practice of reading to attain a coherent text, this 'passage' (Heath) of the audience through the narrative, is not gender specific. It functions as a basis for both male and female viewers to identify with an individual of either gender engaged on a similar cognitive quest within the text itself. Yet in her desire for a subject of identification, 'the woman spectator' watching the investigative male may well be 'stranded between two incommensurable entities, the gaze [of a male subject] and the image [of a female object]'.[51] Identifying with the former, she is trapped by the ideology of the latter.

But occupying the role of inquiring reader is not the only basis for identification. Other modes of identification have other foundations. Social roles responsible for a viewer's experience of problem solving are to be found beyond the immediate context of viewing. 'I mean, you know, it's an escapism. You switch on the telly and you forget your problems, and you concentrate on other problems, other people's problems' (interviewee, *Hotline*, SBS, 5.30, 27.10.91). Establishing a coherent sense for the events constituting the 'text' of a viewer's life allows an individual to identify with subjects engaged in similar activities in the programme itself.[52]

For both audience and character, what is important could be said to be involvement in an integrated flow of often concurrent narratives, private and public stories of domesticity, work or leisure.[53] Narratives of success can be regarded as 'units of meaning' where the achievement of anticipated goals defining those units (for example, a happy marriage) is sustained rather than disrupted. But often viewer identification is predicated upon experiencing narratives of failure and difficulty similar to those in the text: 'her marriage is not satisfactory, is it! . . . Well I can understand that, you see. Now *that* is a thing, when I'm listening to that, I think, "I can remember I used to be a bit like that." '[54] People 'explain in their letters that the reason they enjoy the serial [*Take the High Road*] is because they identify with the way of life in Glendarroch and recognise the problems experienced by the characters'.[55]

My argument is that the processes of identification in viewing a programme are always centred around sense-making. Identification may arise simply as a result of the work required from the audience to render the text intelligible. But the processes of identification are often more complex than this. The desire to establish sense in life itself may result in a similar framework of understanding and hermeneutic role being appropriated by both character and viewer. Here television, whether 'factual' or 'fictional', acts as a source of information on which the audience can base its assumptions about living: media use becomes 'constitutive of ongoing social interactions and relationships'.[56] Identification may move as a 'nomadic subjectivity' (Grossberg) from locating oneself with a subject on the basis of understanding a text to identifying with other characters on the basis of making sense of a life.

Viewers, that is, often use television's narratives to comment upon and come to understand events in their own lives, thereby providing themselves with a certain pleasure and perhaps relief: 'you can then say, "OK these people have got problems just like you. Or, funny things happen to them

just like you." But it's how they *deal* with them that makes the difference'
(*E Street* script editor interviewed on *Hotline*, SBS, 5.30, 27.20.91).

Viewers can identify with a character, permitting his or her perspective
on events to take root amid their own realities. Differences in lifestyle are
open to being reworked as similarities. A viewer can read meaning into a
text, while at the same time extracting out of it a unifying source of
significance for the not infrequently fragmentary moments of daily existence. Adapting a televisual narrative in this way, of course, may provide
only a transitory means of coming to terms with the world.

All identification involves sense-making, a shared involvement in the
processes of manufacturing a coherent 'unit of meaning' (story) out of the
events of a life, a programme or both. Identification is a relationship
between viewer and character or programme presenter, both of whom seek
an intelligible and non-contradictory meaning in what affects them and how
they are, in turn, responding. This is the case even where identification
between audience and character appears highly coloured by emotion. For
emotions are inalienably cognitive, never 'blind', but rather ways of
apprehending the world. Story building, therefore, can function as an
attempt to overcome indeterminacies in a life as well as a programme.

The processes of identification may lead to the distinction between the
diegetic and the extra-diegetic becoming blurred where audiences find that
the stories of one can be employed in the other. For one viewer the school
featured in the BBC's *Grange Hill* is so 'much like the school where I work
that I could write an episode from my experiences'.[57] A father watching the
Australian series/serial *A Country Practice* with his daughter tells her, 'all
you're going to learn is what you end up experiencing in your own lifetime
anyway'.[58] Another viewer responds in precisely this way to *Sons and
Daughters*: 'this is more the story of my life'. Or as a soap opera enthusiast
threatens her husband: 'Right! See, this happens to you if you don't pay
attention to me!'[59]

Identification with characters in soap opera can provide an audience with
narrative formulas upon which to base future action or insights into life.
These stories are used to generate a sense of normality, placing problems in
perspective:

J.R. tricks people. This is interesting because it is the only way to succeed.
I, for instance, am going to do the same thing myself. I am going to
accumulate money, acquire land and use my cunning.

I would say that somehow we enjoy it because the problems the Ewings
have evoke some of the dark secrets which exist in every family. I used to
say that my family was a zoo until I discovered that every family has
different animals but everybody has a zoo at home.[60]

A lot of the problems they experience [in *A Country Practice*], we have,
every character is believable and even some of the problems Shirly has
with Gabe I have had with my own daughter.[61]

To care about the world with a soap opera character is to identify with a form of sense-making through which events are rendered intelligible for both audiences and dramatic subject. Similar social roles, rationalities and relationships as well as shared perspectives of understanding will be played out in both the text and the lives of viewers. Events in the daily existence of the elderly people interviewed by Tulloch 'were firmly placed within a routine of organisation and caring' : 'similarly their favourite programmes were about professional organisation and caring. In that sense, soaps became part of their practical consciousness, their competence in caring or being cared for.'[62] More specifically, representations of caring in US television's *Cosby Show* can motivate caring in everyday life across the generations. Cliff Huxtable's parents, asserts a viewer, 'were just like my grandmother . . . If I just sent my grandmother a photograph or if I just sent her a letter, my grandmother would be the happiest person in the world.'[63] Clearly, this reader has not perceived the behaviour 'to excess' which disturbs identifications aligning an audience with the humour of situation comedy.

Meanings established in a programme may be reread, used by viewers to shed light on their own lives, producing a pleasurable significance which otherwise would be lacking. 'Respondents said, for instance, "the people in *The Dales* sometimes have problems that are like my own" and "it sometimes helps me to understand my own life" '.[64] Here, particularly, identification presupposes an experience of the text as realistic. Without this its meaning will not be read as 'referential', as applicable to the viewer's daily experience of living. However, Seiter et al. record the 'ability of experienced viewers to commute with considerable ease between a referential and a purely fictional reading'.[65] In the latter the audience self-consciously occupies the role of reader, and the textuality of the text (its fictionality, constructedness) becomes evident.

The patterns of similarity and difference constituting 'identification' are such that the narratives produced by readers to make sense of their lives as a consequence of identifying with a textual subject may be very different from those with which they are involved in the programme itself. News stories may be 'rewritten' by an audience, producing private rather than public meaning. A marriage within *Dallas* can enter the life-world of the viewer either as a story in which a lack (the husband) is overcome, or as a story in which a lack is created (loss of independence).

At this point a distinction may be made between the 'manifest' and 'latent' functions of a character's actions. (I use these terms in a sociological rather than psychological sense.) Apparently contributing to the preferred reading of a text (their manifest function), such activities may have a latent function for the viewer in allowing him or her to generate rather different narratives which provide a certain reconciliation with difficulties in life. So, for instance, a male viewer of the American *All My Children* established 'an analogy between Phoebe's disapproval of Ted and Hilary's affair and his own great aunt's severe standards in sexual matters – standards from which he himself and his girlfriend had suffered'.[66]

More generally, Hodge and Tripp note that Australian children watching *Prisoner: Cell Block H* adapt its stories to provide an interpretation of their subjective experience at school, allowing them a limited rebellion.[67] Likewise, Walkerdine shows how a male working-class viewer of *Rocky II* uses it as a basis from which to generate narratives guiding his own struggle 'against the system and *for* his children'. Watching is a process of active 'creation': this man wants 'to have the fight on continuous and instant replay forever, to live and triumph in that moment'.[68] These textually generated narratives of interpretation involve, in Tulloch's phrase, 'subcultural negotiations of power'.[69]

Myriad uses of television can be theorized as conforming to role-related needs and interests. For an audience to rewrite television narratives in a process of self-interpretation is for it to exercise its status as 'active', even in the case of a viewer entering hospital. 'So then all the *General Hospital* things that went on, that I had seen, sort of became real to me. I couldn't believe that I was in the hospital playing the part of a very, very sick man.'[70]

Fiske describes cases where identification results not only in new ways of making sense of the world for the audience but also in reconstructions of the text. Aborigines establish a novel kinship system for Rambo and in identifying with Indians in Westerns find the Indians' defeat at the hands of the white settlers less than inevitable. Here narratives of life are fed back into the text.[71]

Identification produced through sharing an experience of interpreting life, then, may occur despite what seem to be great differences between the viewer and subject concerned. As Hobson argues in her book on the soap opera *Crossroads*, 'differences in class or material possessions seem to be transcended in the realization that there are problems in everyday life which are common to all women and their families'.[72]

In his cross-cultural analysis of the *Dallas* viewer Massing notes how an 'older housewife sees in the "disparity between the splendid façade of the Ewings and their inner turmoil" a replica of her own situation . . . she is troubled to maintain a social front despite inner feelings of inadequacy and insecurity'.[73] Here identification continues to draw on a perception of similarity, though it is not easy to regard the problem-solving roles in the programme as echoing those in the woman's social experience. The similarity might be said to verge on the 'counterfactual', its recognition a consequence of this viewer's creative insights rather than resting on an obvious analogy between situations within and outside the text. The sentiment that, despite their many differences, both the Ewings and the 'older housewife' are faced with managing the role of the socially troubled is a product of the latter's work on the text. Her viewing involves a process of moving from one role to another, a process whose engine is desire, and whose consequence is the ability to 'explore other situations, other identities, other lives'.[74] This is the imaginative exploration of her problems by a member of the television audience, using the possibilities of solution to be found within another's experience. Such complex processes of identification imply at least a passing belief in the 'realism' of events in the programme.[75]

Identification accompanied by a rereading of television's narratives so that they apply to often very different conditions in the life of the audience is not restricted to television drama. Rath writes of the 1981 Italian news coverage of a little boy falling into an uncovered well in Vermicino, near Rome. 'For two days and two nights Italian television devoted three channels to uninterrupted reporting of the rescue work which failed . . . Significantly it happened at a time of national political–economic crisis . . . "Saving the child" also meant saving one's own way of life.'[76]

Identification, then, often has a complex and multiple basis in role management. It may be produced not only from the subject's and reader's fundamental experience of establishing coherent meaning in the text but from the involvement of each in following a wide range of other rule-governed practices. Identification with a subject is frequently on the basis that both are incumbents, at one and the same time, of a set of roles (investigator, father, tourist, etc.) in all of which the assigning of meaning is implicit (cf. Tom Vernon's role of 'tourist' in *Fat Man Goes Norse*). Hence the account in these sections of a central process constituting identification – that of coming to understand – does not, as I have noted, exclude other activities from being involved in each of these roles. Caring with a subject in the text is not simply to be analysed as attributing meaning: it revolves around hoping, despairing, looking and loving.

As the readings examined above indicated, the experience of similarity necessarily underwriting identification, often itself the product of a viewer's work on the text, can be the basis for projecting new meaning in the life-worlds of programme or audience. Although identification revolves around appropriating a subject's hermeneutic role of sense-making, the subsequent horizons of understanding with which an audience comes to terms with events may be quite distinct from those associated with that character. Viewers of *Dallas* or *Rambo* may approach their lives with fresh insight: they do not live out the determinations of a fictional construct. But it is worth remarking that where a text functions to permit a viewer a sense of superiority in outlook or lifestyle (as some argue is the case with soap opera), it is unlikely to function also as a source of narratives for the 'real world'.

Narratives produced by a viewer from the processes of identification may be narrative 'sketches' rather than fully fledged stories. The concept of 'narrative sketch' reworks an idea suggested by the philosopher of science Hempel. Scientific explanations, he argued, often omitted a full indication of the natural laws upon which, for positivist philosophy of science at least, they were always based. Instead, rendering physical or chemical processes intelligible took the form of providing 'explanation sketches'. 'Such a sketch consists of a more or less vague indication of the laws and initial conditions considered as relevant, and it needs "filling out" in order to turn into a full-fledged explanation.'[77]

I do not intend to suggest that fully formed narratives originated by an audience (or indeed narratives of any other variety) need to make reference to laws. Narratives and laws bear no necessary relationship. My claim is, rather, that the concept of a 'narrative sketch' is helpful in analysis, and that some indication of its possible use can be established by considering Hempel's account of an 'explanation sketch'. 'Sketches' of either character, for instance, can occur where there are 'background assumptions that may have been left unstated because they are taken to be understood in the given context'. 'The filling-out process . . . will in general effect a gradual increase in the precision of the formulations involved.' A fully fledged viewer-centred narrative will disclose a paradigmatic similarity between events at its commencement and at its termination. The rewriting of television narratives in the respective life-worlds of the audience can be seen as an act of empowerment, an activity open also to a reversal of dominant hierarchies.

Occasionally, television texts fail to articulate a basis in speech from which role-governed processes of identification and narrative production can operate. The screenplay *Christine* (BBC2, 9.25, 23.9.87), for example, was set among the activities of juvenile 'suburban junkies', heroin addicts and pushers. A naturalistic camera followed the 'heroine' from home to home, as she supplied the drug to her 'customers'. Since her conversation provided the viewer with only the most minimal understanding of her surroundings, the documentary shooting style raised (unrewarded) expectations of a 'hermeneutic' voiceover. This discourse would have mediated between the viewer and the sometimes unintelligible, often 'difficult' interchanges of the individuals concerned: it would have functioned to allow identification between those in the extra- and intra-textual roles of assembling meaning in the text.

I am not arguing that the use of textual narratives to interpret aspects of an audience's life-world is a necessary and invariable response to a programme. (That would be to reinvent structuralism.) Clearly, viewers may produce no new stories with themselves at the centre. Rereadings of textual narratives, while providing insights into existence, can themselves be non-narratival in structure. Liebes has analysed in detail an audience's 'retelling' of events in *Dallas*. She indicated that (as phenomenology would anticipate) while the response is interest related, it may be to seek from a story a 'theme, or message, to sum up the "moral"' of an episode. In the case of a Jewish Russian group, for instance, a thematic decoding is motivated by an interest in political persuasion: *Dallas* 'is actually advertising – or, more accurately, propaganda – for the American way of life'.[78]

Recognition, Hall notes, is central to identification: it 'is crucially important in securing that circuit of understanding between audiences and messages'.[79] Identification begins, I have been suggesting in this section, with the detection of similarity, sustaining a movement from the role of reader to a role within the text. For one of Morley's interviewees, the UK situation comedy *Only Fools and Horses* 'doesn't seem like a show when you're watching. It's just you're in it with them and they just . . . I think you identify with them a bit, sometimes, when you see, like, you – you sort of identify with them.'[80] And in the recognition of similarity which initiates identification with a textual subject the time and space is also made available in which narratives for a viewer's life can be produced.

But in an equal and opposite movement away from the text, the reader may be prompted by an awareness of difference to set out on a return to the role of viewer. Involvement with events in the time and space of a programme is a continually evolving process, 'a constant to and fro movement between identification with and distancing from the fictional world as constructed in the text'.[81]

3.3   Serials, Sense and Identification

The pattern of shifting identifications which occurs throughout reading is a process in which the audience as 'nomadic subject' locates itself in a series of textually defined social roles. As Radway indicates, 'multiple, publicly constituted discourses call to social subjects who, in turn, through complicated processes of identification, actively locate themselves within at least several of those discourses'.[82] A continuous serial on television may be deliberately constructed to contain the widest possible variety of such positions, with the intention of allowing many readers to recognize its subjects' problems and rule-governed activity as akin to their own. For the implied audience, 'the other presents himself so much in terms of our own selves that there is no longer a question of self and other'.[83]

Turning momentarily to 'authorial' statements, the producer of Channel Four's *Brookside*, Phil Redmond, acknowledges this to be the policy he follows when introducing textual subjects and roles with which he hopes an audience can identify. The programme contains the views of 'old-age pensioners in society' and several characters represent a 'kind of working-class view of society'. It examines the social role of the redundant 'middle-management figure', 'the role of the . . . career woman in society', the social type of a 'good strong working-class guy' with a 'socially aspiring' wife and so on (*The South Bank Show*, ITV, 10.30, 13.4.86).

Each of these social roles can be read as a source of personal development for the subject and of textual narrative for the reader, stories to which speculation and the attempt at a coherent understanding are appropriate responses. For the viewers to recognize a role within the text as similar to a role they already inhabit is for them to regard its occupant as subject to the same irreversible process of change as the world to which they belong. It is this irreversibility and daily repetitiveness of life within the drama which both sustain the 'reality effect' of the text.

To identify with a role in a soap opera is to appropriate an element of the life-world of which that role is a part, 'playfully' engaging with its social practices in a willing suspension of disbelief while being ever open to a return to the role of reader. A viewer of *Coronation Street* notes the experience of this: 'you get involved in the characters. As though living their lives. Almost become [them].'[84] But as Fiske appears to suggest, the 'pleasures of identification' are role related: 'non-American ethnic groups viewing *Dallas* can frequently find the pleasures of identification with the Ewings in the domain of kinship, while simultaneously distancing themselves from the Ewings as bearers of Americanness'.[85]

According to Modleski, soap operas 'tend, more than any other form, to break down . . . distance': distinctions between the diegetic and the extra-diegetic become blurred.[86] Audiences refer to their sense of a cognitive distance between viewed and viewer returning at the end of involvement in the text: 'it's almost being there yourself, watching it, 'cos you just lose yourself in the programme. And then, of course, at the end, you're on a real downer, aren't you, when the programme's finished and you think . . . aahh . . . you've got the washing up to do' (*Watching You Watching Us*, ITV, 7.00, 6.4.87). To identify with a role is to accept as appropriate its associated rationalities, evaluative preferences and cognitive interests. Here, simultaneous occupancy of different roles may generate conflict.

Identification with another's social role in a programme can occur on the basis of its similarity to a role occupied by the viewer solely in that person's imagination. But again there is a movement from the role of viewer to that of participant in the text. Some interviewees in *Watching You Watching Us* indicated the 'counterfactual' nature of their enjoyment. Their pleasure rested, that is to say, on being prepared to efface, in a willing suspension of difference, the gap between their 'real-life' roles and those offered by a programme. Similarity, functioning still as the basis of identification, characterized the relationship between textual roles and those which were the object of the viewer's fantasy: 'people . . . wish they'd got all the things that all these people have got . . . hundreds of dead animals to wear and . . . things like that'.

Likewise, Massing describes the pleasures of viewer identification as sometimes resting on a proximity between a role enunciated by the text and one occupied pre-textually only in the masculine imagination. In the case of some viewers in a group of *Dallas* watchers, J.R. 'sparks their admiration for a macho ideal. They would like to dare being as unscrupulously cunning and aggressive and get away with it as he does. They are not like him but wish they were.'[87]

An extended analysis of social roles and the activity through which they are maintained, often in a construction of 'moral consensus about the conduct of personal life',[88] is a common feature of the discursive interchanges ('gossip') of subjects in the continuous serial. These analyses 'mirror' discussions among viewers, themselves engaged in critically analysing the 'management' of a range of social roles by the text and its producers. 'We always sit down and it's "Do you think she's right last night, what she's done?" Or, "I wouldn't have done that," or "Wasn't she a cow to him ?" '[89] *Right to Reply*, the Channel Four audience response programme, dealt on one occasion (6.00, 20.12.86) with the channel's representation of the unemployed in its 'soapie', *Brookside*. The serial's deployment of characters in social roles involving unemployment was argued by members of its audience to be both inadequate and sexist: 'Why don't we see any women . . . on the dole ?' Constraints on the text's ability to present social roles as well as constraints on individuals' behaviour within those roles are clearly a regular feature of dramatic productions.

A soap opera offers a plurality of possible identification figures, each confronted with the need to resolve enigmas within the 'texts' of their existence (like the viewer confronted with the text of the drama itself). Where an enigma appears in a particular story, each subject in that narrative is likely to be allowed to speculate on or anticipate its resolution, providing a variety of hermeneutic strategies for the reader. In this way texts attempting to establish patterns of identification among their audiences assume the viewer implied by hermeneutic theory.

Episodes of soap operas leave at least some of their stories inconclusive. Meaning is always open to revision, never final, with readers frequently postponing its assessment until events in succeeding episodes have been viewed. Despite this, each episode is to be regarded as a 'text' which, as such, can be submitted to analysis. For no text has a 'final meaning': the meaning of each and every text, whether televisual or otherwise, can be reassessed by a reader with new information.[90] The short sections or brief 'segments' from which each of these episodes is composed are also frequently to be found constructed around, or ending on, an assertion of the open-ended and uncertain.[91] Enigmas may range from the trivial to eventualities which could threaten the continued existence of the serial.

These points can be illustrated by referring to a particularly 'moralistic' edition of British television's soap opera *Brookside* (C4, 5.05, 23.8.86). It was preceded by the continuity announcement that 'for the Grants . . . there's yet more private agony in Brookside'. The Channel Four logo was accompanied by a voiceover, a 'textual shifter' (Bennett) moving the episode in the direction of social documentary: 'Now on Four, facing the sometimes uncomfortable and often unpleasant problems which seem unavoidable in modern life [pause] *Brookside*.'

The segments following the programme's title sequence (a kind of 'as the crow flies' arrival in Brookside Close, Liverpool) exhibited a series of uncertainties which varied greatly in their importance:

First Segment   Karen Grant (Shelagh O'Hara) to her father, Bobby Grant (Ricky Tomlinson):

Karen: Do you know what I think would be best for me mum right now?
Bobby: Yeah, a nice holiday.

3   Brookside Close, the setting of *Brookside*

Karen: Well, there is that, but there's something else . . . encourage her to carry on with her education.

Second Segment   Annabelle Collins (Doreen Sloane) to her husband, Paul (Jim Wiggins):

Annabelle: And the condemned man ate a hearty breakfast.
Paul: What?
Annabelle: I could be having my meeting with the Clerk of the Justices while you're getting locked up in a cell underneath me.

Third Segment   Doreen Corkhill (Kate Fitzgerald) to her husband, Bill (John McArdle), about the possibility of Annabelle Collins coming to her clothes party:

Doreen: All right, if she comes – which she will – you let me fix you an appointment with [the dentist] for tomorrow morning.
Billy: And if she doesn't.
Doreen: I won't buy anything at the do . . . Right?
Billy: You're on.

Fourth Segment   Bobby Grant to his wife, Sheila (Sue Johnston):

Bobby: Come on love, it's all over now.
Sheila: It isn't over, Bob, I'm pregnant.
Bobby: From the rape?
Sheila: Yes.

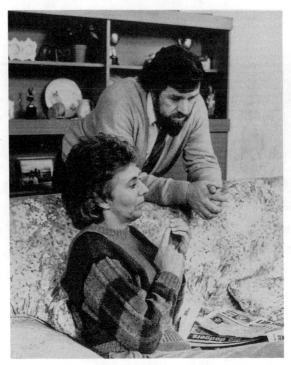

4   Bobby Grant (Ricky Tomlinson) and Sheila Grant (Sue Johnston) in an episode from *Brookside*

Each of these segments establishes an enigma whose solution will be delayed in the episode. In some cases it is not revealed until a later programme. Particular segments can be submitted to detailed analysis indicating how they elaborate the enigma around which they are structured. The extract from the second segment above shows Annabelle convinced that there is a clash of interest between her attempt to become a JP and Paul's intention of taking part in a (probably illegal) demonstration. This theme is reworked and re-argued throughout the segment : 'I'm going on a demonstration . . . not rob a bank' ; 'You're breaking the law on purpose' ; 'They have a just cause and I want to help them with it . . . What I'm doing shouldn't have any bearing on your chances of becoming a magistrate' ; 'It shouldn't have, but it's bound to . . . especially if you've got a criminal record.'

Intention, prediction and moral judgement are in conflict. Projections of sense, attempts to generate a meaning for the 'text' of an individual's life, are clearly at odds with one another. This produces a pattern of shifting and conflictful identifications for the audience engaged in its turn in attempting to understand the drama.

The processes of identification involved here align reader and subject in their respective pursuits of a coherent account of a story. Elsewhere these same processes of identification may be undermined when dramatic action or character construction indicate that an individual has assumptions about the world which are fundamentally flawed. Such a subject is to be read as an unhelpful partner in speculating on the course of future events in the text, as ethically or in other respects unreliable. Characters are endowed unequally with an ability to discern in advance the outcome of events in a soap opera. For even in the relatively non-hierarchical continuous serial some are allowed to 'produce' more sense and truth than others (cf. Sheila Grant and Harry Cross (Bill Dean) in *Brookside*, a soap opera which is 'open' but not too open to the egalitarian statement of ideological variety).

Disagreements about action, about what is to be done, disagreements likely to be based on a struggle between opposing moral assessments, work to develop and complicate the uncertainty in segments in the continuous serial. As a result these segments often display an intensity marked by a considerable lack of unity. Such inconclusiveness produces 'enigma' for both subject and viewer, allowing them to identify in a hermeneutic project, the discovery of their respective stories.

'The role of the reader emerges from this interplay of perspectives, for he finds himself called upon to mediate between them.'[92] The relatively 'open' nature of the soap opera text allows the audience to weigh the different merits of the opposing moralities at work in segment and episode. Viewers adopt different positions, seeking to close the story in a way which affirms a particular moral perspective. While segments are often characterized by an absence of information about the future, soap opera's narrative construction is organized to allow the intended viewer to produce unified and completed stories. Without this the reader's hermeneutic activities would be largely futile. Narratives are frequently constructed around the emergence of extended debate on and resolution of an enigma drawing on conflicting moral values. The comments of one of Ang's *Dallas* viewers are symptomatic: 'who knows, perhaps Pamela will start an extramarital affair (I must admit she's really beautiful); that would be something to smack your lips over'.[93] Enigmas of this nature are engaged with, repeatedly returned to in and across a series of segments, functioning to allow the intended viewer to unify and relate them as segments concerned with one story, one moral dilemma.

Brookside's centring of stories around ethical issues was illustrated in its dramatized examination of morally appropriate responses to sudden and serious brain damage or to the murder of Sheila Grant's youngest son. Sometimes the *TV Times* story summary of *Brookside* resembles a list of the week's ethical enigmas in the Close: 'while Ralph asks Harry for help, Chrissy has a meeting with Growler's pastoral head. Elsewhere, difficult decisions face Geoff, Dorothy and Jonathan.'

The subject matter of soap opera, then, is often an extended and elaborate negotiation between moral points of view. The events and action of a story set the debate in motion, providing it with its subject matter and finally permitting a moral perspective to prevail, allowing the intended reader to end that particular narrative. As Brunsdon argues in her paper on the continuous serial, in this narrative form moral and ideological frameworks 'are explored, rehearsed and made explicit for the viewer in the repeated mulling over of actions and possibilities'.[94]

The continuous serial's narratives are to be read by the intended viewer as characteristically (if only eventually) conclusive. This is not to deny that the events of a story may be much interrupted by 'ever more complex obstacles between desire and its fulfilment'.[95] Nor is it to forget that a narrative, once ended, may nevertheless be referred to later in the serial, sometimes in considerable detail (for example, the death of Sheila Grant's son in *Brookside*). But in the context of these contemporary moral fables the intended audience completes a story with the recognition that the events sustained by its central enigma have been brought to a conclusion. Here, a narrative generally ends with an expression of its subjects' awareness that a dilemma has been resolved, a dilemma usually with an ethical dimension. Unlike the dilemma continuing from episode to episode of a television series (often whether or not the central group of characters will remain together), ethical dilemmas associated with the continuous serial are finally decided. Even in the relatively egalitarian text of the soap opera, at these points a particular moral position is favoured. This is an ethical position often with implications regarding the integration or disintegration of the familial.

In one episode of *Brookside* (C4, 5.05, 1.3.86), for instance, Lucy Collins (Maggie Saunders) and her father, Paul, acknowledge the ending of her affair with a married man : 'I don't know how you could imagine it'd end any other way ... Lucy! See things how they are. Don't fantasize for God's sake !' Paul is allowed (for once) the voice of realism, a discourse of moral insight : 'I do think you're using us. All we were was a convenient base so you could carry on seeing *him*.'

The ideal viewer of the continuous serial is 'feminine'. The text is constructed for a cognitive interest which is concerned not only with factual eventualities (as a means of producing a coherent narrative) but with issues of value and welfare. 'Soap operas appear to be the one visual art which activates the gaze of the mother – but in order to provoke anxiety ... about the welfare of others.'[96] Distinct from this is the 'masculine' cognitive interest in a closure of the hermeneutic circle of understanding around a sustaining of power and social hierarchy.

MTM's *Hill Street Blues* extends many of the discourses of the continuous serial into the hybrid form of an action series/serial. In these texts the role of 'podium sergeant' functions as a point of identification for the viewer attempting to construct a coherent sense for the drama. Considered in relation to the needs of the text, the sergeant organizes, anticipates and sets in motion a series of narratives, 'making assignments, turning out the shift ... Let's roll !' Unlike many police action series, here the nature of 'justice' is not unproblematic. As narratives concerned with both power *and* morality, these stories address both masculine and feminine cognitive interest among the viewers: 'Esterhouse was the law up here and now that he's dead I feel like everything's gonna unravel'; 'It's your job and mine to see that it doesn't.' As Curti puts it, *Hill Street Blues* 'witnesses a certain feminization of a male paradigm'.[97]

The role of 'commander of the watch' or podium sergeant is that of initiating sequences or 'episodes' (Harré) of rule-governed behaviour in which others also act out roles. While some of these sequences remain enigmatic, resisting the viewer's hermeneutic attempts at their understanding, the role of commander is generally a source of meaning, familiar discourse ('Let's do it to them before they do it to us') and reliable truth. It can be read as a valid source of cognitive frameworks for ordering (and mostly) understanding the events of the drama: as the audience scrutinizes the visual and verbal complexities of the text, the sergeant reads the 'roll-call of *Hill Street Blues*'.

Deming suggests that 'the squad room is reminiscent of an old-fashioned kitchen, where family and friends exchange news and gossip, argue, and offer advice'.[98] Opportunities are taken, as in the continuous serial, for ethical reflection upon the management of social roles. *Hill Street Blues* establishes 'moral issues as a hermeneutic game'[99] to be pursued in its storylines. Esterhouse's farewell message emphasizes one aspect of this ethical 'play': 'find something of worth in each person, something to care for in each situation ... Though the Hill is generally considered the wastebasket of this city's law-enforcement minions I have found its denizens to be the fairest, most courageous and hard-working I've been privileged to know'.[100]

Much is made of differences in role-management, for it is through the statement of such difference that an imagery of policing is delivered to the programme. But these are differences inseparable from contradiction. The Hill Street police are both the enemy of conflict and its source. Disorder within the station can be the disorder of sexism, with the series/serial 'mapping' issues of gender on to issues of authority.

Unlike many earlier British series, where the police were the undisputed arbiters and agents of the law, 'reducing policing to a fictional pursuit of natural justice',[101] the role of 'peace-officer' in *Hill Street Blues* is opened up to reveal contradiction in attitude and behaviour. These conflicts complicate the drama's pursuit of the imperatives of melodrama and soap opera, where 'the good must be rewarded and the wicked punished'.[102]

The role of police officer embodies both a support for and a subverting of law, justice and morality: in one episode (C4, 10.00, 24.11.84) 'a rookie officer – who was the victim of some sexual hijinks at an off-duty cops party the night before – hangs himself' (*TV Times*). There are other differences from earlier British series. Beyond the public life-world of policing (structured by familiarities both for those who inhabit it and those who view), in *Hill Street Blues* the private sphere of leisure is on display.

Finally, an interest in the resolution of ethical issues is not confined to the continuous serial or its variants. In the internationally conscious documentary of 'personal' reflections, *Everyman*'s 'No Easy Road : Michael Buerk's South Africa' (BBC1, 10.20. 18.10.87), Buerk displays an ethical dimension to the role of reporter, his hermeneutic concerns addressing (in this sense) a feminine viewer. This liberal humanist is 'no gung-ho war correspondent whose nostrils twitch at the smell of cordite . . . [but] the journalist who seared the minds and touched the hearts of people all over the world with the fierce compassion of his reports' (*Radio Times*). The investigation of apartheid by 'No Easy Road' clearly has the status of a moral quest, however uncertain Buerk is of his ability to handle 'complex questions of good and evil, power and survival'. The viewer intended by the programme is, likewise, a morally responsible viewer (who may also be bringing a religious perspective to bear on the text). He or she is prepared, for instance, to consider the ethical justification proposed for the programme's showing a violent murder (or, as the continuity announcer puts it, a 'harrowing sequence . . . crucial, we believe, to the film's purpose').

This viewer is positioned with Buerk both morally and cognitively, engaged like him in assembling an adequate and coherent sense for a country, for a programme. A related article in the *Radio Times* accurately conveys the hermeneutic mission in which the text is involved : 'Buerk's struggle [is] to pull together all his experiences in South Africa, as BBC correspondent for four years, and make some final sense of them, refining a jumble of memories into a television essay for the *Everyman* programme.'

Notes

1   Eco, *The Role of the Reader*, p. 49.
2   De Man, Introduction to Jauss, *Toward an Aesthetic of Reception*, p. x.
3   T. Asad, 'The Concept of Cultural Translation in British Social Anthropology', in Clifford and Marcus, *Writing Culture*, pp. 141–64.
4   Elsaesser, 'Narrative Cinema and Audience-oriented Aesthetics', p. 273.
5   Ibid., p. 280.
6   Ibid., p. 279.
7   Bordwell, *Narration in the Fiction Film*, p. 52.
8   Bordwell, 'Adventures in the Highlands of Theory', p. 78.
9   Bordwell, *Narration in the Fiction Film*, p. 31.
10 Ibid., p. 34.
11 Bennett, 'Texts in History', p. 76.
12 De Man, Introduction to Jauss, *Toward an Aesthetic of Reception*, p. xii.
13 Jauss, *Toward an Aesthetic of Reception*, p. 143.
14 Gadamer, *Truth and Method*, pp. 236–7.
15 Ibid., p. 98.
16 Ibid., p. 259.
17 Ibid., p. 94.
18 Ibid., p. 95.

19 Weinsheimer, *Gadamer's Hermeneutics*, p. 105.
20 Gadamer, *Truth and Method*, p. 92.
21 Ibid., p. 259.
22 Ibid., p. 261.
23 Ibid., p. 110.
24 Hobson, 'Soap Operas at Work', p. 165.
25 Indeterminacies of meaning are primarily to be found within a text's release of the information allowing a viewer to assemble a diegesis or dramatic narrative. However, despite its implicit claims to 'completeness' of description, the mimetic text (discussed in section 4.3) can also be read as indeterminate by a real viewer.
26 Iser, *The Act of Reading*, pp. 167, 166.
27 Carr, *Interpreting Husserl*, p. 257.
28 Gadamer, *Truth and Method*, p. 340.
29 Hans, 'Hermeneutics, Play, Deconstruction', p. 311.
30 Root, *Open the Box*, p. 28.
31 J. Corner and K. Richardson, 'Documentary Meanings and the Discourse of Interpretation', in Corner, *Documentary and the Mass Media*, p. 146.
32 Iser, *The Act of Reading*, pp. 128, 133.
33 Corner and Richardson, 'Documentary Meanings', p. 146.
34 Eco, *The Role of the Reader*, p. 8.
35 Fiske, *Television Culture*, p. 64.
36 Root, *Open the Box*, p. 21.
37 Buckingham, *Public Secrets*, p. 49.
38 R. C. Allen, 'Reader-oriented Criticism and Television', *Channels of Discourse*, p. 81.
39 Iser, 'Interaction between Text and Reader', pp. 106–13.
40 Freund, *The Return of the Reader*, p. 81.
41 Tulloch, *Television Drama*, p. 211.
42 Ricoeur, 'Appropriation', *Hermeneutics and the Human Sciences*, p. 186.
43 Barwise and Ehrenberg, 'Television as a Medium', p. 5.
44 Brand, 'Intentionality, Reduction and Intentional Analysis', p. 198.
45 Nicholls, *Ideology and the Image*, p. 205.
46 Silverstone, 'The Agonistic Narratives of Television Science', p. 85.
47 Iser, *The Act of Reading*, p. 109.
48 In Lyotard's terms the narrative shows Levin himself to be a 'hero' undergoing a 'positive apprenticeship', characterized by 'successes ... greeting the hero's undertakings', in which 'criteria of competence' are being defined for the viewer in terms of the appreciation of music, art and 'what Europe could be' (*The Postmodern Condition*, p. 20).
49 Gadamer, *Truth and Method*, p. 111.
50 Austin, 'How to Do Things with Words'.
51 De Lauretis, *Alice Doesn't*, p. 144.
52 Ricoeur argues for the concept of 'text' to be applied at the level of 'meaningful action'. See 'The Model of the Text: Meaningful Action Considered as a Text', *Hermeneutics and the Human Sciences*, pp. 197–221.
53 Narratives are 'teleological' units of meaning, sequences of events whose

narration is directed by a concern to show how they brought about a particular conclusion. Sometimes the significance of these conclusions for a life is established by relating them to a personal 'fable'.

54 Woman respondent in Hobson, *Crossroads*, pp. 134–5.
55 J. Watt, 'Heather-scented Soap', *Glasgow Herald* (24 Dec. 1987).
56 Lindlof and Meyer, 'Mediated Communication', p. 13.
57 Day-Lewis, *One Day in the Life of Television*, p. 205.
58 Tulloch and Moran, *A Country Practice*, p. 238.
59 Tulloch, 'Approaching the Audience', and E. Seiter et al., ' "Don't Treat Us Like We're So Stupid and Naïve" : Towards an Ethnography of Soap Viewers' in Seiter et al., *Remote Control*, pp. 196, 241.
60 Liebes and Katz, 'On the Critical Abilities of Television Viewers', pp. 209, 217.
61 Tulloch and Moran, *A Country Practice*, p. 233.
62 Tulloch, 'Approaching the Audience', p. 191.
63 Press, *Women Watching Television*, p. 85.
64 Tulloch, *Television Drama*, p. 197.
65 Seiter et al., ' "Don't Treat Us Like We're So Stupid and Naïve" ', p. 236.
66 Ibid.
67 Hodge and Tripp, *Children and Television*, pp. 183–7.
68 Walkerdine, 'Video Replay', pp. 180, 171.
69 Tulloch, *Television Drama*, p. 213.
70 Seiter, 'Making Distinctions in TV Audience Research', p. 64.
71 J. Fiske, 'Moments of Television : Neither the Text nor the Audience', in Seiter et al., *Remote Control*, pp. 60, 61.
72 Hobson, *Crossroads*, p. 131.
73 Massing, 'Decoding *Dallas*', p. 98.
74 Ang, 'Melodramatic Identifications', pp. 83, 84.
75 The complexities of identification might be a basis for challenging Caughie's comment about the 'absurdity' of Hare's expressed intention in respect of writing 'Dreams of Leaving' that he 'wanted to write something which a mass audience would recognise as a situation in which they'd been' ('Rhetoric, Pleasure and "Art Television" ', p. 12).
76 Rath, 'Live Television and Its Audiences', p. 89.
77 Hempel, *Aspects of Scientific Explanation*, p. 238.
78 Liebes, 'Cultural Differences', p. 285.
79 Hall, 'The Narrative Construction of Reality', p. 14.
80 Morley, *Family Television*, p. 67.
81 Ang, *Watching 'Dallas'*, p. 50.
82 Radway, 'Reception Study', p. 364.
83 Gadamer, *Truth and Method*, p. 268.
84 Hobson, 'Soap Operas at Work', p. 164.
85 Fiske, *Television Culture*, p. 174.
86 Modleski, 'The Rhythms of Reception', p. 68.
87 Massing, 'Decoding *Dallas*', p. 97.
88 Brunsdon, '*Crossroads* : Notes on Soap Opera', p. 79. Other texts examine other roles. The *Arthur and Phil Go Off* (C4, 9.25, 16.12.85, and C4, 11.00, 18.7.87–1.8.87) series of dramatized documentaries looked reflex-

ively at the role of the documentary maker: 'we gotta do that bit about the *essence* of Spain before the signature tune, you know'.

89 Morley, *Family Television*, p. 156.
90 Each episode might be regarded as a 'work', with the viewer relating it to other episodes or works to form, eventually, a story (the text). But it would be difficult to maintain an account of understanding as 'playing' with a 'work'.
91 By 'segments' I mean the series of consecutive 'times and spaces' within a programme. These spatio-temporal segments, while following on from one another, often contain events which have no cause and effect relationship with those in the succeeding segment. Ellis argues that the characteristic mode of television narration throughout both 'factual' and 'fictional' serial and series is 'segmental': the 'basic unit' of 'the vast quantity of broadcast TV's output' 'is the segment, with segments following on from each other with no necessary connection between them' (*Visible Fictions*, pp. 116–17). The sequence or flow of segments which forms the characteristic episode of a soap opera exemplifies the non-causally connected sections of programme to which Ellis refers.
92 Iser, *The Act of Reading*, p. 33.
93 Ang, *Watching 'Dallas'*, p. 14.
94 Brunsdon, '*Crossroads*: Notes on Soap Opera', p. 79.
95 Modleski, 'The Search for Tomorrow in Today's Soap Operas', p. 12.
96 Modleski, 'The Rhythms of Reception', p. 70.
97 Curti, 'Genre and Gender', p. 10.
98 Deming, 'Control over Chaos', p. 24.
99 Boyd-Bowmann, 'The MTM Phenomenon', p. 85.
100 Other texts also address a feminine interest in puzzle solving which demonstrates the importance of ethics or 'caring'. For instance, in the *Open Space* programme 'A Nice Way to Treat People' (BBC2, 7.25, 12.8.87) Dr Hilary Allison mediated between the viewer and the 'down-and-outs' of her Oxford surgery, explaining their difference in a discourse of caring: 'they are just very ordinary people with ordinary problems, perhaps some of them are a bit extraordinary, the problems I mean, but they are just *totally* normal, ordinary people'.
101 Hurd, 'The Television Presentation of the Police', p. 68.
102 Modleski, 'The Search for Tomorrow in Today's Soap Operas', p. 184.

4

Viewing and the
Veridical Effect

The processes of identification establish themselves in a 'fusion of horizons' around the construction of meaning in a text or life-world. As I have suggested, this can involve an audience producing narratives, sense-making stories resolving problems of understanding a programme or the circumstances of daily existence.

Identification is role related, generating role-dependent interests and horizons of understanding. The investigators of television fiction, for instance, have an interest in establishing the truth, and 'read' events as contributing to or postponing that knowledge. In identification, roles, interests and outlook are appropriated. Subjective perspectives such as those of an investigator are mediated through the horizons of understanding associated with the reader who comes to identify with a character in the text.

In this chapter I examine what I shall refer to as the audience's 'horizons of expectation'. Distinct from horizons of understanding, these are an audience's assumptions about generic practices, routine camera work and appropriate ways of behaving, assumptions which they bring to the context of viewing. These horizons are particularly important in generating an experience of the television text as being easy to consume and as providing a transparent access to the world. Horizons of expectation are constituted by the audiences' anticipations, which arise in turn from a long history of viewing. As I shall argue, an experience of the image as transparent is a precondition of the processes of identification taking place.

4.1   The Audience's Horizon of Expectations

The 'act of appropriation' expands 'the conscious horizons of the reader by actualizing the meaning of the text'.[1] In understanding a text, 'what I appropriate is a proposed world . . . that which the work unfolds, discovers, reveals'.[2] The horizons of understanding belonging to reader and textual subject consist of the cognitive frameworks through which they interpret the world. As I indicated in Chapter 2, these sets of assumptions are brought together in mediating 'play' by the appropriation of meaning which supports identification. 'This placing of ourselves is not the empathy of one individual for another, nor is it the application to another person of our own criteria, but it always involves the attainment of a higher universality that overcomes, not only our own particularity, but also that of the other.'[3]

But Gadamer also notes that 'all understanding presumes a living relationship between the interpreter and the text, his previous connection with the material that it deals with'.[4] The reader engages with the text in a complex cognitive context : this involves not only horizons of understanding but horizons of expectation. These are assumptions about how a programme will develop and present its content, assumptions based on past experience of others of its type. 'Reading the text' occurs 'with particular expectations in regard to a certain meaning'.[5] Such anticipations are central to the activity of viewing and may be foregrounded for study. Some ethnic groups may lack the appropriate horizons of expectation in respect of particular forms of television (or film). Michaels asserts in his Australian research that Aboriginal people 'were unfamiliar with the conventions, genres and epistemology of Western narrative fiction. They were unable to evaluate the truth value of Hollywood cinema, to distinguish, for example, documentary from fiction.'[6]

A multiplicity of horizons of expectation must be regarded as underwriting the experience of different genres and different forms of television. At the most fundamental level, being aware that anticipations which are appropriate to the end of serials are inappropriate when directed at series is central to the role of viewing, at least as television is currently constituted. Audience expectations may be classified on the basis of their level of decreasing generality as (a) inter-generic (for example, assuming spatio-temporal continuity), (b) intra-generic (for example, concerning appropriate behaviour for a detective) and (c) programme specific (for example, anticipating activity as appropriate to a particular character).

Horizons of expectation involve a form of knowledge derived from inhabiting a role through time. As Jauss remarks about reading literature, at different levels of generality a text 'awakens memories of that which was already read . . . and with its beginning arouses expectations for the "middle and end"'.[7] Horizons of expectation inform an understanding of television form and genre, constituting a knowledge of differences which (one might remark incidentally) the teaching of media studies aims to make explicit. It is just not the case that, as Meyrowitz puts it, when 'you know how to watch and listen to one television programme, you essentially know how to watch and listen to any television programme'.[8]

Encountering a programme as a semiotic process which conforms to viewers' horizons of expectation based on a knowledge of television form and genre is implicit in an audience's experience of viewing. It is responsible for the reader's sense of constructing a unified and appropriately completed reading of a text. Anticipations of information typically provided have to be satisfied. The closing stages in the weekly episode of a television detective series provide generically relevant information which, despite its always being limited, is usually experienced as resolving any indeterminacies of meaning.

It is an audience's horizon of visual expectations which (when confirmed by a text) produces the effect of a 'veridical' sequence of images, an apparently unmediated and reliable presentation of how things are. The truth of these images is preserved from doubt by the near transparency of the access they provide to the 'real', articulating television's 'characteristics of "liveness", presence, and immediacy'.[9] Here the relationship between signifier and signified is 'barely code at all', and 'television looks and sounds much more like reality than sentences and paragraphs do'.[10] While giving an account of this, I shall use the term 'veridical' in a conscious attempt to transcend the uncertain trinity of 'realism', 'naturalism' and 'illusionism', which I discuss below. In the absence of the veridical image, identification with a textual subject cannot occur. But where the image appears transparent, as a Morley interviewee puts it, 'I am there in the action, feeling every blow, running every mile.'[11]

Horizons of expectation supporting a unified reading of a programme, a reading which has known what to expect and found it, draw particularly on an awareness of genre. For genre is an important aspect of audience knowledge as well as of textual formation, producing a sequence of expectations within the hermeneutic process of understanding a text : genres are 'systems of orientations, expectations and conventions that circulate between industry, text and subject'.[12] Both 'fictional' and 'factual' pro-grammes are generically inscribed : assumptions of structure and order govern the reception of a television news bulletin. Even in less obviously generic pieces a viewer anticipates and assembles a consistent sense for the text in accordance with a knowledge of its accustomed 'internal rules'. 'Regular *Minder* viewers all appreciate that the newest Arthur Daley scheme will somehow collapse : it is the anticipation of the event through the twists and turns of the plots which is delightful.'[13]

It is equally possible for a viewer to operate with the wrong horizon of expectations, to treat a serial, for instance, as if it were a series (or vice versa). An audience can anticipate a resolution of enigmas at the end of an episode only to be disappointed when none occurs. Gripsrud indicates this to have been the case with Norwegian viewers of *Dynasty*, explaining it in terms of 'their previous aesthetic experiences, their lack of experience with the soap opera format'.[14]

Horizons of expectation also draw on the viewer's knowledge of 'act-action' structures (Harré), of typical patterns of activity, such as greeting another or saying goodbye.[15] An awareness of these routines supports anticipations of meaning in the text which are likely to be confirmed by events. In Harré's theory such structures range from the formal and explicitly ritualized (for example, the act of worship with its integral actions of prayer, blessing, etc.) to the informal and only implicitly rule bound (for example, the 'act' of conversation, with its constituent activities of listening and hearing). Whatever their degree of formality, 'the unifying principle for a series of actions is the identification of them as the performance of a certain act'.[16]

A viewer's knowledge of a particular act-action structure can be elicited, producing a horizon of expectations, by a subject's discursive expression of an intention (for example, to murder or to obtain revenge). The process of reading may confirm the accuracy of those expectations. Act-action structures are of a less macroscopic character than those which typify genres: yet they are more substantial than the actions of which they are composed. As an intermediate level of meaning in the text these act-action structures are customarily integrated as sequential (or concurrent) elements within a story, while constituted themselves by particular mental and physical activities (or their absence).

To establish a narrative is, then, to relate together a set of act-action sequences. Activities brought together by the reader within a single act-action structure in the process of constructing an intelligible programme are read as 'units of meaning' with their own spatio-temporal unity. The viewer's task may consist of assembling that unity from the fragments of activity available within the text. 'One of the many possible ways in which a principle of unity can give structure to a sequence of happenings in which human beings interact . . . [is where] the sequence constitutes a set of actions in the performance of which a certain act is carried out.[17] But within a particular text some of these act-action sequences will be resolutely open-ended or incomplete in some respect, as in the many episodes of the continuous serial which resist closure. Some may make only a particular, limited kind of sense.

An audience's horizons of expectation (whether associated with a knowledge of genre or act-action structures) serve to unify an evening's viewing, bringing together items and programmes as instances of types such as situation comedies. Raymond Williams's concept of 'flow' can be read as drawing attention to the way in which one section of programming influences the horizons of expectation brought to bear on another. Continuity announcements, for instance, offer appropriate descriptions of impending textual activity: 'many particular items – given our ordinary organization of response, memory and persistence of attitude and mood – are affected by those preceding and those following them'.[18] An audience's horizons of expectation, like media personalities, repeatedly return within the viewing of particular programmes, to be sustained (or occasionally reworked) while simultaneously providing 'anchors' for recognition and a sense of continuity. Generic anticipations are regularly confirmed, contributing to the reassuring sense of unproblematic familiarity characteristic of an evening's entertainment. Root argues that current audience behaviour provides evidence for thinking that flow is now 'viewer controlled'. The individual's experience of programmes relating together across an evening's viewing is actively produced by the viewer's moving frequently from one programme or channel to another.[19]

At a more detailed level of 'watching', where the viewers' expectations of the image in front of them are confirmed by the text, it will often seem to give an unmediated, 'transparent' access to the apparently real. Television is generally characterized by camera movements, editing and images which belong to the mundane and unexceptional. As a result, the audience's horizon of expectations is that of the likely ordinariness and everyday quality (in this respect at least) of much of its viewing experience. One viewer of the former UK soap opera *Crossroads* (now terminated) put on record for Hobson a degree of displeasure at the unusual blurred camera shots intended to suggest a character's subjective point of view of a hospital ward after an eye operation: 'they've been doing more of that lately, different sort of camera things ... I didn't think that was *Crossroads* actually.'[20]

But where this anticipation of the commonplace is confirmed, it produces the experience of what I shall call a veridical sequence.[21] Here the function of the image as sign is realized. In Gadamer's words, the function of the sign is 'to point away from itself ... It should not attract attention to itself in a way that would cause one to linger over it, for it is there only to make present something that is not present, and in such a way that the thing that is not present is the only thing that is expressed.'[22] The transparent ordinariness of the 'veridical effect' undermines any fetishistic relationship to the complexities of an image which exists in its own right.

The veridical sequence is a series of images disclosing the apparently 'real' as unproblematically present to the viewer: 'the generalized fantasy of the television ... image is exactly that it is *direct*, and direct for me'.[23] Television's electronic orthodoxies of 'showing' often allow a near transparent 'window' on its content, an apparently immediate 'looking in on reality'.[24] The time of the veridical image is that of the viewer, giving the appearance of 'live' television. Denying their status as selective appropriations of meaning, veridical images resist a reading as other than truthful accounts of the world by a viewer whose horizon of expectations has been easily confirmed. Variations in the relationship between image and signified are generally limited by convention. Finding only what is anticipated, the audience notices little of the camera work or editing responsible for setting these images within what is experienced as an uninterrupted sequence: 'the human or cultural agency in the process is masked'.[25]

The experience of the veridical is a visual registering of image content sutured into place in a near seamless and transparent flow. It is an experience of Todorov's 'vraisemblance': 'one can speak of vraisemblance of a work in so far as it attempts to make us believe that it conforms to reality and not to its own laws'.[26] In the language of phenomenology, horizons of visual expectation are based on past knowledge ('retentions') allowing 'protentions' regarding future camera work. Where these protentions are confirmed without difficulty, the viewer's experience becomes that of the veridical.

In the veridical sequence the text appears unconstructed, 'bringing it to you as it really is'.[27] As Bob Ferguson asserts of the 'realistic' television programme in an episode of a UK schools' television series, 'Making It Look Real', *Media File: Inside Television* (BBC2, 12.20, 12.5.89): 'we aren't conscious of the way it's put together. We're not asking ourselves, "oh, there's a close-up, there's a long shot, that shot was twice as long as the one before it".' Equally, the reference of the veridical sequence, its content, is to the apparently 'real', a realism whose existence is ultimately a function of audience recognition : 'this has gotta be real because you can see it's so exactly the way it really is in real life.' Situation comedies develop this recognizability to excess, undermining their own 'realities'.

My use of 'veridical' is intended to point to the often near transparency of a text as a product not only of its visual practices but of an active audience reading which is informed by a particular horizon of expectations. The veridical effect occurs where anticipations are confirmed. While such 'transparency' is the condition of identification, it is an achievement by a viewer with knowledge rather than, as Ferguson implies, a mark of audience passivity : 'we expect to be able to be sucked into the programme, deliver ourselves up to it and just watch, and not ask any questions'.

Television, then, frequently allows its viewer an apparently veridical access to the world, an access which seems to be both unmediated and truthful. The image (as image), the television camera and the editing are forgotten in a reading in which the content of the image is perceived directly rather than through 'the mediation of editing and form of presentation'.[28] The viewer sees for much of the time not a restrictive electronic screen but an unproblematic presentation of a coherent spatio-temporal reality. The veridical image appears self-evidently truthful. As far as the viewer is concerned, it supports its own claims to validity rather than possessing a truth status which relies, for instance, on the prior knowledge of the audience that what it shows is the case.

Television (whether factual or fictional) typically sets into play practices which encourage such a veridical effect as well as support a conception of the relaxed and easy pleasures of uncomplicated viewing. 'Television production textbooks warn students about the need for simplicity in the image.'[29] Allowing the experience of a 'transparent' sequence involves both continuity editing and a careful use of the camera : the veridical occurs at the 'zero point' of minimal television style. Editing is made as unobtrusive as possible in a 'smooth pictorial flow' with the aim of avoiding a fragmented series of images.[30] A voiceover may unify the disparate nature of what is seen, hiding cuts. Offering the individual in the role of viewer desired activities of observation and gaining information, edits from shot to shot pass relatively unnoticed or, if not, are rarely experienced as visually constraining. Cuts from medium-long shot to medium shot (or closer) can retain a continuity as solutions to an indeterminacy of sense in which the audience is interested. They merely show the viewers what they want to see. Editing between segments whose content is not related as cause and effect (as in soap opera) is more likely to attract the audience's attention since it interrupts the viewer's attempt to assemble a story. But its mundane and repetitive sequencing (as in a news programme) customarily allows a sense of disclosing the 'real' to be preserved.

A continuous flow of television images is an 'unwritten' (MacCabe) bearer of truth; the marks of producing this communication of the 'seeming-real' are effaced. Writing is articulated as 'marks of material difference distributed through time and space'.[31] But in many texts for much of the time the articulation of the television image is not experienced as the distribution of difference. Rather, 'compositionally matched (matched cuts)' produce a flow of similarity, in which the presence of editing is left undeclared.[32] In the 'unwritten' discourses of television, reality simply appears.

Often in television, cutting is used to register an intersubjective play of looks during a conversation in a series of shots from positions distinct from those which can be occupied by the single cinematic film camera. In the three-camera television studio the cameras are situated not in the immediate space of the dialogue (allowing over-the-shoulder shots) but in less intimate 'third person' positions. This produces a shot/reverse-shot sequence which observes the conversation, looking on as it occurs. A sequence of this type might be termed television's 'match on speech' in which the cameras register the flow of discussion, moving from one contributor to another in a motivated editing which preserves continuity. Television's 'most typical image is a mid-shot or close-up of someone talking or reacting'.[33]

This 'match on speech' is responsible for a visual structure in which one image registers a subject's glance or gaze with a second image showing its content (usually another subject, from an angle which avoids a direct address to camera). This sequence of shots hides the cut between images to the extent that it is scarcely noticed: the construction and resolution of uncertainty establishes for the intended viewer a veridical 'looking'. The audience response to the visual indeterminacy of the first shot is likely to be a speculative projection of meaning (he or she is looking at/talking to X? X's reaction is . . . ?). The subsequent shot imitates the look which would 'naturally' occur to ascertain the truth of this speculation. At this point, the viewer's desire to see is satisfied and therefore unconstrained. For the implied viewer, at least, this produces the experience of a smooth and continuous flow of images, a near invisible edit. In this context, two-shots (or shots showing the conversational group assembled) function to resolve indeterminacies concerning the location of the social interaction.

Such conversational interchanges normally conform to viewers' horizons of expectations, allowing them to assemble a unit of meaning, an act-action sequence from a series of events in the text (for example, A promising to do something for B, agreeing to meet B, etc.). In the segmental story-telling of television the audience is often assisted in separating this sequence off from others by a gap in narration. The content of successive segments (in the serial at least) is rarely related as cause and effect. But here, as with all production of meaning, coherence and the integration of events is attained by a viewer rather than derived from the text. In this sense hermeneutic theory reverses the relationship between viewer and viewed proposed by structuralism and discussed in the Introduction.

The reading of a sequence of images as veridical is likely to occur with an audience's recognition of an act-action structure which has been predictably (and therefore unproblematically) displayed in the programme. The often repetitive editing of popular television drama ('a purely functional routine') conforms to the audience's horizon of visual expectations, allowing a near transparent viewing of conversational exchanges in which 'the viewer instantly appreciates' the meaning and identity of what is seen.[34]

The veridical effect of an apparently unproblematic visual truth is also held in place through the television camera's repertoire of shots, generally more restrained than those in films primarily intended for cinematic exhibition. Here the camera resists drawing attention to its own activity : where movement occurs it is often motivated (and therefore made less conspicuous) by the need to follow a subject's movement in space. In popular drama at least (for instance, situation comedy), camera work is frequently limited to providing 'visual support for the verbal and is subordinated to the needs of the "actors" speech'.[35] The camera's 'look' (like that of the human being) moves at the end of a statement to register the response.

As I have indicated, television camera work usually permits the viewer's (perhaps preconscious) expectation of an 'ordinary' point of view on events to be confirmed. Tilting shots or shots at a pronounced angle to the action which upset television's visual restraint are uncommon. Even subjective point-of-view shots are unusual, at least in the multi-camera set-up of a studio. Most shots have a counterfactual aspect, observing events from 'normal', unproblematic positions which might have been occupied by participants (but are not). They are shots which disclose events to a hypothetical human glance or gaze, a look which is available to be appropriated by the viewer. The camera takes up the perspectives of an 'embodied subject' to disclose its meaning : like the 'lived body [it] moves in a world of privileged perspectives organized around the projects of that body and the given significance of its milieu'.[36]

The infrequently occurring zoom, extended pan or tracking shot, however, is usually both noticed and read as producing a non-transparent image. These camera movements declare themselves to be selective constructions of how things are. The possibility is made manifest that the images for which they are responsible are not veridical, that they provide a distorted account of the world. Nevertheless, in documentary or drama, the transparency of the image may be somewhat preserved where a prolonged tracking shot or pan resolves an indeterminacy of meaning in the text (for example, an off-camera noise). In allowing the viewer's uncertainty and desire to see to be satisfied, this camera movement may be able to resist being read by the audience as an artificial intrusion into the flow of images in the text. Alternatively, the movement of the camera may be masked by the movement of its location (as in a tracking shot from a plane).

This situation is to be distinguished from the obtrusive cutting and shooting associated with the location footage accompanying news or current affairs (where a sudden zoom may draw attention to the presence and selectivity of the camera in its very concern to show important events). Here, the truth of the image is 'guaranteed' by the immediacy of the response (and perhaps by the reputation for accuracy belonging to a news agency such as the BBC or SBS's *World News* team) rather than by what seems to be an unmediated experience of its content. While the veridical sequence possesses apparently self-authenticating truth, other televisual sequences may be accepted by an audience as expressions of truth for a different reason.

The veridical effect is founded upon repetition, upon the unproblematic confirming of the viewer's horizon of visual expectation. Camera positions are endlessly reused, constructed therefore as seemingly necessary and without alternative. Like myth, the veridical effect 'naturalizes' a way of seeing: 'in order to make it innocent ... it is immediately frozen into something natural'.[37]

These production routines of editing and camera work might be described as a 'naturalism' in which the television audience, anticipating such practices, is forgetful of the text's mediations. But the concept of 'naturalism' has, as I have indicated elsewhere,[38] an 'ambiguous philosophical and literary past and present'. In addition to its use in referring to accustomed television practice, the term 'naturalism' has denoted an ideologically questionable 'reproducing' of 'whatever manifests itself immediately and on the surface' of society (Lukács), a 'consensus-reinforcing trap' (Woodhead), an ' "authentic" evocation of the "non-dramatic" tempo of everyday living' (Hill) and the view that character and action are 'affected or determined by *environment*, which especially in a social and social-physical sense had then to be accurately described as an essential element of any account of life' (Williams). 'Naturalism' is also used by critics to refer to 'bad and boring realism' (Caughie). It has even been used indiscriminately across television news, drama and film, despite the differences involved, to denote their varying practices of attempting to construct an 'unmediated reality': 'news is not the only network program to conceal its symbolic fabrications in naturalistic film. Most movies and most television series and even most commercials also present themselves as *unmediated* reality' (Gibson).[39] Given these many uncertainties and divisions in its understanding, I shall not rely on the term here. Furthermore, 'naturalism' marks, however indefinitely, a set of features belonging to the text. My interest is rather in a term ('veridical') which can be used to denote a certain form of experience available to the audience in which a text functions in a perfectly ordinary way.

The 'veridical effect', then, is a product of the viewer's assumptions and of the programme's conformity to those beliefs. Expectations, often never explicitly formulated, about likely camera practices in a text are a function of an audience's beliefs about the sort of television they are viewing. The camera work required to confirm those varying horizons of expectation will not be identical, but will allow a veridical experience to emerge in different ways. This theory of the veridical applies equally to such aspects of television *mise en scène* as lighting and quality of the image. Horizons of expectation which are continually confirmed allow the visual environment in a text to pass without conscious scrutiny. The experience of the veridical image is of a near transparent (and hence apparently truthful) presentation of an intersubjective reality.

This experience of the 'veridical' is the televisual equivalent of the cinematic experience of 'illusionism', which, like the 'veridical' is sustained by repetition and conformity to a horizon of visual expectation, even if in the case of film the spectator's anticipation is of a less restrained camera practice : 'any classical series of shots will include several identical camera set-ups . . . Such repetitions encourage us to ignore the cutting itself and notice only those narrative factors that change from shot to shot.'[40]

My use of the term 'veridical' is intended, in part, as a productive rereading of the ambiguities of meaning associated with discussions of 'realism'. While the veridical effect is a feature of the 'realistic' television text, the filmic 'classic realist text' of cinema is illusionistic. In the latter case, 'film depends to a greater or lesser extent on the illusion of unmediated vision, on a transparency of form and style . . . [and] a spectator who forgets the camera'.[41] While the veridical is undermined by a departure from the restrained and orthodox, illusionism is compatible with more varied modes of camera use. 'A device such as an unmotivated camera movement, which would probably go unnoticed in the average Hollywood film, is such a departure from the norm in soap opera style that its use immediately privileges the content of the shot for the audience – the viewer "reads" this device as "something important is about to happen".'[42] Since cinematic filming is oriented towards the representational needs of human action rather than speech, extended tracking shots, tilts and pans are more common and therefore less conspicuous than similar sequences in (for instance) a television serial drama. Television's veridical images are less likely to give an elliptical account of events (particularly conversations) than cinematic film, which often requires the spectator to make assumptions about what has not been seen. 'The lack of spatial or temporal ellipses augments the impression of "simple recording" characteristic of the [Metz's] "scene".'[43] The ellipses of filmic representation require that illusionism adopt specific devices of concealment (for example, matched cuts).

Television predominantly offers the experience of the veridical image, but clearly the codes of illusionism occur in the cinematic films it screens for a largely domestic audience. There are other texts which, while produced for television screening, contain a visual regime more akin to that of cinematic film. *Dallas* is untypically shot in a film studio or on location with financing and technical help which is uncharacteristic of television. The increasing production of drama with a single-camera set-up may extend the number of texts which emulate the cinematic image and disrupt the viewer's anticipation of the orthodoxies of the veridical.

The veridical image, as I have noted, is likely to involve a familiar 'matching on speech' (although it can also involve a 'matching on action'). Television, to a greater degree than cinematic illusionism, obtains emphasis and support from the verbal in its veridical effect of presencing the world. A brief but characteristic BBC trailer (BBC1, 10.19, 18.10.87) for the following day's current affairs programme *Panorama* commenced with two shots : the first showed a missile taking off from its silo, the second a missile reaching its target and exploding. These shots were accompanied by a voiceover confirming their appearance of conveying the real, directing attention from the image to the world and emphasizing television's impression of veridical looking : 'Cruise missiles like *these* will be abolished from Europe if the superpowers sign the proposed new INF agreement.' Unlike the illusionist sequence, a veridical series of images occurs in a communicative context which frequently acknowledges in speech its own status as discourse, as an enunciation of meaning from a source to a recipient.

The veridical television sequence is generally maintained in play through the use of different strategies from those of filmic illusionism. Additionally, a television institution may propose different conditions of viewing for the broadcasting image from those associated with the cinematic exhibition of film (or even film watched on a hired or purchased video). Continuity announcements, for instance, may be read as denying permission to treat the text as veridical, as giving an unproblematic access to reality. In doing so, as I show in section 6.2, they are likely to be following television's pluralistic requirements of 'balanced' reporting in the areas of the political and controversial.

4.2　Identification and the Veridical Effect

Images read as veridical (producing a firm belief in what can be immediately seen) sustain the truth of a subject's (character's or presenter's) discursively established interpretations, upholding them as verbally expressed insights into the evidently real. In documentary the presence of the images, 'the visible evidence they offer of an event, authenticates the carrier of the meaning – the commentary'.[44] A text which provides visual support for a subject's verbal discourse is one in which the time and space has been opened so that identification can occur between viewer and viewed. Here an audience can appropriate a subject's horizons of understanding the world as valid.

But the veridical experience of an image supports the ontological moment of identification as well as the cognitive. With the appearance of an unmediated access to 'reality' viewers are able to 'read' themselves into the text, moving from the hermeneutic role of reader to that of a subject in the time and space of the programme. Mechanisms of identification (cf. Chapter 5) in the text itself may support and assist this process. In the words of a male viewer of *Dynasty*, 'I don't know what it is about it but you just, you end up . . . it pulls you in, like you're almost right there. You feel . . . you can feel it.'[45] Whereas a television image must be read, an individual in the text sees *simpliciter*.

The discursive status of the television reporter as a source of truth, for instance, is authenticated by the unproblematic relation of what he or she says with the viewer's near transparent perception of its topic. An experience of the world whose mediation by an electronic image is likely to be almost imperceptible supports both the cognitive and ontological moments of identification with the role of 'investigator'. The intended viewer appropriates this role, acknowledging its incumbent as a source of information. And in the time and space of the programme the reporter can also identify with the audience, allowed as he or she is to ask questions on behalf of the ideal viewer. The reporter 'does not merely ask a common-sense question, but claims to do so on behalf of us; we are the viewers – those "other people" who "want to know"'.[46]

The experience of a veridical image may be at one and the same time the experience of a subject's visual field. A shot of an individual looking (off camera) at an object which cannot be seen by the audience constructs an indeterminacy of vision for the viewer. The reverse-shot (giving the content of the look) sustains the veridical effect for the audience by providing it with the information it needs to resolve its speculations. The intended viewer can identify with the subject. In television situation comedies or continuous serials these sequences are rare and unusual occurrences, perhaps only used to mark a moment of heightened intensity in the drama.

But subjective sequences marking out a character's 'looking' can also disturb the apparently unmediated character of the televisual experience. They may include a particularly 'angled' vision of events (as in a shot tilted downwards from eye-level), which is likely to draw attention to itself as unusual in the midst of the 'ordinary' images of television. Where this occurs it suspends the audience's experience of a veridical sequence as giving an apparently uncontrived access to the world. The image itself is declared. It is a televisual paradox that the visual mechanisms of aligning the audience with a subject in the text sometimes disconnect the flow of images, intervening with their own artifice. Camera work at such points becomes noticeable, repositioning the viewer in the role of reader. Identification demands an image which is truthful to the point of invisibility, a transparent aperture on the 'real' itself.

A self-evidently constructed marking out of a subject's perspective on events occurs in a variety of contexts. In drawing attention to itself, the image loses its unproblematic status as an expression of truth. Television video is an electronic technology with a capacity for quick and easy (if not 'anarchic') editing which is celebrated in the postmodernist music video. But sequences of complex editing may also be found in television drama where the camera establishes individuals' 'looking' in a swift succession of images articulating the 'glance' of the subject (cf. *Dance with Me*, a Globo TV Brazil production, transmitted on Channel Four and SBS). As in the music video, a compilation of images of this character never articulates a 'transparent' access to the world.

Extended tracking shots, zooms or tilts may be visually or verbally defined as articulating a subject's field of vision, often as a prolonged gaze rather than a glance. The camera may tilt upwards, for instance, to record what we are told in voiceover is a subject's looking. These are unusual occurrences in television's regime of vision. For this reason, as I have indicated, they are likely to draw attention to the operations of the medium, undermining the transparency of the image. This is particularly so if these assertions of subjective looking hold an indeterminate content devoid of specific objects of interest. In shots such as these marking out an unrewarded visual 'search', little remains within the image to distract the viewer's attention from its framing. Given television's generally restrained visual practice, these subjective camera movements constitute almost inevitable disruptions to our experience of the near-transparent representing of a textual content. The use of subjective travelling shots to align the audience is examined further in section 5.3.

But in the relationship between text and viewer which constitutes identification the mediation of reality by an image is 'forgotten' in favour of reality itself. This allows a movement from the role of viewer to that of participant in the space and time of the programme, where the separation from the text implied in the former position is discarded. Yet the visually unexpected (for example, a zoom marking out a subject's visual field as in Globo TV's production *Dance with Me*), or simply cutting from segment to segment, is in turn likely to lead the viewer to disengage from the illusion of unmediated access to reality.[47]

'Identification' between audience and programme may mark a sustained positioning of the former in the life-world of the latter in which, as I noted in the last chapter, 'you concentrate on other problems, other people's problems' or 'you're in it with them'. But, more often, the relationship between television and its viewer is one in which the audience engages with the text in a continuous establishing and suspension of the veridical effect which is presupposed by the processes of identification. The viewer moves 'to and fro', playing with a text which may not always collaborate in the construction of the 'transparent' as visual expectations are confirmed or undermined. This is a movement from a counter-to-factual denial of textuality to a reassertion of the text as text in a reading which is aware of the operations of the image. The conventions of shooting which sustained the veridical experience of an immediately available reality may begin to become apparent, freeing themselves from merely confirming the viewer's horizon of expectations. 'Camera things', as the *Crossroads* viewer put it, are noted.

This movement between an apparently self-authenticating veridical access to reality on the one hand and awareness of an image which is open to question on the other will vary from text to text. A drama is more likely to engage its audience in an enjoyment of the image as near transparent than a much edited and elliptical news sequence with abruptly changing camera angles. Involved in this to and fro 'play' of viewing (to awareness of the image as image, from a denial of textuality) is an active relaxing, the viewer's response to the text's varying success in constructing the conditions of a transparent reading. This is the experience of an 'ease of play, which naturally does not mean that there is any real absence of effort'.[48] But in the to and fro movement of an audience's relationship with a programme, the viewer's position as an involved observer of its 'realities' (rather than as a reader) may constitute an ironical 'role play'. Here there is a particular consciousness of playing coloured by an awareness that involvement in the role rests on forgetting its source in a text.

Subject to the constraints imposed by the aesthetic forms of television, professional practice attempts to produce an unproblematic flow of images, an entertainment-led distracting and extracting of those watching from the role of the viewer :

> Where quite dissimilar shots are intercut, your audience may have some difficulty in appreciating continuity or relationships. But you can establish an immediate connection through :
>
> 1 *Dialogue* – introducing or implying the next shot's substance.
> 2 *Action* – establishing a cause – effect relationship.
> 3 *Common Reference Points* (a person) in both shots.
> 4 *Audio continuity*.[49]
>
> You can often make a cut smoother (and therefore better) by making sure that the points which attract the eye in neighbouring shots are in the same section of the screen.[50]

Yet the experience of the (real) audience is frequently, as I have noted, that of a movement into and out of an awareness of textuality. The concept of filmic 'illusionism', where it is allowed to imply that the experience of watching film is of a seamless whole, confuses the intended with the real spectator. Similarly, the intentions of those behind the television camera must not be taken as an account of the actual experience of watching, of a 'playful' encounter with a reality which on occasions must appear heavily mediated.

In this 'play on the veridical', being aware of a distance between text and audience is a necessary condition for criticism. The relationship between viewer and programme is not generally sustained as one or other extreme in the opposition between involvement and disengagement. It is rather a continuous movement, back and forth, over the distance between roles within and roles beyond the text, generating an assertion or denial of textuality. The return to the role of viewer provides the time and space for distanciated criticism of a programme (cf. my Conclusion). This is an opportunity which may or may not be translated into practice.

4.3   Producing the Veridical Effect

'Veridical' is a historical concept : rules which underwrite the production of transparency will change through time. The transparent experiences of the 'real' which support identification have no essential nature. Television forms of drama and documentary, for instance, not only vary in their respective setting into play of the image but allow viewing experiences of the veridical which rest on different textual practices. This section examines the veridical effects associated with drama and documentary, leaving on one side other forms of television.

Drama and documentary television assume different relationships between the text and the non-textual. Drama is first and foremost the production of a diegetic space and time constructed around narrative. Documentary, however, foregrounds a space and time employed in mimesis, a copying of the pre-textual. This results in different camera practices and routines of image production with, as a consequence, different possibilities for their audiences of experiencing an apparently unmediated access to reality.

The distinction I am pursuing here between the 'mimetic' and 'diegetic' forms of the veridical must itself be distinguished from other uses of these terms within the literature of film and television studies. Silverstone, writing about television science, contrasts 'mimetic' and 'mythic' discourse, identifying the former with 'science'. But science is as much a deliberately selective enterprise as it is (at least in intention) mimetically descriptive of detail : a history of science is, importantly, a history of reasons for particular choices of investigative topic. Additionally, Silverstone's 'mythic' refers, he indicates, not to 'narrative' *per se* but to 'Lyotard's narrative', a concept of story-telling which emphasizes the existence of a particular, justificatory dimension to the practice.[51]

Like Silverstone, Bordwell's distinction between 'mimetic' and 'diegetic' rests on a particular theory of narrative. But here it is confusing to learn that the mimetic itself is a form of narration. Mimetic accounts of cinema, apparently, understood the discourse of film narrative as a series of visual perspectives associated with an 'attentive observer'. 'By framing the shot a certain way, and by concentrating on the most significant details of the action, the director compels the audience "to see as the attentive observer saw".[52]

Diegetic theories of narration, on the other hand, understand film discourse as either 'literally or analogically' a language. Narrative is the play, often hierarchical, between statements in this language, 'a telling. This telling may be either oral or written.'[53]

The distinction I wish to make between 'diegetic' and 'mimetic' opposes narrative to non-narrative (here, the descriptive). The veridical images of drama are predominantly narrative images of events. The audience can establish a story in which its fictional or diegetic locations are defined as the times and spaces of individuals and their actions. 'The diegetic is the implied spatial, temporal, and causal system of the characters.'[54] In this way spatio-temporal references become relative to a viewer's projection of a meaningful life-world for the text in which the events of the story occur.

The pre-text of dramatic narrative (as opposed to that of documentary description) is subjective and ideational rather than public and 'real': it is justified as a basis of narrative by its 'worthwhile' difference from other possible sources of a drama. Even where the story to be constructed by the intended viewer is based upon 'real events', only those aspects of the latter which easily conform to the needs of the narrative are permitted to enter the text.[55] The story, indeed, may reorder these events, an option which is not open to the text with mimetic ambitions.

In dramatic narratives the construction of the discursive precedes and determines the selective appropriation of the non-discursive. The narrative camera is interested in allowing the viewer to establish cause and effect sequences (perhaps of some complexity) and not in their detailed visual description. These sequences involve events, action and individuals' verbal responses to each other. The customary practices of visual narration allow the 'transparent' image to emerge. The needs of a *Brookside* story, for instance, produce the necessary arrangement of the actors, the cameras and a *mise en scène* which draws on a particular Liverpool close. It is the planned regularities and repetitions of these arrangements which result in turn in the viewer's experience of the veridical image, a (paradoxical) forgetting of textual artifice as he or she assembles the story.

Distinct from drama with its centring around narrative is the predominantly descriptive or mimetic mode of documentary, a 'privileging of description as against plot, of reporting on nature and on the environment as against a strong narrative and dramatic line with a fully elaborated resolution'.[56] The veridical images of documentary television, with their foregrounding of description rather than narration, are 'mimetic' in the sense with which Plato endowed that concept. Mimetic images owe their selection not to the functional requirements of a narrative but to the need to allow the viewer to construct a detailed perception of a public time and space which existed pre-textually. The selective image of television is re-presented as non-selective, showing rather than narrating. The mimetic often appears to have no clear criterion of the 'important'. Here the non-discursive precedes and determines the discursive, producing particular forms of camera practice (for example, prolonged shots involving pans and tracking movements).

The images of mimetic television can be read as engaging in the pursuit of the impossible, a perfect correspondence to what is represented. But to attain this correspondence would result simultaneously in their becoming identical with the 'reality' they seek to display. Nevertheless, like Plato's portrait painter, the producer of descriptive television may lead the viewer to believe erroneously that 'his picture was a real carpenter' rather than a selective image.[57] The veridical sequence is in play. The mimetic ambition characterizes the verbal as much as the visual; that is, it is evident in the voiceover attempting to describe as well as the image. Plato asserts that in mimesis the poet speaks through his characters, imitating their 'voice' and position, trying 'to make his manner resemble that of the person he has introduced as speaker'.[58] The mimetic discourses of television, of course, often function more widely than this, describing the inanimate as well as the animate. And in a 'speech' in voiceover the content of what is said, rather than the gestures and manner accompanying its saying, will be the sole vehicle for the mimetic ambition.

Within Plato's account of visual representation the Forms always exceed or are better than those images or descriptions which seek to represent them. Similarly, that which is imitated by the discourse of documentary television always exceeds that which imitates. Language, both verbal and visual, is inevitably restricted to a perspectival appropriation of the 'real'.

The mimetic ambitions of documentary presuppose a pre-textual reality of events undetermined by the needs of the programme. 'Documentary-makers wish to communicate with audiences by using the medium to "show" them aspects of reality, to "access" them with maximum immediacy to real circumstances, events and issues as discovered by the programme's exploratory eye.'[59] The camera following rather than anticipating action is a frequent occurrence. In documentaries (unlike drama) characters have an autonomous existence from the programme and its construction: they exist before the text rather than for the text. The textual plane of the mimetic intersects with that of the 'real world'.

The mimetic camera may show events (rather than places), but its showing is detailed, and visual descriptions often interrupt the representation of a causal process. These intervening descriptions may have the effect of separating events into groups, allowing them to be read as discrete causal sequences. Such mimetic camera work can produce extended pans and tracking shots which undermine the transparent, self-authenticating quality of the television image. These operations of the camera show themselves to be contingent, to belong to a system of inclusions and exclusions: they include visual information which might have been omitted, inevitably excluding other images. That which is shown no longer bears a self-validating truth.

But, as I have noted, camera pans or tracking shots may retain something of the transparency of the television image where they function as apparent responses to indeterminacies of meaning in the text. Here they mimic the human look of inquiry which might investigate an off-camera voice or on-camera activity. Travelling shots are also frequently motivated by the need to illustrate a voiceover, resolving its uncertainties of reference. The truth of what is seen is, in turn, confirmed by the truth of an authoritative verbal address to the viewer, providing 'powerful guarantees of authenticity'.[60] Where a voiceover occurs, sound takes precedence : the mimetic function of the documentary is discharged through what is heard, with the text's images providing corroborative visual evidence. Editing itself is effaced by the continuous flow of a commentary, uniting together extended series of often very similar 'short takes'. In these ways documentary images attempt to 'present themselves as a reflection and embodiment of the reality and truth of a taken-for-granted world'.[61]

The 'unsmooth camera movements' of 'fly on the wall' (*cinéma vérité*) photography often found in documentary television, while appearing as a response to events in the world, also enunciate the inevitably selective sight of the camera.[62] The unproblematically given truth of the veridical image is a function of its conforming to the viewer's expectation of the visually ordinary. But the truth associated with 'fly on the wall' documentaries relies on other memories : 'it is precisely the presence of these marks of enuncia-tion . . . that convinces us of the scene's authenticity, for we associate them with reportorial work on live, actual, unpredictable events'.[63] The 'hand-held camera, the cramped shot' have a 'prior association with truth and neutrality'.[64] But precisely because they are 'clearly marked' they signal that they are (however neutral) also limited in what they show. Similarly, the slow-motion shot is conventionally coded as disclosing a certain non-transparent truth. It has 'an aura of scientificity' while (as slow motion) it both distorts its content and denies representation to other events.[65] Hand-held camera sequences and slow-motion shots represent 'variations on the veridical'. Here, though not transparent, images can be read as signifying their own 'truth' : unlike others produced by conspicuous operations of the camera, they are not easily open to doubt.

Documentary foregrounds description of the extra-textually 'real' rather than the telling of a story. But it can be inflected by the narrative ambitions of entertainment, establishing in the process a diegesis with a varying degree of pre-textual existence : 'forms that are not ostensibly fictional entertain-ments, but rather have other goals – description, education, persuasion, exhortation, and so on – covertly tend to use narrative as a means to their ends'.[66] At the beginning of the Channel Four *People to People* documentary ('Get It Shown', C4, 8.00, 5.12.84) about the UK miners' strike of 1984, people complain that an Independent Television current affairs programme *TV Eye* which showed their village during the strike failed to depict the 'normal people', 'the social life in the village'. 'They spent a whole day with us one Thursday and they put nothing on about that.' 'Individual, weren't it ? They kept it a lot to individuals.' 'It were one against the other.' 'They didn't portray . . . the village as a whole.'

These complaints suggest that *TV Eye*'s representation of the village had departed from its mimetic, descriptive ideals as documentary to operate instead in terms of entertainment and the concepts of the diegetic. The result was an emphasis on 'spectacle', on the story and dramatic conflict of individuals. With their activity abstracted from a description of its context in the history of a community, the strikers appeared 'not right in their heads, really'.

Just as the television of descriptive documentary can be influenced by the individualistic preoccupations of narrative, so television drama can be inflected within the horizons of the mimetic. Narration of cause and effect yields to the description of context. In the first episode of the Scottish television serial *Grey Granite* (BBC1, 10.10, 21.3.88) Chris (Vivien Heilbron) commences the story of her 'first months in Duncairn', a fictitious town somewhere in the north-east of Scotland. She refers as she does so to her preceding years in the village of Seggat, which ended with her husband's death.[67] Here the viewer identifies with Chris and is located with her in a position from which the (hermeneutic) unity and closure of those years can be perceived : 'all ended. Put by. Robert himself no more than a name. I'd loved him so deep. For the day he died something had broken in me. Something went numb, still, and stayed so.'

This first Duncairn episode begins and ends in the 'silence' of the Windmill Steps with Chris reflecting on past, present and future in long passages of descriptive voiceover which both initiate and draw the narrative to a (temporary) close :

in the stillness of the steps I was suddenly aware of the silence below [pause] as the whole [speech unclear] shrouded town also stood still, deep breathing in the curl of the fog. No need to hurry [speech unclear] in the peace of the ill-tasting fog. In the blessed desertion of the Windmill Steps so few folk used in Duncairn town [pause]. Rest for a minute in the peace of the fog. Or nearly a peace but for its foul smell. Like the faint ill odour of that silent place where they'd taken Robert's body a few months before.

Notes

1   J.B. Thompson, Introduction to Ricoeur, *Hermeneutics and the Human Sciences*, pp. 18–19.
2   Ricoeur, 'The Hermeneutical Function of Distanciation', *Hermeneutics and the Human Sciences*, p. 143.
3   Gadamer, *Truth and Method*, p. 272.
4   Ibid., p. 295.
5   Ibid., p. 236.

6   Michaels, 'Hollywood Iconography', p. 9.
7   Jauss, *Toward an Aesthetic of Reception*, p. 23.
8   Meyrowitz, *No Sense of Place*, p. 76.
9   M.A. Doane, 'Information, Crisis, Catastrophe', in Mellencamp, *Logics of Television*, p. 225.
10 Meyrowitz, *No Sense of Place*, p. 75.
11 Morley, *Family Television*, p. 151.
12 Neale, *Genre*, p. 19.
13 Root, *Open the Box*, p. 23.
14 Gripsrud, 'Watching versus Understanding *Dallas*', p. 13.
15 Harré and Secord, *The Explanation of Social Behaviour*, *passim*. Horizons of expectation, unlike horizons of understanding, are explicitly future directed.
16 Ibid., p. 11.
17 Ibid., p. 163.
18 R. Williams, *Television*, p. 95.
19 Root, *Open the Box*, p. 30.
20 Hobson, *Crossroads*, p. 121.
21 'Veridical' is defined in the *Concise Oxford Dictionary* (1980) as 'truthful; (Psych., of visions etc.) coinciding with realities'. The philosophical employment of the concept most notably occurs in Austin, *Sense and Sensibilia*. Austin uses 'veridical' in the context of examining the empiricist question whether or not our 'sense-perceptions' or 'sense-data' inform us accurately about material things, that is, are veridical. According to this empiricist account of seeing, 'whenever we "perceive" there is an *intermediate* entity *always* present and *informing* us about something *else* – the question is, can we or can't we trust what it says? Is it veridical?' (*Sense and Sensibilia*, p. 11.) The empiricist analysis of perception rests on a theory in which 'sense-data' are conceived of as 'things', psychic entities interposed between the mind and reality. This theory is, as Austin indicates, erroneous, but yields the useful concept of 'veridical'. For 'veridical' sense-data are asserted to possess the properties of being both accurate representations of the world beyond and, *qua* sense-data, virtually invisible to all but the analytic vision of the philosopher. We (appear to) see, most of us, for most of the time, not sense-data but the world. In a similar vein, I am applying 'veridical' to television images which are experienced as giving near transparent access to the 'real'.
22 Gadamer, *Truth and Method*, p. 134.
23 Heath and Skirrow, 'Television', p. 54.
24 Kozloff, 'Narrative Theory and Television', p. 61.
25 Fiske, *Television Culture*, p. 21.
26 T. Todorov, 'Introduction, le vraisemblable', *Communications*, 11 (1968), pp. 1–4, quoted in Silverstone, 'The Right to Speak', p. 146. (Cf. discussion by Caughie of Todorov's 'verisimilitude' in 'Adorno's Reproach', p. 146.)
27 Feuer, 'The Concept of Live Television', p. 14.
28 Richardson and Corner, 'Reading Reception', p. 490.
29 Seiter, 'Semiotics and Television', p. 25.
30 Millerson, *The Technique of Television Production*, p. 112.

31   MacCabe, 'Realism and the Cinema', p. 218.
32   Millerson, *The Technique of Television Production*, p. 113.
33   Fiske, *Television Culture*, p. 149.
34   Millerson, *The Technique of Television Production*, pp. 112, 113.
35   T. Wilson, 'Depressing Stories with Inconclusive Endings ?', p. 24.
36   Schenck, 'Merleau-Ponty on Perspectivism', p. 309.
37   Barthes, *Mythologies*, pp. 125, 129.
38   T. Wilson, 'Depressing Stories with Inconclusive Endings ?'
39   Lukács, 'Realism in the Balance', p. 33 ; L. Woodhead, 'On Television . . .
     Under Drama-documentary' (interview), *Monthly Film Bulletin*, 50, 593
     (1983), p. 155 ; Hill, 'Scotland Doesna Mean Much tae Glesca', pp. 103–4 ;
     R. Williams, *Keywords*, p. 182 ; Caughie, 'Scottish Television', p. 119 ;
     W. Gibson, 'Network News : Elements of a Theory', *Social Text*, 3 (1980),
     p. 103, quoted in Stam, 'Television News and Its Spectator', p. 34.
40   Bordwell et al., *Classical Hollywood Cinema*, p. 58.
41   Caughie, 'Progressive Television and Documentary Drama', pp. 342–3.
42   Allen, 'On Reading Soaps', p. 100.
43   Flitterman, 'The *Real* Soap Operas', p. 90.
44   R. Collins, 'Seeing Is Believing', pp. 130–1.
45   Schroder, 'Cultural Quality', p. 14.
46   C. Brunsdon and D. Morley, 'Everyday Television : *Nationwide*', in
     Bennett et al., *Popular Television and Film*, p. 132.
47   Viewing frequently occurs in a social situation. Aspects of the audience's
     life-world (e.g. interference by others) may also cause a lapse of involve-
     ment with the veridical text. The life-world of the 'real' viewer is discussed
     in the Conclusion.
48   Gadamer, *Truth and Method*, p. 95.
49   Millerson, *The Technique of Television Production*, p. 114.
50   Watts, *On Camera*, p. 83.
51   Silverstone, 'The Agonistic Narratives of Television Science', p. 86. But
     note his discussion of the mimetic as a 'selection' in 'Narrative Strategies in
     Television Science', p. 387, and 'The right to speak', p. 139.
52   V. I. Pudovkin, *Film Technique and Film Acting* (London Grove, 1970),
     pp. 70–1, quoted in Bordwell, *Narration in the Fiction Film*, p. 9.
53   Bordwell, *Narration in the Fiction Film*, p. 3.
54   Branigan, 'The Spectator and Film Space', p. 61.
55   According to Genette, when a narrative text takes as its subject matter a
     series of 'real' events, they become a 'story', the text's 'signified or narrative
     content (even if this content turns out, in a given case, to be low in dramatic
     intensity or fullness of incident)' (*Narrative Discourse*, p. 26). The writer
     elaborates the story through its 'discursive' construction. Speech is attrib-
     uted to textual subjects ; a relationship between text, reader and narrator
     arises and may be discursively indicated ; changes in temporal sequence and
     tense may occur ; and differing perspectives on those events are discernible
     within the text. Television characteristically adds segmentation. (Cf.
     Martin, *Recent Theories of Narrative*, p. 108.)
56   Caughie, 'Progressive Television and Documentary Drama', p. 337.
57   Plato, *The Republic*, bk X, paras 600 and 598.

58 Ibid., bk III, para. 392.
59 Corner, 'Documentary', p. 30.
60 Flitterman, 'The *Real* Soap Operas', p. 91.
61 A. Kuhn, 'The Camera I, Observations on Documentary', p. 82.
62 Ibid., p. 76.
63 Stam, 'Television News and Its Spectator', p. 35.
64 Caughie, 'Progressive Television and Documentary Drama', p. 343. Note also the sections of drama which bear a 'documentary look' in *Hill Street Blues* (MTM). Because of their unexpected presence within drama they are 'easily visible'.
65 Morse, 'Replay and Display', p. 49.
66 Kozloff, 'Narrative Theory and Television', p. 43.
67 The television serials *Sunset Song, Cloud Howe*, and *Grey Granite* were based on the trilogy of novels of the same name by L. Grassic Gibbon (published as *Scots Quair*, Jarrolds, 1963), a fictional record of the life of a young woman growing up on the north-east coast of Scotland.

5

Mechanisms of Identification in Film and Television

Identification rests on an experience of the image as veridical, as apparently providing unmediated access to the world. Where this occurs, processes of identification involve the reader's taking up a subject's social role(s) and interest-related horizons of understanding. For a character's behaviour, I have been arguing, can be understood as an enactment of social roles, displaying their status as a generative mechanism for activity and discourse within the television programme. In this way Tom Vernon's behaviour in *Fat Man Goes Norse*, for instance, conforms to the role (*inter alia*) of tourist.

Identification requires an appropriating of sense and meaning, a particular way of understanding the world. Where it articulates a role associated with inquiry and the construction of meaning, a text provides a moving focus for identification by an 'empirical' reader engaged in the hermeneutic activity of delivering sense to the programme. But, as I have noted, identification can imply following other rules, subscribing to other rationalities and satisfying other interests in addition to those concerned with sense-making (for example, those related to caring).

Additionally, television possesses a range of mechanisms of identification, variations on a character's 'look' and discourses of speech. These align the implied audience, at certain points in its reading, with a subject's role-related articulation of meaning. They include the televisual point-of-view shot, the 'subjective travelling shot' (as I have chosen to refer to it), spoken discourse in voiceover and direct address to the viewer. In respect of all but the last of these mechanisms, what is seen by the audience usually occurs in a context where the verbal discourses of the text (a character's speech, for instance) provide an interpretation of visual content.

In this concern with processes of identification my argument is not, of course, that an audience's identification with a character is ever forced or determined by a text. Real viewers identify (or fail to identify) in any way they choose. A group of Indian viewers in *The Neglected Audience* points out that when watching European films set in India, 'our identification is with the Asian characters and environment, and not with the main white stars'.[1]

5.1 The Filmic Point-of-view Shot

In his book *Rhetoric of Filmic Narration* Browne asserts that a point-of-view shot is 'authorized by a certain disposition of attention of one of the characters' in the film. Its content is assigned to an individual's glance by preceding or following the shot with a close-up of the subject's 'looking'. Here the character's look authorizes or motivates the shot; he or she is foregrounded as a significant agent in the plot, as a potential source of order or disorder.

The point-of-view shot (POV) cognitively aligns the spectator with the character whose glance it records. It can be said, with a certain metaphorical truthfulness, to 'position' the audience in the space occupied by the subject in the text. The shot 'gives the spectator a point of view and a position within the fiction as a subject of its world'.[2] Metz argues that when this occurs, the spectator's 'look' is no longer 'hovering' (where 'the spectator can do no other than identify with the camera').[3] Instead, 'the framing of the scene corresponds precisely to the angle from which the out-of-frame character looks at the scene'.[4]

For Bordwell also, point-of-view sequences construct 'optical subjectivity' as a 'glance' by 'placing the camera in the spatial position of the character': 'the first shot shows the character looking at something off-screen; the second shot shows what the character is seeing, but more or less from the character's optical vantage point'.[5] Bordwell's definition of the point-of-view shot in terms of the subjective 'glance' is important. For these shots are to be distinguished from the marking out of a subject's 'gaze' in extended tracking movements, pans or tilts. Point-of-view shots are usually brief, with minimal camera movement; the others are of longer duration and involve altering the position of the camera (or camera 'head'). (This distinction between 'glance' and 'gaze' is developed further in section 5.3.)

Branigan also defines the point-of-view sequence in terms of the subject's 'glance', though he allows for 'permutations' on the sequence which involve camera movement. In point-of-view sequences the first shot establishes the subject's 'point' or location in space and an 'off-camera object by glance'.[6] In the second 'we see what a character sees from his or her point in space':[7] 'the POV shot is a shot in which the camera assumes the position of a subject in order to show us what the subject sees'.[8]

The point-of-view shot can be read as founded upon negation, Heath's 'separation in identification'. It assigns a field of vision which is within the text, denying the subject's capacity to look out of the film or programme and at the audience. The filmic point-of-view sequence excludes the familiar look at the audience so prevalent, for instance, in segments of television news.

The spectator's appropriation of meaning in a point-of-view shot is constituted internally as a fusion of (cognitive) horizons in which the viewer's look 'goes through' the subjective looking of an individual in the text. 'The spectator's look . . . must first "go through" – as one goes through a town on a journey, or a mountain pass – the look of the character out-of-frame.'[19] To insist on an audience's involvement in a point-of-view sequence as consisting of a mediating fusion between the cognitive horizons of different 'looks' is important. It acknowledges (along with anti-empiricist philosophers of perception) that an individual's perceptual experience is inflected by a 'cultural capital' of assumptions and expectations : 'what observers see, the subjective experiences that they undergo, when viewing an object or scene is not determined solely by the images on their retinas but depends also on the experience, knowledge, expectations and general inner state of the observer'.[10]

The film camera marks out its own or a subject's visual field. The practices in which this camera engages (for example, shooting angle) or a subject's accompanying verbal discourse indicate the cognitive horizon in whose terms what is seen by the spectator has been understood within the text. An upward-tilting camera angle connotes authority. What characters say signifies a sense for what is shown. In the processes of spectatorship this cognitive horizon is itself read through the framework of horizons of understanding brought to the text by its reader. Reading is a 'fusion of horizons' : the 'positioning' of a spectator everywhere occurs through the audience's active negotiation of meaning in the text.

The term 'horizon' is being used to refer to an aspect of cognition. It refers neither to the spatio-temporal limits of a shot nor to any spatio-temporal relationship between its contents. This is to relinquish one use of the concept found in phenomenology : 'the image of the *horizon* that shifts according to one's position and that can expand and shrink as one moves through the rough countryside'.[11]

'Horizons', as I noted in Chapter 1, provide a context of understanding as 'frames' of meaning rather than spatial 'frames' of seeing (though, like those which mark out spatio-temporal dimensions, they are often neglected in favour of what is in the foreground of attention). Here, they refer to cognitive, rather than perceptual, limits on the 'look', which are often effaced or regarded as unproblematic because of their very familiarity to the discursive subject. For both audience and individual in the text they are the shifting categories in terms of which the contents of perceptual subjectivity (or verbal discourse) are identified.[12]

Cognitive horizons set the processes of seeing or hearing within a context of presuppositions, mediating the audience's awareness of the objects to which its attention is directed by the text. Where identification occurs, the processes of film spectatorship involve a fusion of the cognitive horizons of textual and extra-textual subjects. A character's understanding and perception of what he or she sees is reread and 'reviewed' by the audience. For both this is a perspectival appropriation of meaning in which some aspects of what is seen or referred to are marginalized and others foregrounded.

The horizons or forms of understanding which underwrite cognition inevitably emphasize particular items of experience and result in silence or 'blindness' over others. In *Mildred Pierce* Mildred's perception of her daughters' personalities, for example, privileges those aspects she can recognize in herself (such as Veda's 'femininity') and ignores much else. As the film proceeds, these preferences are themselves the subject of a selective reading by an audience. They place varying emphases on what they see and hear as a consequence of bringing to bear on the text horizons of understanding inflected by different interests and experiences.

The use of 'horizon' as an epistemological tool to investigate language and perception, that is, implies a 'field of understanding' beyond which aspects of the text are ignored by subject or reader involved with the processes of making sense (for instance, events to which reference is not necessary in constructing a coherent meaning). Just as in perception, so in speech perspectival appropriation of the world occurs : phenomenology 'shows that speech manifests the same figure/horizon structure as perception. Every explicit linguistic meaning carries its horizon of implicit and latent significance.'[13] I shall discuss this relationship between speech, vision and the world in later chapters.

Alignment of spectator with character in a point-of-view shot, then, cannot manufacture an identity of vision. An audience's appropriation of the contents of a subject's looking will draw on the horizons of experience (the semantic regime) it has brought to the text, operating an interpretative logic in response to the visual rhetoric of the film. Containing such varieties of reading, point-of-view shots establish a spectator's identification with a subject in ways which are both spatial and conceptual. Identification allows the spectator to be 'drawn into the narration itself' : occupying the place of a subject who is trying to make sense of events leads to 'a resolution of the narrative in which all the ends are tied up' being 'in certain ways pleasurable for the spectator'.[14]

To identify is to take up many of the activities appropriate for a subject in the film. According to Browne, the cavalry officer's wife in John Ford's *Stagecoach* (1939) enacts a 'kind of central consciousness that corresponds to a social and formal role'. As the bearer of an assured cultural knowledge she is the source of information that can serve as the basis of making the film intelligible. Identifying with her, the spectator becomes able to 'make the depicted space coherent and readable'.[15]

Point-of-view shots are sometimes cognitively elaborated by a subject's description of their content, manufacturing particular identities for what is shown in a construction of meaning which is partly visual and partly verbal. Here an individual's way of understanding his or her social context is made explicit for the audience, contributing to the preferred reading of the text (cf. section 5.4). An (actual) audience may appropriate only part of the interpretation attached by the subject to what is seen, dissenting from other aspects of the description or evaluation. Identification may, in other words, be limited.

Point-of-view sequences are often claimed to produce 'empathetic' identification with a subject in the text : they 'may even, perhaps, encourage the viewer to empathize with' a character.[16] If this is the case (and I shall indicate that it is open to dispute), the processes of identification involved continue nevertheless to be informed by a cognitive appropriation of meaning. The experience of emotion is simultaneously an apprehension of the world ; empathy, while predicated upon the 'sharing' of emotion, is not thereby cognitively 'blind'. To empathize with another is to appropriate that other's horizons of understanding. In Lovell's phrase, there are 'structures of feeling'.

Cooke, writing in the British Film Institute study notes accompanying the film *Psycho* (directed by Hitchcock, 1960), asserts unequivocally that point-of-view shots produce empathetic states of mind. In the course of the film we are positioned with Norman Bates (Anthony Perkins), allowed access to his looking in a point-of-view shot which shows Marion Crane's (Janet Leigh) car sinking in the swamp with her body in the boot : 'when the car briefly stops sinking into the swamp we not only see Norman's anguish but experience it from his POV. When the car eventually sinks out of sight we experience Norman's relief.'[17]

In the first place this interpretation of 'our' experience as an empathetic identification with Norman can be questioned. The tension ('anguish') and release ('relief') which characterize the spectator's enjoyment of this scene may be produced not by the point-of-view shots but, on the contrary, by the reverse-shots of Norman looking. For these shots function to postpone the spectator's knowledge of whether or not the car has sunk in the swamp. The audience's experience of tension (and release) while watching these events is, arguably, produced quite differently from Norman's. Its source is a series of images (his looking) to which he has no access. Both Norman and the film's audience experience an indeterminacy of meaning which is emotionally charged, but that experience is not the same for subject and spectator. More generally, the point-of-view structures which allow identification may also induce emotional states for the spectator ; but these offer no guarantee that empathy has occurred.

Secondly, despite this objection, some analyses may continue to assert that empathetic identification characterizes the relationship between audience and text in this and other instances. Even if this is the case, 'empathy' cannot be regarded as the experience of 'mere' feeling. As I have noted, emotion is a way of perceiving the world ; it provides an epistemological purchase on 'reality'. If, for instance, as a result of a series of point-of-view shots, the audience of *Psycho* experiences something like Marion's fear when pursued by the law, this experience has a cognitive aspect. It implies understanding the policeman concerned as 'embodying' a threat.

My argument for an account of 'empathy' as a mode of cognition rests on the phenomenological thesis that the experience of emotions generates particular cognitive apprehensions of reality. Fear produces the experience and evaluation of the world as threatening. If a spectator empathizes with a character in a film, then there occurs not only a similarity of emotions but a fusion of horizons whereby the audience also understands the world at that moment in a similar (yet also different) way.

Sartre argues that emotions are intensional ; 'emotion is a phenomenon of belief'. The experience of emotions contains the 'projection of affective meanings upon the world'. Consciousness *'lives* the new world it has thereby constituted – lives it directly, commits itself to it, and suffers from the qualities that the concomitant behaviour has assigned to it . . . "I find him hateful *because* I am angry." '[18] 'The emotion is a specific manner of apprehending the world', generating anticipations ('protensions') of the future : 'thus, in every emotion, a multitude of affective protensions extends into the future and presents it in an emotional light'.[19]

5.2 The Televisual Point-of-view Shot

The televisual point-of-view shot establishes a visual identification for the intended audience with a subject whose social role(s) and horizons of understanding what is seen are likely to have been verbally constructed prior to the shot's taking place. Here, as in film intended for cinematic exhibition, a subject's visual field is given as the content of a glance. Displaying the visual indeterminacy of an individual's looking, followed by its resolution, effaces rather than draws attention to the editing processes involved.

The point-of-view sequence is a not infrequent aspect of the discourse of advertising, in which viewer identification with a textual subject is likely to be a desired effect. In a Du Pont 'Antron Stainmaster Carpet' advertisement (C4, 10.00, 12.4.88), for instance, the first seven shots included what appeared to be two point-of-view sequences. In the second the shots occurred in reverse order, showing the content of the look followed by an image of the subject's 'looking' in anxious concern. In this short story of near disaster the narrative moved from an equilibrium involving a relaxed group of party guests, through the disequilibrium of a nearly damaged carpet, to the re-equilibrium of the relieved onlookers. Unusually for television, the time of the action was drawn out to allow a complex series of images to occur. A single sentence in voiceover accompanied the first five shots : '*Recently* Dupont discovered people with *great* carpets have to make *great* saves' ; sound of crowd (at football match ?).

Shot A *(objective)* : small boy at a party holding a plate full of cake
Shot B *(objective)* : the expression on the face of one of the female guests registers concern as she looks in the boy's direction
Shot C *(subjective)* : this reveals the content of the woman's glance to be the cake falling off the boy's plate

Shot D (*objective*) :   the woman rushes forward through the guests to prevent the cake from reaching the immaculate white carpet
Shot E (*objective*) :   the woman's feet, surrounded by carpet
Shot F (*subjective*) :   the cake falling
Shot G (*objective*) :   the woman diving forward into the air, her look fixed on the cake (defining the content of shot F as her visual field) (See Figure 5.)

If the function of a point-of-view shot is to produce an easy identification with an individual in the text, an extended series of such shots edited together with reverse-shots in rapid succession is likely to be self-defeating. Directed at the hermeneutic activities of the viewer, its visual complexity will nevertheless subvert any experience of its images as transparent disclosures of the 'real'. This complex textuality draws attention to itself as different ; 'in most TV productions editing is simplistic . . . creating a feeling of consecutiveness and order'.[20] Such an experience of visual difference disturbs the veridical effect of the image and undermines the process of identification. It repositions the viewer in the role of reader rather than participant in the text.

One variation on the point-of-view sequence is particularly televisual. Unlike most dominant cinema, television permits apparent eye contact between viewing and textual subjects in its direct visual address to the audience.[21] The enunciation of a subject's field of vision in a point-of-view shot may therefore include the 'return look' of another individual in the drama (or documentary). This individual directly addresses in visual, if not also verbal, terms both the intra-textual subject and the extra-textual audience. He or she becomes a subjective source as well as an objective content of the 'play' of glances between text and audience. The (intended) viewers are here the focus of multiple positionings. Through the point-of-view shot they share the visual field of a subject in the text, a visual field in which another individual appears as object. But equally, and in an opposite direction to this looking, the viewers themselves become an ('implied') object within that individual's glance at the camera.

In television documentary the 'return look' within a point-of-view sequence is unusual. The subjects with which the text is concerned rarely have their visual fields recorded for the audience unless they happen to occupy the position of presenter. The presenter's looking, fixed momentarily through a point-of-view shot for the viewer, may include one or more individuals, subjects who are thereby looked at. But these subjects, unlike those of drama, are rarely allowed to displace the camera's and presenter's look, to acquire in their turn a visual field displayed for the television audience. There is, in this sense, no 'relay' of looks in the documentary text ; the 'documentary look is a look at its object, fixing the object rather than putting its look into play'.[22] The 'object's' look, let alone direct address is excluded.

Only occasionally does the documentary presenter transfer his or her control over the 'look' in a text to an individual who has previously been

5 In this excerpt from Du Pont's advertising literature the shot in the top row, second from the left, is a reconstructed version of Shot G in my analysis. Other images indicate the intended audience.

fixed in place as the object of documentary scrutiny. The UK *This Week* documentary and current affairs programme 'Death on the Rock' (ITV, 9.00, 28.4.88) investigated 'the death of three IRA terrorists in Gibraltar' (*TV Times*). Carmen Proetta, 'our second witness', announced the presenter, 'had a different view [from other witnesses] with what seems to have been a more complete picture of the shooting'. During the course of her interview a point-of-view shot reconstructed for the audience something akin to her original 'look' at the roadway below. The human activity present within her glance on the first occasion was absent from this image, but it was retrospectively manufactured in speech for audience and interviewer: 'I looked out of the window and all of a sudden I saw a car, police car. It stops, all of a sudden, the doors will [*sic*] open, all of them, the four of them and three men came out dressed in jeans and jackets, jumped over the intersection barrier in the road, guns in hand.'

5.3 Televisual Identification and the Subjective Travelling Shot

The rhetoric of the televisual point-of-view shot, when not asserted to excess, effaces the presence of the camera by attributing the image to the look of a textual subject. This constructs an unproblematic flow of images which is articulated around a swift subjective glance and likely to be read as veridical. Distinct from this sequence, however, is the visual rhetoric which produces a subjective gaze. Unlike the construction of a glance, it is likely to indicate to the viewer the technical presence of a camera. In part this is because the shots by which a subject's gaze is often marked out draw attention to themselves as untypical of the restrained vision of television. Zooms or tilting camera actions belong to this category. Equally, extended pans or tracking movements in drama 'offend' the viewer's established horizons of expectation concerning the repetitive and ordinary, the settled anticipation of television's everyday images. The sustained representation of another's visual subjectivity in a panning shot often begins, in addition, to seem artificial, drawing attention to the image as construction.

Branigan refers to a pan or tracking shot which provides a filmic subject's visual field as a 'continuing POV' shot or 'subjective travelling shot', 'where one character looks at several objects'.[23] But because these images signal rather than mask the operations of technology within the television text, they cannot be read (in Branigan's terms) as involving mere 'formal permutations' of the point-of-view shot. Rather they must be understood in terms of their difference.

The visual discourse of what I shall refer to as the 'subjective travelling shot' is varied. It consists of shots requiring camera movement, either of the camera 'head', as in tilting and extended panning, or of the entire camera, as in prolonged tracking shots (and 'zooms', as 'simulated' camera movements). While drawing attention to the work of the camera, the subjective travelling shot is also motivated by accompanying shots of a subject's looking out of frame. In this way it functions, at one and the same time, as an expression of a look whose source is both an object and a subject. In television's subjective travelling shots involving movement of the camera (as in tracking) the slowly changing view of what is seen implies an alteration in space of the subject as well as the camera.

As I have indicated, the edit from a glance to the object of the glance in the paradigmatic POV sequence discussed above sets up a structure of visual indeterminacy and resolution whose effect is to hide the cut, sustaining in place the veridical (or illusionistic) effect of the image. This marginalizes the camera's presence with a subjective look, providing a 'fictive alibi' (Flitterman-Lewis). It elides and excludes the symptoms of television's production from the text itself : 'the directional eye movement at the end of the shot . . . has the effect of motivating the cut in a way which masks its presence as a technical intrusion into the continuity of the world'.[24]

But the two-shot sequence involving a cut from look to 'object' of the look may register the latter in a tracking or panning shot of some duration. This discourse of subjective gazing subverts the effect of the veridical associated with television's ordinariness and reasserts the status of the image as construction. In the subjective 'surveying pan' 'the camera slowly searches the scene (a crowd, a landscape), allowing the audience to look around at choice'.[25] But for that audience this is a knowledge-providing shot which (however encompassing) also signals its own production by a camera. This effect is particularly noticeable when associated with a hand-held subjective shot in a drama.

A subjective travelling shot may even include its source, the subject. The pan, zoom or tracking shot celebrates a flexibility of camera use which encourages not a cut from look to subjective content but an unbroken movement. This is an emphatic statement of the continuities of space and time in which both subject and field of vision are enclosed. Here it is difficult to distinguish between that part of the shot which signifies the ownership of the look and that which informs the viewer of its content.

In *To the End of the Rhine*, as I noted earlier, Bernard Levin is our 'guide'. His position in the text is defined from time to time by sequences of images which, while registering his visual field, cannot be regarded as straightforwardly involving point-of-view shots. In the opening segments of the first episode an image of the snow-covered mountains above the Rhine initiates a slow reverse zoom. The camera pulls back to a position which includes Levin, indicating that the first stages of this shot marked out his gaze at 'these hills', 'these majestic views'. The viewer, like the camera, undergoes a process of visual adjustment in which the technology of a zoom lens is used in a notably constructed (and rather imprecise) definition of subjective looking which here includes the subject himself.

At the end of the final programme (UK first transmission, 21.11.87) Levin departs for England on the ferry. 'I looked up at the Red Ensign and realized that I would soon be home.' In support of this announcement the camera tilts conspicuously and slowly upwards to reveal Levin's field of vision, the Red Ensign flying above his boat. This gaze is 'anchored' both in subject and object, experienced as 'given' by a technology as well as by the look of an individual in the text.

In comparison with cinematic film, television images could be thought commonplace and even dull. In this context the camera practices generally associated with marking out the gaze of textual subjects might be considered a 'return of the repressed', a 'remembering' of visual technology as a source of innovation. Here the logic of the shot or sequence which establishes the gaze is *inclusive* : not only a subject's perceptions but also the 'looking' of technology. It is the explicit enunciation of a subjectivity constrained by the objective possibilities of the camera. The logic of the point-of-view sequence establishing a glance, on the other hand, is *exclusive* : not the camera but the 'look' of the subject.

In 'We're Not Mad, We're Angry' (C4, 8.15, 6.9.87), a documentary drama in the Channel Four *People to People* series referred to in the previous chapter, these visual discourses of identification around the 'gaze' are further complicated. Prolonged sequences of shots, some consisting of camera tilts and pans, mark out for the television audience the subjective gaze of several members of a group of psychiatric patients during their admission to hospital and subsequent stay. At certain points in the text a nurse and psychiatrist return the look of patient and viewer in an authoritative direct address to camera (see Figure 6). Here the intended audience is simultaneously 'positioned' both as object and subjective bearer of an inquiring gaze, a gaze which is also that of the camera :

> *Psychiatrist (in direct address to patient, viewer and camera)* : Now we like all our patients to take a bath and to change into their night clothes. It's more comfortable for them. Just for today.
> *Alice, a patient (in voice only)* :   But it's lunch-time.

5.4   Discourses of Speech in Voiceover

The point-of-view sequence is constructed in a series of shots which visually define an image as the 'glance' of a textual subject. Likewise, the subjective travelling shot is experienced as marking out the visual field of both character and camera simultaneously. A shot expressing a subject's visual field, however, may be signalled as doing so not by a preceding (or succeeding) image of an out-of-frame look but by speech. An individual, in what I shall call the role of 'presenter' (commentator, reporter, narrator, etc.), refers to the image in voiceover, picking out its content for attention. 'This is the house where the artist was born . . .', and so on.

6   A psychiatrist addresses patient, camera and viewer in 'We're Not Mad, We're Angry'

In documentary, news and current affairs texts (and occasionally elsewhere on television) an image may be anchored to the time and space of a 'presenter's' gaze through the spoken discourse of voiceover. During standard point-of-view sequences of the type already discussed both object and source of the look are located in the same spatio-temporal framework. But a presenter who is in the text only as voiceover occupies a position beyond the space of that upon which he or she looks and comments.

In the paradigmatic case of this mechanism of identification no reverse-shot occurs throughout these extended visual sequences to anchor the images in a subject's looking. Instead, the image is often indicated to occupy the visual field of a presenter by the appearance of demonstratives (for example, 'this' or 'here') in the voiceover. The use of such linguistic correlatives of pointing also 'places' the intended audience within the spatio-temporal framework occupied by the presenter by assuming both to share a similar look. 'Here we see the scene of the historic defeat of the Scots', etc.

The function of a discourse of identification is to produce a fusion of horizons (and social roles) between textual subject and ideal viewer. During the experience of watching television the spoken discourses of a voiceover will align the intended audience in terms of a proposed interpretation of what is seen, determining what is of interest and how it is to be regarded. Here, cognitive horizons of speech are constituted as horizons of understanding the visual. The ideal viewer appropriates the meaning which has been verbally articulated by the presenter ; located together in a hermeneutic role, they engage with the sense of the text. In this process a close proximity is established between the structure of foreground and background within the look of textual subject (presenter) and (intended) audience alike. Description in voiceover suggests what is to be noticed, to be regarded as more or less important. While there are inevitable differences in understanding, agreement between subject and intended audience on what is noteworthy is reached. In this mechanism of identification associated with the voiceover, the speech of a presenter relates to an image through discourses of position and interpretation.

5.4.1   *Discourses of position within a voiceover*

In a discourse of position 'ostensive' or 'denotative' reference to the image suggests it to be the object of a subjective look. Talk of 'this' or 'that' item of interest in the frame implies its visibility to the gaze or glance of the presenter. The evident conformity by objects, or events, to the presenter's references in voiceover appears to confirm that he or she is 'now' looking at 'these' images. A discourse of position establishes the presenter and intended audience in an implied spatio-temporal relationship to what is seen : 'on that hill in 1337, the battle commenced . . .'

On the one hand, in this shared (if not precisely determined) 'here' and 'now' of the presenter and audience they are both absent from there, the space of those aspects of the programme other than the voiceover. On the other hand, the television image 'presences', creating an apparent simultaneity between the time of content, voiceover and viewing.

A television picture discloses the referent of a voiceover to presenter and audience in a context of perception and understanding centred on the text. Here, the use of demonstratives positions viewer and presenter in a shared space and time established with respect to images. But the presenter may cease to occupy the spatio-temporal position associated with his or her voiceover, that of a 'heterodiegetic' (Kozloff) narrator. He or she may appear instead 'homodiegetically', within the image itself, perhaps subsequently engaging the audience in visual and verbal direct address. The presenter's knowledge is now seen to be authenticated by on-the-spot experience, as in John Blunden's references in his UK Open University programme to the 'house behind me' : 'after the dissolution of the monastaries, Henry the Eighth gave these lands to Anne of Cleves when he divorced her, and the house behind me still bears her name' (*The Changing Countryside*, BBC2, 1.05, 23.4.88).

Each item to which a voiceover refers is available to the 'look' of presenter and viewer. *To the End of the Rhine* (C4, 6.30, 17.10.87, and subsequently SBS) allows Levin to position himself with the audience (and the audience with him) by means of a voiceover which, in its references, presupposes a similarity of look and comprehension : 'I swooped memorably low over these savage rocks in the blinding fiery sheet of the . . . glacier.' But a presenter may be heard on voiceover and seen in an image at one and the same time. At this point in the text Levin becomes visible : objective images form around a 'split subject'. He is *here*, as the source of a voiceover in what is implied to be the time and space of the viewer outside the image. Yet he is equally *there*, seen in the accompanying shots which emphasize his on-the-spot experience and right to speak. The electronic immediacy of the television picture appears to allow Levin to exist simultaneously, in the present, within both the space of the voiceover and the image.

A subject may, then, appear visually in the text while his or her spoken discourse continues as a voiceover to fulfil the role of presenter. The image which results can possess a certain objectivity, for when positioned in front of the camera, the subject's immediate control over it is conspicuously denied. But the opposition between a presenter's being seen there (in the image) and heard here (in voiceover) generates an uncertain reference for his or her words. In this context the use of demonstratives in voiceover is read, I would suggest, as an attempt to position viewer and presenter not with respect to a two-dimensional image but in terms of its three-dimensional content. Here, a visual alignment between audience and presenter looking at the image can no longer be assumed, for the latter has demonstrated his or her presence among the things themselves.

More generally, what 'this' or 'there' refers to will clearly vary depending on the location of the individual who is talking. Where the subject is a presenter speaking in voiceover outside the space and time 'displayed' in the image, the implied reference will be to that two-dimensional representation of 'the world'. This suggests in turn that audience and presenter occupy a common (if indeterminate) space and time (usually the present). Both presenter and intended viewer engage with the text as a set of images in a similar look structured by a similarity of cognitive interest.

However, as I indicated, the presenter may appear within the time and space of the image itself. Denotative references accompanying shots of this spatio-temporal location, even those heard in voiceover, are read as 'pointing to' a three-dimensional 'reality'. At this point, again, between (ideal) viewer and textual subject there will be a fusion of speech-determined cognitive interests in 'this' or 'these' items of concern. But for this merging of cognitions to be translated into visual alignment in the perception of an object, other mechanisms, such as the point-of-view shot, will also be required. It is worth noting that, asserted within the image, demonstratives may also function to anticipate a cut to a new image, an image which registers a content of subjective looking at the world in a point-of-view shot.

Voiceovers in television news are often ambiguous as to whether their reference is to an electronic image or the 'real'. In a UK ITV *News at Ten* item (ITV, 10.00, 21.4.88) on the Kuwaiti airliner hijacking of April 1988 Simon Cole comments in voiceover on a sequence showing the freed hostages leaving Algeria by plane to return home : 'here, a member of the Kuwaiti royal family. Despite threats to her life by the hijackers, the Kuwaiti government had refused to give in.'

'Here' appears to position reporter and viewer in the same time and space from which images of 'these Kuwaitis' are visible. But subsequent remarks undermine this impression. While Cole does not appear on camera, his later references to 'foreign diplomats *here*' (my italics) signal to British viewers the distance between his space and theirs. This distance allows uncertainty to emerge concerning whether his commentary is directed at a sequence of images or at events themselves. However, his time, like that of the viewers, remains the present, with his function that of relating past, present and future in a discourse of narration : 'and so the freed hostages left Algeria to be reunited with their families, to tell their stories and then to try to forget their two weeks of terror'.

Other forms of television are often clearer as to whether their positioning references in voiceover locate the 'presenter' with respect to image or a three-dimensional 'reality'. In this context there is generally a difference between how a voiceover functions in news and documentary on the one hand and drama on the other.

Ken Loach's now classic early documentary drama for the BBC, *Cathy Come Home* (BBC1, 16.11.66), has become a central reference point for writing about UK television. Cathy's (Carol White) plight as a homeless single parent is foregrounded throughout the text for the viewer's concerned attention. In the opening sequence her voice functions as a discourse of position and presentation in voiceover, introducing the audience to her predicament. But this section of text also contains a series of point-of-view shots (approximately) marking out Cathy's perception of the world through which we see her passing. The intended viewer shares not only her time but the dramatic space of her look. Cathy's narrative inserts aspects of her life, little dramas, into the text, relating them to 'that' house and 'this' street, the objects of our (collective) looking back in time. This is the discourse of intimate recollection, its displaced location in the voiceover to be read as a mark of privacy rather than (as in documentary) a positioning of the subject outside the image : 'that house over there, yeah, that one with the broken steps, that's where I went for a room. And the fella kept touching me. Where did I get a room in the end ? Oh yeah, down there, Mantua Street, three pounds a week. That's where I got my first job, petrol pump girl. Mad.'

These denotative references align Cathy and the viewer, and are in part responsible for the experience of the text as transparent which supports these identifications. They prompt and structure the audience's look, pointing out items of importance, 'that house over there' or 'down there, Mantua Street'. This constructs the viewer's desire to see, a desire immediately rewarded in the veridical effect of the text, drawing the onlooker into the documentary drama and an unquestioning involvement in its world. Accompanied by the references in Cathy's voiceover, these images take on the status of presenting 'obvious' objects of attention, their choice and editing unproblematic, escaping conscious scrutiny by the audience. That details of images do not correspond to the voiceover, that the 'broken steps' of 'that house over there' cannot be seen by the viewer, is a nearly invisible reminder of the text as construction.

The use of these demonstratives of pointing and vision emphasizes the spoken, familiar qualities of Cathy's discourse. As in a conversation, they position speaker (Cathy) and listener (the audience) in a shared location in time and space, the 'present' of recollection, looking down from the top of a bus on Mantua Street or across the road at the house with the broken steps. This alignment of understanding in speech sets in motion an emerging pattern of identification with Cathy in the text. For a moment one of the women in Mantua Street looks back at the camera/Cathy/the audience. We are caught looking, our 'look' is established.

Other television dramas use voiceover as a mark of intimacy between subject and viewer. In 'Ploughing' (BBC1, 10.10, 18.1.88), the second episode of *Sunset Song* (part of the Gibbon trilogy referred to in Chapter 4), Chris becomes increasingly aware of her alienation from much around her. She describes in voiceover the men of the farms at the evening meal after the threshing is over and her response to their rejection of 'education'. The viewer shares her thoughts about the workers surrounding her, but the cameras, while showing her to be present (see Figure 7), do not give access to the content of her look (all the shots are objective):

Shot A :   Chris gazes around the table
Voiceover : For a moment, I saw the ill-natured grin from the faces of them.
Shot B :   cuts from face to face as the men eat
Voiceover : Suddenly, I hated the lot. The other Chris of the books came back into my skin and I saw the yokels and clowns everlasting, dull-brained and cruel.
Shot C :   wink from one of the men to Chris
Shot D :   Chris's return look, smiling
Voiceover : Then I was 'shamed
Shot E :   shows two of the men talking
Voiceover : as I thought, Chae and Long Rob they were, my clowns and yokels,
Shot F :   Chris, looking
Voiceover : the poorest folk in Kinraddie.

This is a verbal discourse of specific reference (to 'them'). In spoken commentary Chris aligns the viewer with her response not to an image but

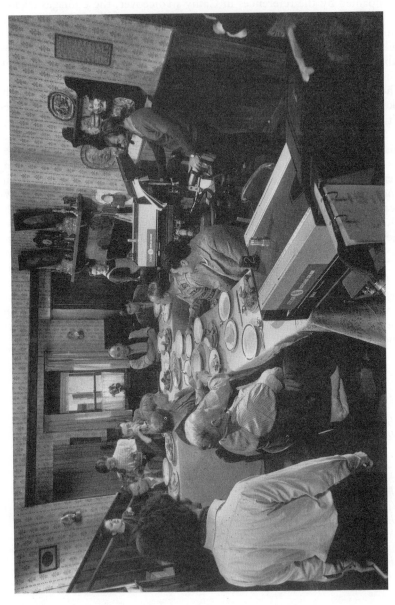

7 The evening meal from the second episode of *Sunset Song. Back, third from left*: Chris Guthrie (Vivien Heilbron).

8   Ake Ogilvie (Alec Heggie) in *Cloud Howe*

to the 'real'. But in this segment of text from *Sunset Song* the audience cannot identify with Chris's subjective vision. There is no shot displaying her look.

Similarly, in 'Stone Circle' (BBC1, 10.00, 4.4.88), the final episode of *Grey Granite* (the last in the trilogy of Gibbon's *Scots Quair*), Chris is shown having her evening meal in the boarding house where she 'helps out'. Her 'inner' reflections on the marriage proposal she has just received from Ake Ogilvie (Alec Heggie) are heard in voiceover. They allow her to 'present' a meaning for what she sees, though the prolonged shot of Ake eating does not align the viewer with her looking : 'oh, the beast, the beast, with his sneering half kindly, half bull-like face, the face of the Howe throughout'.

5.4.2   *Discourses of interpretation within a voiceover*

The spoken discourses associated with a text's presenter also relate to the television camera's articulation of visual perspectives through contributing a discourse of interpretation, analysing and accounting for what is seen. This discourse establishes the sense of an image for the implied audience, an image sometimes given in 'pans' or 'trucking' movements, which move 'across the scene, parallel with it. Trucking becomes associated with an attitude of inspection, critical observation, expectancy, intolerant appraisal.'[26]

The cognitive categories (such as those of 'discovery' or 'gaining insight') implicit within a discourse of interpretation are horizons of understanding whose apparent validity, at least in television current affairs and documentary, is likely to be confirmed by their ease of comprehension. Contained in the voiceover, they engage with the cognitions of the viewer to produce the frameworks of knowledge traversing the processes of audience looking. These horizons of understanding mediate the relationship between reader (his or her perception of the text) and what is seen (the perceived text).

The discourse of interpretation unavoidably imposes a selective dimension upon the already selective look marked out by the camera. Interpretation defines a specificity of perceptual interest in areas of the visual field identified by the discourse of position. Where the discourse of interpretation appears to 'fit' the image, the look of the presenter is confirmed as being 'in play'.

A discourse of interpretation distracts the attention of the viewer from the limits of the image. The opposition it implies between that which is of interest and that which is not of interest within the frame 'mirrors' that between what is included in and excluded from the frame itself. The flow of images allows the audience to define a space, the space of that particular text. Occurring in the context of a discourse of interpretation, the moment of viewing functions as a time of 'named', discursively presented vision.

Interpretation of an image serves to structure the look of the (ideal) viewer in terms of cognitive interests and categories similar to those of the presenter, producing a fusion of horizons of understanding and expectation. For the real viewer, identification may nevertheless be limited, marked by a selective appropriation from the discourse of interpretation. This discourse is important in sustaining a reading of the text as unified, particularly if its visual discourse is in some respect fragmented. In her review of Channel Four's series about television, *Open the Box*, Boyd-Bowmann notes the 'problem of how to construct a coherent discourse in the absence of' the conventions of voiceover (and presentation to camera).[27]

Without interpretation, images may be 'unintelligible': 'the images' significance comes from the context and interpretation provided by speech'.[28] The sense attached by the discourse of interpretation to the images it accompanies may go far beyond their (apparent) immediate significance, evaluating their content in particular ways. A UK 'Broadcasting Complaints Commission Summary of Adjudication' printed in the *TV Times* noted that the Commission had upheld a complaint from a Dr Spooner about *Viewpoint 87*, 'Borderland', a Central Television production broadcast on 8 July 1987. The programme criticized failures in communication between doctors and patients suffering from cancer : 'the commentary was delivered by an individual patient who has not met Dr Spooner. But some of his most critical remarks were laid over shots of Dr Spooner and appeared to be directed at him. The Commission considers that this was unacceptable and unfair.'[29]

Alterations in a discourse of interpretation may produce a different sense for the image. A particular visual content can have its significance 'reversed' by a new commentary. In Marker's film *Letter from Siberia* a 'series of images just seen by the audience is replayed twice with different commentaries which totally reverse the ideological meaning of the sequence as first shown'.[30]

A discourse of interpretation (and its accompanying images) is, as I have indicated, selective. It may relate cause to effect (and effect to cause) in the construction of a narrative. Or it may resist selection to a degree that allows it the appearance of a mimetic description of detail, inclusive rather than exclusive. Discourses of position and interpretation, together with their accompanying images, may denote action in a series of briefly established frames. Or they may reveal place in long pans or tracking shots. The 'Wonders of Ellora' (the 'rock-cut temples' of western India) contained, and the programme about them displayed, 'the most extraordinary sculpture of *all* which unites in one, three contradictory aspects of Shiva, as creator, preserver and destroyer' (*Footsteps*, BBC2, 9.30, 3.11.88). The construction of action and place, of the diegetic and mimetic (as I noted in Chapter 4), can both occur in the same text, with the one giving way to the other. 'Exposition (description) and narrative . . . are not exclusive.'[31] Chris's voiceover in *Sunset Song* (BBC1, 10.10, 18.1.88), for instance, allows an announcement of events to yield to description : 'there was nothing but the corn growing and the peewits calling. Summer coming. Marching up each morning with unbraided hair.'

Discourses of position and interpretation are enunciated in voiceover by subjects who are documentary, news or current affairs presenters. The task of the presenter is to 'presence' the text's significances in the time and space of the audience, mediating them through discourses of narration and description. Television, of course, can be read as 'presencing' in the absence of a voiceover, its electronic immediacy suggesting that what is shown is occurring now. This process is sometimes in conflict with the real time of the events with which the text deals. Constructed around memories of the Queen's Coronation, '*The Spongers*, broadcast on 24 January 1978, is able to take the Jubilee as history, but the mode of its narrative, constructing the *presence* of events, contradicts this'.[32]

The 'presencing' capacity of documentary voiceover can be used to unusual effect. *The Luddites* (ITV, 10.35, 19.4.88) was 'made as if it were a contemporary documentary' belonging to the early nineteenth century (*TV Times*). Its topic was industrial struggle over the introduction of new machinery. The voiceover addressed an audience in the 'present' of 1812, referring to the Combination Laws of 'thirteen years ago' (1799) which made 'trade unions illegal'. 'These men cannot openly defend their trade.'

Finally, a relationship may exist between discourses of identification in voiceover and a further visual mechanism of identification to be found in certain documentary and current affairs texts. 'No Easy Road: Michael Buerk's South Africa' was referred to in section 3.3. The images of South Africa which Buerk interprets in voiceover are interrupted on several occasions by a brief return to the editing suite of a television studio (in London?). Here Buerk is watching a bank of monitors on which the images the viewer has just seen are plainly visible. As the programme cuts from South Africa to the studio, Buerk turns from the monitors to speak to the television audience in the authoritative voice of direct address (see Figure 9). Clearly the implication of this visual rhetoric is that the viewer and Buerk have together been watching the images of South Africa which constitute so much of the programme.

It is this visual inscription of Buerk's discourse space in the present which is a central difference between the aesthetic form of 'No Easy Road' and many other television documentaries with voiceovers. In the former the spatio-temporal location of (most of) the text's discourses of interpretation and position in voiceover is determinate. Their space is distinct from the viewer, within the text if necessarily outside the content of its South African images. The time and space of South Africa is almost always of the past, the time and space of the post-production suite always the present. Buerk's voiceover confirms the images as the content of his looking: 'that little boy was a Bantu black ... But as that endemic violence burst out into what looked like the first splutterings of revolution my problems as a reporter got worse.'

In this personal documentary the return to the studio demonstrates an ownership of the image which is only verbally asserted in a documentary voiceover. These images of Africa are 'his', Buerk's, in two senses, separated in meaning by their different temporal reference. They are his in so far as they are the result of processes of production or 'authorship' in which he played a major part as a journalist, processes forming his awareness of past 'realities'. But they equally appear to function as the content of his perceptions as well as the viewer's in the present, in the process of re-viewing which constitutes the *Everyman* text. This ambiguity of the image in 'No Easy Road' is responsible for a certain complexity of tense in the discourses of position and interpretation with which Buerk is associated. This is most noticeable in voiceovers for extracts from news programmes where, as a television journalist, he had already provided a commentary during their original transmission by the BBC. Buerk's voiceover for 'No Easy Road' refers to the content of these images in the past tense. But in his

9 Michael Buerk and monitors in 'No Easy Road:
Michael Buerk's South Africa'

role as the news journalist in South Africa responsible for the pictures (voiceover shown in italics), his references are in the present: 'Everywhere we went whites were afraid. *In the Transvaal the white Afrikaners that have voted Mr Botha's National Party into power for forty years are worried now* . . . [BBC News, 22.5.86]. *Alexandra may be quiet now but this week's trouble, so close, has made Johannesburg's whites nervous . . . [they] now feel black anger is a real threat* [BBC News, 21.2.86]. Pets were often trained to go for blacks.'

'No Easy Road' articulates for the British viewer the space and time of South Africa, a world defined for those who belong to it by the familiarizing of apartheid as 'administrative routine'. For the whites this was 'a lulling, cosy world'; for the blacks in Soweto 'twenty-five domestic murders a weekend were routine'.

'The sun that had flamed into dusk over the Limpopo rose again behind London's soft drizzle, a night away but a world apart.' If these descriptions of 'a world apart' are to make sense to the reader, Buerk's discourses of position and interpretation must address that reader's conception of 'different' behaviour. 'This', when directed at an image, marks a focus of cognitive interest for viewer and textual subject alike. The discourse of interpretation must elaborate that interest intelligibly if the text is to succeed in communicating with its audience.

Here I anticipate Chapter 7. If the voiceover is the point at which the presenter enters the life-world of familiar meaning inhabited by the ideal audience, then it is equally the entry point into the text for the audience of empirical study. In the voiceover sense begins, to be subsequently elaborated and completed by the 'real' viewer: 'when the line of reasoning of the narrator bridges sequences, threading its way through the entire film, it usually promotes the verbal sound track to a position of dominance, organizes the remaining tracks (location sound, music, image and graphics), and provides the viewer's point of entry to the expository whole'.[33]

5.5   Discourses of Speech in Direct Address

A subject's direct address from the television screen, that is, his or her (apparently) looking at and speaking to the viewer in a simultaneous conjunction of activities, is familiar. Its implied audience establishes an identification with the particular version of the role of knowledgeable individual which that subject inhabits. This mechanism of identification is associated with a group of television subjects (presenters, reporters, etc.) produced by their institutions as both authoritative and familiar. The range of people permitted direct address is extensive. In one American laundry product advertisement, a housewife's 'direct address to the spectator is meant both to elicit identification on the part of the female spectator and to speak with the authority of common wisdom about the importance of whiteness'.[34] Generally this address to the viewer is 'embodied' in expressions of familiarity evoked by tone of voice, smile and prolonged (apparent) eye contact. Unlike the self-enclosed space and time normally constructed by cinematic film, 'television's foremost illusion is that it is an *interactive medium*'.[35] Communication changes the viewer, the implied object of a presenter's look, into an implied subject of address. Here, the person who is addressed comes to identify with the person who addresses.

Direct address occurs in what Morse refers to as an imaginary 'discourse space', a space in which an 'I' 'calls for intersubjective relations with a "you" in the here and now'.[36] The discourse space is imaginary, an absence, because the technical presence of the camera and television screen is such that the addressee cannot respond directly to the 'I' of the communication. The impression of a shared space and time is illusory. Such a 'discourse space [of direct address] is an imaginary construct based on denying the look of the camera. Neither narrator nor narratee are present to each other – the narrator addresses an empty lens. The narratee then can feel "looked at" only by denying the camera's mediating look.'[37]

The spoken discourse of television's direct address is, in this respect, closer to written discourse in its inability to respond to real questions from a real reader (as opposed to those directed at it from an assumed and anticipated viewer). For much of the time 'television . . . has the appearance of dialogue but the reality of monologue'.[38]

Discursive direct address initially positions the viewer as implied addressee of the text. But the effect of the discourse, if successful in maintaining its truth claims, is ultimately to reposition the intended audience with its source, the presenting subject him- or herself. This fusion of cognitive horizons realizes the 'reciprocal perspective' contained in another's speech. Both intra-textual and extra-textual subjects now *know*.

Sometimes (as I suggested in section 5.2) television combines direct address to the viewer with shots indicating that the audience shares the visual field of an addressee in the text. This notably occurs in advertisements where these sequences reinforce an identification between the extra-textual and intra-textual addressees. Clearly, the processes of identification in such advertisements are complex. For the ideal audience, at least, an initial visual alignment with the addressee concludes in cognitive alignment with the speaker.

In a studio discussion, direct address is permitted the chairperson. Other contributors are unlikely to be more than accidentally allowed to engage the viewer in an authoritative direct look. As I argue in section 6.2, these are individuals seen by the pluralist text as articulating simply possibility. But visual aspects of the studio such as graphics displays also possess the authority which characterizes the chairperson. The printed word, displayed on a caption board, is encoded as 'truth'.

I noted in Chapter 1 that a familiar, spoken direct address to camera often implies that textual subject and audience share a life-world of spatio-temporal reference and understanding. In a current affairs or 'magazine' programme like British ITV or Channel Nine (Australia) 'breakfast television', the world presents itself to be re-presented to the audience by the seated studio 'anchors' (Mike Morris, Steve Liebmann, or whoever). The views of each are incorporated in a discourse which signifies truth, the direct address of television. But this is also a discourse which is thoroughly infused with familiar informalities. 'Talking back to television' is a not uncommon reaction to this style of communication : the television interviewer 'is probably well known to the public. For many of the regular studio interviewers, particularly those in regional television, their relationship with people watching is almost that of a family friend.'[39] Television may construct the familiarity of its address by drawing on a particular genre of spoken discourse, that of anecdote. A friendly recounting of the past occurs in and supports the social relationships of familiarity. In this context television produces the 'anecdotal effect'.[40]

These familiarities of direct address presuppose that the presenters already share a 'universe of discourse' with the audience, a set of 'knowledges' and interests to which it is possible to refer from time to time in the programme.

This is to assume a view of the world, an often complex horizon of understanding, in which there is some measure of agreement.

Spectatorial identification in the case of television's direct address arises, then, from the use of a camera or studio practice which constructs a domain of authoritative familiarity involving viewer and programme. This relies on a variety of devices, including apparent eye contact between intra- and extra-textual subjects and verbal references which assume a shared spatio-temporal positioning in the present. The intended audience will recognize an accustomed and truth-providing 'friend' with an accent and mode of address known both from watching television and from daily life. In certain sorts of programmes involving direct address, like the news, the regular style and pacing of the segments of information involved does much to support their easy appropriation by the implied viewer. The familiarity of a presenter enhances his or her authority, producing an audience reading of his or her views as possessing 'credibility' : 'the greater perceived credibility of TV is partly due to the personalized nature of the communicator . . . Audience members come to feel they "know" the communicators in an illusion of face-to-face communication.'[41]

Identification occurs with the audience's recognition that the horizons of experience implicit in the direct address to the viewer are similar to their own. In ITV's *Good Morning Britain*, as I have noted, the programme calls upon the (intended) viewer's experience as a member of a family in order to 'remind' him or her that both text and audience possess similar perspectives on the world. An 'easy' identification is intended, with the ideal viewer moving into the role of the appropriately and 'accurately' knowledgeable person, a role already occupied by the presenter. If the presenter seeks to speak for the audience, attempts to put him- or herself in the 'place' or role of the viewer, the process of identification is confirmed.

While current affairs television normally supports such identification, certain studio arrangements can complicate it. A presenter's discourse, with its references to 'here' and 'tonight', may assume a similar spatio-temporal positioning as the audience. But discussants who are present in the studio only as images on studio monitors (for instance, as a result of satellite link-ups) are likely to be unable to make such assumptions with regard to either presenter or audience : 'discussion can be conducted between talking heads in a bank of monitors . . . Interlocutors need no longer be present to each other in the same three-dimensional space.'[42]

In documentary television direct address by the presenter is a common occurrence. What is much more unlikely is that the individuals under investigation by the text will be permitted to address the viewer directly. The documentary camera is an 'invisible' camera whose looking is rarely returned by subjects other than the presenter. But there are exceptions, as in one *Odyssey* (C4, 9.00, 12.8.87) documentary programme : 'the Shilluk villager is drawn by the sound of music. Now he is distracted by the film camera. But far from being intimidated by these white strangers with their mechanized eye, he finds them ever so faintly ridiculous.' At this point the

Shilluk tribesman holds up his hands in mocking imitation of the camera and looks into it in direct address.

Certain television dramas also make use of familiar direct address to position their viewers as recipients of the spoken discourse of conversation. But, unlike the direct address of news or current affairs programmes, this positioning of the implied viewer is not necessarily to be understood in terms of a proposed identification with a discourse of truth.

In the fifth episode of *Sunset Song* (BBC1, 10.40, 8.2.88) Chae Strachan (Victor Carin) tells Long Rob (Derek Anders) of his distress on returning from fighting the Germans to find that his trees have been cut down to provide timber for the war effort. Here the audience is positioned with Strachan as he remembers the response from the landlord's agent : 'it'll be all right, Mr Strachan. The government's going to replant all the trees as soon as the war's been won.' It is difficult to read these words, spoken in direct address to the audience and Strachan, as a discourse of truth. 'That'll console me a bloody lot, I'm sure,' Strachan responds on our behalf.

Notes

1 Sharma, 'Do They think We're Uloo ?', p. 64.
2 Caughie, 'Rhetoric, Pleasure and "Art Television"', p. 27.
3 Metz, *Psychoanalysis and Cinema*, p. 49.
4 Ibid., p. 55.
5 Bordwell et al., *Classical Hollywood Cinema*, pp. 207, 57.
6 Branigan, *Point of View in the Cinema*, p. 55.
7 Ibid., p. 2.
8 Branigan, 'Formal Permutations of the Point-of-view Shot', p. 55.
9 Metz, *Psychoanalysis and Cinema*, pp. 55–6.
10 Chalmers, *What Is This Thing Called Science ?*, pp. 23–4.
11 Habermas, *Theory of Communicative Action*, p. 123.
12 'Horizons', as used here, might be associated with the spatio-temporal limits of the image by arguing that they are 'embodied' in the text's *mise en scène*. If it is read as a discourse about the personalities of subjects in the text, then the *mise en scène* could be said to signify a cognitive horizon in terms of which their action and discourse is to be understood.
13 Spurling, *Phenomenology and the Social World*, p. 51.
14 A. Kuhn, 'History of Narrative Codes', p. 214.
15 Browne, *Rhetoric of Film Narration*, p. 11. Browne argues that while point-of-view shots are attributed to Lucy (the cavalry officer's wife), the preferred reading of the film is not one of identification with her understanding of the social world. Identification 'need not be with the character whose view [the spectator] shares' (p. 12) ; it may be a function of the film's extensive narrative rhetoric rather than of an intensive point-of-view shot. His argument is, regrettably, not sufficiently detailed to be able to assess it properly.
16 S. Johnston, 'Film Narrative and the Structuralist Controversy', p. 244.

17 Cooke, *Psycho*.
18 Sartre, *Sketch for a Theory of the Emotions*, pp. 77–8, 91.
19 Ibid, p. 82.
20 Millerson, *The Technique of Television Production*, p. 112.
21 Branigan refers to a filmic variation on the shot described here. He calls this variation the 'reflexive POV' : 'when the object of a glance is also a person, then it is possible to alternate POV structures – as in a conversation – centred about two, or more, points. This is the reflexive POV. A character need not stare directly into the camera (for this involves another convention) but the eyes must be very near the line of the camera' ('Formal Permutations of the Point-of-view Shot', p. 63).
22 Caughie, 'Progressive Television and Documentary Drama', p. 346.
23 Branigan, 'Formal Permutations of the Point-of-view Shot', p. 62.
24 Caughie, 'Rhetoric, Pleasure and "Art Television"', p. 27.
25 Millerson, *The Technique of Television Production*, pp. 67–8.
26 Ibid., p. 72.
27 Boyd-Bowmann, 'Open the Box', p. 148.
28 J. Corner, 'Seeing Is Believing : The Ideology of Naturalism', *Documentary and the Mass Media*, pp. 130–1.
29 *TV Times*, 132, 29 (1987).
30 McArthur, 'The Narrator as Guarantor of Truth', p. 202.
31 Nicholls, *Ideology and the Image*, p. 173.
32 Stevens, 'Reading the Realist Film', p. 29.
33 Nicholls, *Ideology and the Image*, p. 199.
34 Flitterman, 'The *Real* Soap Operas', p. 91.
35 Feuer, 'Narrative Form in American Network Television', p. 104.
36 Morse, 'Talk, Talk, Talk', p. 3.
37 Ibid., p. 5.
38 Jobbins, 'Lodging an Appeal for Language', *Times Higher Education Supplement* (20 Nov. 1987).
39 MacShane, *Using the Media*, p. 145.
40 Tolson, 'Anecdotal Television', p. 25.
41 Zukin, 'Mass Communication and Public Opinion', p. 373.
42 Morse, 'Talk, Talk, Talk', p. 9.

6

Subverting the Veridical Image

Watching television, the experience of the veridical effect is of the apparently real. The transparent image seems to give access to the world. Constraints of visual mediation by a text are placed on the margins of looking, allowing an unqualified identification with a subject. Moving within the programme, we act and understand like a character. The veridical experience of the documentary, in particular, is one in which a voiceover is likely to join the (intended) viewer in contributing an unproblematically fixed description to what is seen. In certain types of programme, however, the veridical image is subverted.

In this chapter I consider strategies through which a text, or its contextualizing discourses (such as continuity announcements), renders opaque the otherwise transparent access to the apparently real which is associated with the veridical. The first of these strategies provides a programme with contradictory voiceovers allocating opposing characteristics to its content, in this way calling into question its ability to present the 'real' unproblematically. What is seen is made indeterminate. The second strategy suspends the veridical effect of, for instance, a documentary by prefacing it with a continuity announcement casting doubt on the validity of its content. Here the viewer's role is outlined in the context of a 'hermeneutics of suspicion'. The third challenge to the veridical constructs a visual text as postmodernist: its status as a representation of reality is refused. Instead, its reference is taken to be simply to itself or to other images in other texts.

6.1 The Text of Contradiction

Some Marxist cultural critics have supported oppositional texts which explicitly foreground social contradictions, thereby (they claim) fracturing that 'imaginary wholeness' (Coward and Ellis), the pseudo-unity of the reader's subjectivity. The television (and film) 'text of contradiction' produces an experience of the 'real' marked by internal conflict. Accounts of history from the perspectives of both dominant and dominated social classes are presented more or less simultaneously prompting analysis. The text of contradiction calls into question the identities disclosed in a veridical sequence, opening them up to different interpretations drawing upon opposing social theories. To reread MacCabe's words on 'empiricist' television, the inclusion of contradictory preferred readings within a text separates the 'realms of truth and vision' which in the experience of the veridical image are 'elided into the instantaneous moment of sight'.[1]

Central to the theoretical analysis which lay behind what I have chosen to call the 'text of contradiction' was the idea that it would produce a viewer sufficiently distanced from the programme to allow him or her to 'actively' engage in accounting for the discursive tensions in its meaning. But it is important (as I hope I have shown in earlier chapters) to recognize that the audience is always active (whatever the text) in a viewing which brings its own discourses of interpretation to a programme. As I indicate in the Conclusion, the effect of the veridical may be deconstructed as much by the ideological challenge of the audience as by the particular structure of the text.

In his account of the theoretical motives for the 'text of contradiction' MacCabe argues that the relationship between representation and object in progressive film montage is such that the very nature of the object is called into doubt. The existence, for instance, of an essential masculinity or femininity is challenged. The film reveals each representation to be an interpretation of the phenomenon in question, a 'looking' which is open to correction.[2] Montage should not merely offer different aspects of a fixed identity. For a series of images of this kind does not contain contradictory interpretations of a given process or entity in such a way as to disturb their own truth value as visual discourses. Rather, montage 'works through a contest between the identities offered by the different discourses'.[3] The nature of what is seen is both asserted and challenged. Progressive montage disturbs the illusionism of cinema and the veridical effect of the television image (and its editing). It upsets the claim of the image to give access to the incontrovertibly self-evident. *The Dragon Has Two Tongues* (C4, 8.00, 3.4.85), discussed below, denies the possibility of a transparent presentation of a 'real' Welsh history.

MacCabe's 'classic realist text', which he claims as the aesthetic form of dominant cinema or television, contains both an 'object language' and a narrative 'metalanguage'. These are, respectively, the textual discourse in inverted commas (the spoken) and that outside, the visual. The latter acts as arbiter of the truth of the spoken; in turn it 'denies its own status as articulation', for 'the narrative discourse is not present as discourse – as articulation'.[4] What we see provides no basis for its truth to be challenged. Unlike the discourse in inverted commas, the narrative metalanguage does not exhibit itself as open to correction or reinterpretation; 'it cannot be mistaken in its identifications'. The visual metalanguage of dominant cinema excludes the possibility of its own falsehood.

Progressive montage undermines the self-evident status of the visual metalanguage in film and television. The (intended) spectator is no longer uncritically positioned by the indubitable 'truth' of the realities disclosed in a transparent image. For it is the very nature of those realities that is being called into question through representing them in contradictory discourses of vision and speech which draw attention to themselves as discourse.[5] In the text of contradiction 'the identities rest in the discourses'. The progressive force of this arrangement issues from the way in which it establishes a textual process characterized by discursive equality, discourses of speech and vision in equilibrium through contradiction. This is unlike dominant cinema with its hierarchical organization of speech on the basis of verisimilitude to what is shown, or the 'real'. Montage is 'the effect generated by a conflict of discourse in which the oppositions available in the juxtaposed discourses are contradictory and in conflict'.[6]

In the progressive text discourses of apparent truth are also discourses in contradiction, discourses likely to draw on competing ideologies of the social and historical. *The Dragon Has Two Tongues* presents opposing insights into Welsh history. In texts refusing to privilege one or other contradictory account of the 'real' 'one could have an organization of discourses which broke with any dominance and which, as such, remained essentially subversive of any ideological order'.[7]

MacCabe's understanding of 'montage' is, as he indicates, distinct from its original formulation by Eisenstein, the Soviet film maker and theorist. For Eisenstein, montage predominantly involved a conflict between images which was intended to produce an active spectator: for example, 'graphic conflict', 'conflict of planes', 'conflict of volumes', 'spatial conflict' or conflict between the content of images.[8] Montage was not, as it was for Pudovkin and others, merely 'a *linkage* of pieces. Into a chain.'[9]

However, unlike MacCabe's montage (a 'contest between the identities' offered by different visual and verbal discourses), Eisenstein's discursive conflicts required images whose truth value was not itself in doubt; they could be assumed to be accurate presentations of the 'real'. Images in conflict (for instance, of rich and poor) would lead an audience to 'form equitable views by stirring up contradictions within the spectator's mind', producing 'accurate intellectual concepts' which could be used in analysis of the film and society (for example, an idea of the distance between social classes).[10] Film is being used here to establish 'new concepts and viewpoints', 'a dynamization of the "traditional view" into a new one'.[11] The relationship between tradition and innovation is not that the latter replaces the former but that it adds to it in a synthesis representing progress. The old is contained in the new; 'we newly collect the disintegrated event into one whole, but in *our* aspect'.[12] Sustaining this sense of incipient dialectical progress, in 'Methods of Montage' Eisenstein asserts that the montage he describes there is 'not yet the intellectual cinema, which I have been announcing for some years !'[13]

MacCabe's concept of montage as a 'contest between . . . identities' can be illustrated by an example drawn from television. In the experience of a transparent and unproblematic flow of images the space and time is opened for identification in which viewers unproblematically align themselves with a subject's disclosure of the 'real'. But in the text of contradiction the identity of that reality is called into question; the viewer is offered conflicting processes of alignment. In 1985 Channel Four (UK) transmitted an innovative televisual account of Welsh history, *The Dragon Has Two Tongues: A History of the Welsh* (C4, 8.00, 3.4.85). Throughout this series of programmes the presenters, Wynford Vaughan-Thomas and Gwyn Williams, liberal and Marxist historians respectively, engaged each other in narrative, description and analysis. In the final episode they concluded that their debate showed them to 'disagree totally about Wales past, present and future' (*TV Times*). In this way the *Dragon* spoke with 'two tongues', both of which were coded and privileged by the text as discourses of truth offering (opposing) points of identification. Each was supported by camera practices and editing consistent with the viewer's experience of a largely unmediated access to the 'real'.

Towards the end of this final episode ('The Death of Wales ?') a section of videotape is 'played and replayed', showing a series of events in the previous five years of Welsh history. On the first 'playing' the images are provided with a voiceover read by the liberal Vaughan-Thomas. When the tape is replayed, the same images receive a contradictory analysis of their content from the Marxist Williams.

For Vaughan-Thomas, recent events are viewed from the political perspectives of liberal democracy. These constitute a horizon of understanding in which references to the workings of parliament are central. He interprets events as undermining a separate Welsh cultural and economic identity, as pointing to its imminent collapse; 'I know we're in a crisis, there's a nightmare appearing.' If Wales survives, it will be because it has 'this inner secret of survival'.

For Williams, however, the theoretical context of analysis is set by struggle and contradiction between classes, between feminism and a 'macho' Welsh culture and between the state and political movements (the Welsh Socialist Republicans). It is in these terms that the fight to maintain a cultural and economic identity and activity for Wales must be understood. The distinctive character of the political struggle which recent events have represented, he believes, has confirmed the existence of a separate Welsh identity. It will be maintained by continued political 'action' ; 'the life will come if we act'.

As speech placed in voiceover, both analyses are to be read as asserting discourses of truth. Read independently from one another they are categorical statements of the actual, supported by a non-contradictory and non-problematic relationship with the visual ; they interpret and in turn receive

10 Wynford Vaughan-Thomas and Gwyn Williams, who establish conflicting points of view in *The Dragon Has Two Tongues*

support from the images they accompany. As formulations of hermeneutic inquiry they construct positions of identification for the intended viewer. But taken together these are interpretations in manifest conflict, producing a contradiction between two 'given' identities for the nature of Welsh history and politics. As opposing accounts of one and the same set of images these voiceovers generate readings in contradiction whose opposition requires resolution.

Considered as a series of images, the videotape made use of in this section of the programme resembles a standard news or documentary compilation, its editing and camera work unexceptional and unlikely to attract the viewer's attention. With these images related together by a voiceover as an unproblematic visual flow, the likely experience for a viewer is of a sequence of events constituting 'real' history, 'transparently' made available by the text. It is only when both voiceovers are brought together to assert differing interpretations of recent Welsh history in a successive 'play and replay' of the images that the effect of the veridical is displaced by a statement of contradictory identities for the 'real'. Here 'rival projects . . . emerge side by side'.[14] The intended viewer must engage in two conflicting processes of constructing meaning.

Finally, it is worth recording that producing a text of explicit contradiction does not exhaust the possibilities of progressive television. A text which upholds the critique of a dominant politics may be one which confirms an audience in an active progressive position rather than disturbing it through initiating contradictory readings. Instead of constructing a fragmented hermeneutic identity for the (ideal) spectator, these oppositional texts themselves represent a political struggle to establish a social identity concerned with resistance in the face of a dominant cultural hegemony. They seek 'to confirm an identity (of sexuality or class), to recover repressed experience or history, to contest the dominant image with an alternative identity'.[15]

6.2 The Text of Possibility

'A literary work, even when it appears to be new, does not present itself as something absolutely new in an informational vacuum, but predisposes its audience to a very specific kind of reception by announcements, overt and covert signals, familiar characteristics, or implicit allusions.'[16] Assertions about the relationship of 'new' television texts to 'reality' are often to be found in the extra-textual discourses of, for instance, the UK *Radio Times* or the Australian *TV Week* and in continuity announcements preceding programmes. These statements can be read as contextualizing the veridical effects generally associated with the visual discourses of the texts involved. Institutional continuity announcers, in particular, are possessed of considerable powers to allocate or refuse the status of unqualified truth to a subsequent programme (for example, a documentary). Themselves unjudged, these 'supernarrators' 'sit outside and above all the embedded narratives, unaffected by them'.[17]

It is by such extra-textual discourses that television classifies its texts in terms of preferred readings of the veridical. Programmes may be 'fictional', with an 'authored' and possible point of view (drama, continuous serial, situation comedy). They may be 'factual', without an author or point of view, 'objective' treatments of events and places (documentary, news and current affairs). The Australian ABC's *Four Corners* features institutionally resourced 'reports on major local and overseas topics' (*TV Week*).

Programmes may, however, belong to a third, 'hybrid' category of 'nominated' documentary and current affairs television texts. These involve authored ('personalized'), possible, point-of-view accounts of the world. They are either inflected in the direction of entertainment/fiction rather than information/fact or transmitted in the context of institutional unease. Programmes in this category include 'personal viewpoint' documentaries scripted by, for instance, John Pilger or David Attenborough, and drama-documentaries. If *TV Week*'s description is to be relied upon, Attenborough's *Trials of Life* (ABC, 7.30, 12.5.91) has generic associations with the soap opera: 'arguments between animals striving to maintain their position in the community are common, but acts of assistance are rare and remarkable'.

Each of these institutional classifications can be read as prescriptions for viewing, contextualizing an experience of apparently veridical images of textual content in different ways. All texts exist as potentialities for meaning, but only some are (merely) potentially true. The division of programmes is not rigid. A soap opera episode may be preceded by a continuity announcement which, in ignoring the fictional status of its content, conspires with a reading of its images as veridical. Here the 'split reference' of the text to the possible, while appearing to be to the actual, is effaced. UK Channel Four's *Brookside* is particularly notable in this respect. Preceding continuity announcements assert its concern with 'reality', sometimes in a declaration verging on the excessive: 'Well, now on Four, the omnibus *Brookside*, and while for Sheila the nightmare continues, for Heather the nightmare is only just beginning' (11.11.86).

Such pre-textual discourses, particularly in their use of the immediate 'now', sustain the veridical quality of images appearing to give 'transparent' access to the world. Their ideal viewer is almost that of documentary television: 'Now on Four, facing the sometimes uncomfortable and often unpleasant problems which seem unavoidable in modern life, *Brookside*' (23.8.86). This discursive context of transmission helps the viewer to forget that the fictional text of soap opera is, in Ricoeur's words, a 'text of possiblity', asserting only a 'possible world' of meaning and truth: 'the mode of being of the world opened up by the text is the mode of the possible, or better of the power-to-be: therein resides the subversive force of the imaginary'.[18]

In the case of documentaries or current affairs programmes signalled by a pre-textual announcement as being accurate 'insights', the veridical quality of their images is to be read as confirmation that they offer 'in-depth reports'. Discourses of interpretation in the text will be supported as truthful in a non-contradictory relationship with what should unproblematically be seen as real. Continuity announcements enable processes of identification to commence, processes legitimated also by such descriptions in broadcast journals as : '*World in Action*. An in-depth report from the award-winning team' ; '*Women in View*. By women, for women – all over the country ; the current affairs magazine that provides a weekly insight into women's lives and opinion' (*TV Times*). These are documentaries or current affairs texts with 'institutional presenters', relatively anonymous and usually belonging to the company producing the programme. They present the institutional 'voice' in the text in mediations of the world which are 'neutral' and self-effacing.

Continuity announcements associated with 'personal viewpoint' documentaries, on the other hand, can construct them as personal reports, an individual's investigations on the edge of entertainment as in Australia's *Sixty Minutes* (C9, 7.30, Sundays) or the BBC's series *Madness* with Dr Jonathan Miller (BBC2, 8.10, 6.10.91–3.11.91). The presentation of these documentaries in terms of an individual's looking is also likely to occur where the media institution concerned reads the 'personal viewpoint' involved as 'political'. 'Personal viewpoint' texts are referred to by Schlesinger et al. as 'authored' documentaries, where the institutional assigning of authorship represents a denial of responsibility : 'whereas the news and most of the regular current affairs output are so closely identified with the broadcasting organizations as to be seen as "their" products, for which they bear collective responsibility, "authored" documentaries are ascribed to an individual reporter or producer and presented as their particular view of the subject'.[19]

Where, then, the personal viewpoint articulated in the text is regarded as politically controversial, the documentary is usually introduced within a discursive framework of caution (cf. the introduction to contributors in a political studio discussion). For the intended audience at least, this will have the effect of subverting not only the authority of the text's verbal discourse but any reading of its images as innocently veridical. Identification with the text's 'author', a subject in the text, is undermined ; apparent visual support for his or her position is contextualized by suspicion. In this situation an author is assigned to a programme with the intention of undermining its 'author-ity'. Expressing a 'personal viewpoint', as a text of possibility in respect of its capacity to display the world, the documentary is marked by difference.

The pre-textual announcement of such a text as 'personalized' implies that what is about to be seen and heard has the status of an individual's point of view, selected, constructed and possibly 'biased'. The repeated appearance and speech of the presenter must work not to authenticate the image but to weaken its authority. Yet if, as is likely, these images are predominantly 'transparent' in their arrangement in the text, they will continue to produce a veridical effect for the audience. They will threaten in their turn the institution's perception of the programme within a limiting horizon of scepticism and uncertainty.

In the late evening of 19 January 1988 Scottish Television transmitted the second programme ('Secrets') in John Pilger's series on Australia, *Viewpoint Special*, 'The Last Dream' (ITV, 10.35, 19.1.88). Before the programme commenced there were two announcements. The first concerned *Votes for Women*, a discussion among 'one *hundred* women with one *hundred* points-of-view' to be broadcast the following day. This interpretation of a 'point-of-view' as the assertion of individualistic difference was maintained in the second announcement. Here the difference rested in a 'look': 'Well now, Tuesday evening viewing continues as we join John Pilger in a *Viewpoint Special*, "The Last Dream", looking at [pause] the secrets in Australia.' When the programme began, the initial credit sequence further emphasized the message that the text was an individual's point-of-view: 'The Last Dream. A Special Report by John Pilger.' The following Tuesday evening the continuity announcement for the last in the series left no doubt about the programme's status as a personal viewpoint documentary whose (dubious) authoring 'voice' was Pilger's rather than the institution's: 'Now we join John Pilger for part three of his trilogy on his homeland. *Viewpoint Special*, "The Last Dream".'

In the BBC *Everyman* authored documentary 'No Easy Road: Michael Buerk's South Africa', the BBC correspondent (and now newsreader) recounted his experiences in South Africa (cf. the discussion of this programme in Chapters 3 and 5). 'No Easy Road' was preceded by a continuity announcement which implicitly suggested some of the contradictions between institutional unease and collaboration which obtained in the relationship between Buerk and the BBC. Formerly 'the BBC's correspondent in South Africa . . . he was expelled by the South African government'. While evading responsibility for the politics of Buerk's 'personal account', the announcement acknowledged a moral responsibility for the transmission of a 'harrowing' part of the programme: 'This film is [Buerk's] personal account of the country he left. Viewers are warned that the film contains scenes of both verbal and physical violence . . . crucial we believe to the film's purpose. "No Easy Road".'

Buerk carries the institutional perception of the programme as a personal documentary within the text itself, describing it as 'a personal journey back'; its truth is a 'central truth, for me'. He himself undermines the status of the text's images as a veridical insight into South Africa: 'I . . . felt depressed as a reporter because in many ways I think we failed to put across what South Africa was *really* like.' But at other points Buerk claims to assert a universal truth supported by what the audience sees. Viewers 'lucky enough to live sheltered lives' are shown what violence is *'really* like': 'they caught him. You can look away. I couldn't. A single blow rarely kills. But death is certain.'

Where personal viewpoint documentaries are perceived by the transmitting institution concerned to be 'non-political', they are less likely to be announced as 'personal'. Before one of Levin's travel programmes, *To the End of the Rhine* (C4, 7.11.87, and later on SBS), he is referred to as a source of knowledge, 'our guide'. This opens his discursively established roles in the text for identification by the audience. The 'authority' of authorship is retained. The programme is to be read as expressing an explicitly subjective view, but a view which while being particular and individualistic has sufficient authority to be read as a discourse containing truth. Yet whatever the institution's perceptions of his 'innocence', Levin's cultural politics are present in the text: 'we may not, some of us, still be quite comfortable among the Germans'.

Levin's status as informative guide is only occasionally undercut by his idiosyncratic manner, momentarily inflecting the viewer's identification towards assuming a position of ironic distance. Elsewhere in the series its visual discourses apparently convey reality, and Levin's assertions are to be unproblematically appropriated by the audience. Dark and fiery images of the Ruhr steel furnaces illustrate his voiceover, 'proving' the truth of his experience and reflections: 'at the heart of the complex, the monster never sleeps, the blast furnace continually vomits blazing metal' (21.11.87). The series is constructed by Levin himself as not only of public but of individual significance: 'I followed [the Rhine] all the way, but I had, as well as the world's reasons, an extra one of my own' (17.10.87).

In a similar way other travel documentaries are not explicitly classified as 'personal' by their respective media institutions. 'The Travels of "Pong" Barley', *Wideworld* (BBC2, 8.10, 9.3.88), articulates the 'innocent anthropologist's' viewpoint. It allows the audience to share, uncautioned, in Nigel Barley's ethnographic field-trip, the 'uncovering' of Indonesia. And Richard Crane, presenter of what he refers to as 'our stories' in the Channel Four documentary series *Odyssey* (C4, 9.00, 12.8.87), is introduced and supported by the channel with a reference to his experience and ability as explorer. Yet Thailand might want to contest his political description of it as the 'cause of much of the West's drug problems'.

With its continuity announcements that a 'personal' or 'authored' documentary is to follow, television recognizes the myth of the veridical as a transparent communication of the 'real'. For documentary is not a kind of 'reality frozen in the amber of the photographic image' but a 'succession of choices between differences, the continuous selection of pertinent features from amongst the various codes and their intersection'.[20] Where a documentary is announced as 'personal', the relationship between the text's discursive articulations of the visual and 'reality' itself exists for the intended viewer at the level of the speculative and merely possible. In this 'modal logic' of viewing, identification gives way to the appropriation of cognitive possibility in the context of a horizon of suspicion. '"Modality" concerns the reality attributed to a message.'[21]

To claim that in documentaries announced as 'personal' there is a modal logic of mere possibility governing the terms of the viewer–television relationship is to be in conflict with the idea that texts are characterized by a strictly defined (epistemological) hierarchy of discourses, with a dominant discourse of truth, the visual. The effect of the continuity announcement is to separate the visual and the 'real', to dislocate any privileging of discourses in the text grounded in the identity of the one with the other. The support from what is seen for the spoken is bracketed and temporarily suspended. In this context there is no visual statement which can be read as its own guarantee of truth, unlike 'classical fictional cinema [which] . . . has the crucial opposition between spoken discourses which may be mistaken and a visual discourse which guarantees truth – which reveals all'.[22]

But the text of possibility is not to be read as celebrating an ideologically subversive organization of discourse. Nor does it foreground contradiction either in itself or with other texts. For this textual form of the 'personal documentary' is the product of television's ideology of balance around the 'middle ground' of politics, of its assertion of a pluralism of possible viewpoints rather than contradictory truths. It is this ideology of 'even-handedness' which UK Channel Four's *Right to Reply* attempts to maintain, for instance, by examining 'the complaint that TV should do better by the over-60s' (C4, 6.00, 28.11.87). This programme of audience response to television even admits a 'bias towards the viewer' in its pluralistic support for the audience's equality of opportunity to speak, however inexperienced, when confronted with the·'media professionals who regularly appear' on television ; never 'even-handed', 'right from the start the programme was biased . . . an unrelenting bias towards the viewer'.[23]

Pluralistic balance is seen as a virtue. In *Split Screen*, a BBC documentary film series presenting 'both' responses to a question (for example, about sex education), the opposing film makers involved must be described as 'unapologetically partial and one-sided' (*Split Screen*, BBC2, 10.00, 28.1.87). They offer 'two partian views of a controversial issue' (*Radio Times*). The presenter cautiously articulates the voice of balance, the middle ground, between the two 'partial' discourses which produce the 'split' screen : 'as *some* people believe that *order* is important we also toss a coin to decide which film goes first'. The breadth of possible meanings with which such pluralism confronts the viewer may, in their complexity, simply obscure those ideas which could aid political understanding.

While a text of possibility is distinct from a text of contradiction, it may activate contradictions within the (real) viewer. Discourses urging a career-centred life for women, set alongside a discursive assertion of the values of domesticity, can constitute a text's display of its commitment to pluralism. But these discourses of possibility may be read by the audience as a reminder that the 'traces of the value systems and ideologies we once held are still there, contradicting the newer ones that our changed social experience has brought'.[24]

The text of possibility constituted by the televisual form of 'personal viewpoint' documentary is, like fictional drama, 'authored' (even if that author is constructed by a media institution in terms of his or her lack of 'author-ity'). Buerk wrote and narrated his own 'story'. This television form may be considered analogous to drama-documentary. In personal viewpoint documentaries presenters move 'out of the normal roles of observer and reporter and into the role of "author", a role they share with the creators of television fiction, and more particularly with the writers of single plays'.[25]

It is because of their character as authored documentaries, as texts which are forced explicitly to acknowledge their source in subjectivity, that these programmes can articulate positions of authorship in the text itself. The author may enter the space of his or her programme to provide an 'anchor' for perspectives which are verbally expressed, either from a time and space which is visually constructed or from outside that space in voiceover.

Like some drama-documentaries, 'authored' documentaries, if perceived by the transmitting institution to be political, exist on the edge of what is acceptable. Such 'authored' documentaries will be 'provocative', a term which Caughie applies to certain drama-documentaries.[26] The framework of reservation and doubt in which 'authored' documentaries are contextualized is to be contrasted with, for instance, the unqualified assertion of textual ownership which precedes the BBC's lunchtime news : 'The One O'clock News from the BBC, with Michael Buerk.' There is, therefore, a certain (unintended) irony in the title of the BBC documentary series *Horizon*. While clearly perceived by the institution to be a 'neutral', 'balanced' programme of scientific interest, its title suggests the reality : that it, like any other text, enunciates a selective and perspectival understanding of the world.

References to 'personal', 'authored' or 'viewpoint' documentaries, documentaries 'written and presented by' someone, represent an unstable mapping of elements belonging to the dramaturgical (and authored) on to the genre of the documentary and non-authored. As I have noted, sometimes this constructs the documentary as entertainment, and sometimes as 'political'. Signifiers of an individual's perspective on the world are assembled in the text alongside signifiers of (apparently) objective presuppositionless truth. Authorial voiceover coexists with the monochrome pictures of past witnesses and interviews with those who are clearly to be read as speaking with the authentic voice of experience. The 'objective' camera of documentary (motivated by no one's look) is undermined by a continual return to its dramaturgical placing, 'subject-ively', with the author in the text.

The project of the 'personal documentary' often has the effect of reducing the social and political to the individual and psychological, with the experience of the individual being reproduced in turn as a social universal. Using a framework of preferences and values associated with human choice, authored documentary (like documentary drama) reworks the objective analysis of the document as the subjective experience of drama. This allows the text to impose its individualistic solution on the social disruption exposed by the documentary. In the final moments of *To the End of the Rhine* Levin boards the overnight ferry at the Hook of Holland and goes home.

In an earlier programme in that series (17.10.87) political contradiction was reduced to ethical dilemma when Levin visited the tax-free investment haven of Liechtenstein. There he 'was tempted to emulate Mr Maxwell and go into business in Liechtenstein quite legally myself'. This 'temptation' was constructed as a moral issue with the effect of positioning Levin and the viewer outside politics. 'Our' moral qualms can be resolved by Levin's decision on our behalf, through the experience and action of the individual subject of the text: 'when I left . . . I felt happier that . . . I wasn't actually setting up a company in Liechtenstein to pay less tax in my own country'.

But in an equal and opposite movement from the individual to the universal the documentary aspect of the text functions to support the validity of Levin's experience and discourse. His status as 'guide' is confirmed with the use of hand-held cameras signifying truth and the presence in the text of monochrome images authenticating his histories: 'the rhetoric of the documentary establishes the experience as an experience of the real, and places it within a system of guarantees and confirmations'.[27]

Unlike the documentary drama, an analogous confronting of the documentary with the dramaturgical, the 'authoring' of a documentary does not establish an 'experiment', a hypothetical scenario within the framework of the text. Implicit in the reporting 'voice' of the documentary author is the claim that his or her presence in the time and space of its topic has not disturbed the passage of events. Reporting leaves everything as it is. This is in contrast with documentary drama which 'seems to produce its analysis by setting in motion a dramatic experiment within the world observed and constructed by the documentary look'.[28]

But like the documentary drama, the personal documentary is a text whose authorial presence has removed it from the status of mimetic to permit it to acknowledge its selective mediations of reality from a particular perspective. As McArthur writes of Peter Watkins's documentary drama *Culloden*, 'it does not present itself as a simplistic "window on the world" of 1746: it is a programme with a clear position on the events it describes'.[29] The unity of the explicitly authored text is the apparent unity of an individual's account of the world: a reference to 'the essential subjectivity of the person seeing the events being filmed [is] necessary for the unity of the film'.[30] The density of mimetic documentary description, where it occurs, is contained within a construction of meaning directed by the selectivity of personal insight.

Dennis Potter's first documentary film for television was the autobiographical *Between Two Rivers* (1960, excerpts in *Arena*, BBC2, 9.30, 30.1.87). It displays the systematic ambiguities associated with the category of 'authored documentary'. 'Written and narrated by Dennis Potter' (caption), its account of the Forest of Dean is 'a story of my discovery of things here to respect and of my anxiety about the *kind* of Forest of Dean *she* [his daughter] will see as *she* grows older'. Authored narrative competes for space with the passages of dense description appropriate to mimetic documentary. Potter speaks of 'my father, who spent most of his working life in the pits of the Forest of Dean. For the green forest has a deep, black heart beneath its sudden hills, pushing up into slag heaps and grey, little villages clustering around the coal.'

Potter acknowledges what he sees as the documentary's failure, 'the way in which it *failed* to deal with what I knew to be there', his 'seeing what was on either side of the camera and wasn't *on* the film'. *Between Two Rivers* marks the presence of a selective vision as a 'look', shared with the viewer, and signalled from time to time in the script as the authorial and audience's 'looking' : 'that's Margaret, my wife . . . And my mother . . . And my father . . . Doing homework like *this* boy . . . this miserable pile of dull villages . . . these drab, untidy old houses.'

6.3   The Postmodern Image*

The veridical effect is constituted by the apparently unmediated viewing of a transparent 'window on the world'. The postmodernist sequence or analysis subverts this effect. Identification as appropriation of a subject's account of the 'world' is excluded. For what is shown or described to the viewer is never a reality independent of the text. The image exhibits only itself or a reworking of other images. Here, the experience of the text is detached from a knowledge of the real : 'postmodernist experiments in visual perspective, narrative structure and temporal logic . . . all attacked the dogma of mimetic referentiality'.[31]

This remark points directly at the implications of postmodernism for the study and analysis of television. From a postmodernist perspective the visual 'layers' of a text are 'open' and indeterminate with respect to the truth or falsity of the verbal discourses which accompany them. They provide no evidence by reference to which the veracity of what is said may be judged. What is seen by the viewer is discredited as a transparent display of a non-discursive reality, a reality 'beyond' the text : 'the screen . . . makes everything circulate in one space, without depth'.[32] Instead, the flow of visual images represents only itself.

Such a 'failure' of the visual is a postmodernist suspension of the veridical effect. To investigate the 'transparency' of the image is modernist, but to undermine its reference to reality is to engage with the aesthetics of postmodernism. While modernism may be regarded as a detached 'scientific' (Brecht) scrutiny of the means of representation, postmodernism raises the question of the very possibility of representation itself. 'Modernist theory presupposes that mimesis, the adequation of an image to a referent, can be bracketed or suspended, and that the art object itself can be substituted (metaphorically) for its referent . . . Postmodernism neither brackets nor

---

* A more detailed version of this section, together with a critique of postmodernism, may be found in my 'Reading the Postmodernist Image'.

suspends the referent but works instead to problematize the activity of reference.'[33]

In terms of the cognitive horizons of such radical doubting directed at the veridical quality of the viewer's experience, that experience itself (paradoxically) begins to constitute the only reality with which the audience can engage. In a postmodernist ontology of television and the world, 'reality' for the viewer is to be identified with a conjunction of images. In this 'denial of difference' (Callinicos) television is 'a world of simulations detached from reference to the real, which circulate and exchange in ceaseless, centreless flow'.[34]

Postmodernist philosophy concerns a world increasingly reduced to simulacra. 'The new postmodern universe, with its celebration of the look – the surfaces, textures, the self-as-commodity – threatens to reduce everything to the image/presentation/simulacrum.'[35] This is to reject the empiricist account of truth as representation, an account resting on a dualistic separation of image and reality in which the one corresponds to the other. It is postmodernism's philosophical contribution to assert that such a separation can no longer be made, for with the 'transformation of older realities into television images' (Jameson) the picture has become reality itself. Apparently successful in its erstwhile functions of representation, the image is now thrown back on 'play', limited to the continual renovation of its own history.

In this context the modernist faith in the visual as a source of information about an independent world is challenged and rejected. The postmodernist suspicion of the image is shared by the feminist, for whom it often consists of representations of the world by a male subject, limiting the possibilities of identification by the unreality of what it discloses.[36] Clearly, accepting these arguments for postmodernism is incompatible with simultaneously maintaining the possibility of 'identification' as appropriating an account of reality mediated through the images of a text.

The last programme in *State of the Art* (C4, 8.15, 15.2.87, and subsequently on SBS), a 'series about the visual arts today (and their relationship with the world in which we live)' (*TV Times*), examined *inter alia* the postmodern experiences of 'lostness' and radical contingency. The failure of the subject's visual or spatial orientation is argued to be in part responsible for generating a non-representational art of pastiche. In the opening segment, a sequence of images later identified as showing Sydney harbour, a woman's voice is heard asking in voiceover : 'Where am I ? It seems like a nice place. What's [speech unclear] special about it ? Why do all these places look the same ? I wonder what was here before. What's missing ? Does it have to be this way ?' In denying a knowledge of reality, this voiceover refuses to provide a focus for the processes of identification by other than the schizoid subject of postmodernism.

As a television series *State of the Art* was itself clearly influenced by a postmodernist aesthetic, for 'the very foundation of postmodernity consists of viewing the world as a plurality of heterogeneous spaces and temporalities'.[37] It eschewed a reading of its 'speech' as a hierarchy of discourses in which those at the base are mistaken while those at the apex bear a simple relationship of correspondence to a visually defined reality. Instead it aimed at an underdetermination of verbal truth by visual image. Many of its complex artistic images could not be read as veridical, were not transparent and unproblematic communications of the 'real', providing support for discursive truth. As its director John Wyver put it on *Right to Reply* (C4, 6.00, 14.2.87), the series 'doesn't have one particular line, one particular didactic formula, as it were, into which it wants to *fit* all the ideas and all the artists with which it tries to deal. It's not trying to do a kind of Robert Hughes type survey where his *certainty* is able to encompass everything that you're shown.'

The 'smooth operational surface of communication', postmodernist non-representational or 'nonreflecting surfaces',[38] are as likely to be said to be those of everyday series and serials as of 'art' television. Postmodernism is both an aesthetics of mass culture and of high art, of the 'little narratives' as well as the 'metanarratives'.[39] Popular television's 'play and replay' of the types and forms of situation comedy, soap opera and talk show is read as postmodernist pastiche, an exploration of the possibilities generated by the simulacra of generic variation rather than the representation of social reality. Often, as Caughie points out, this is economically motivated with an 'institutional as well as an aesthetic logic'.[40] At least in a postmodernist reading, the processes of identification as an appropriation of the extra-textual must also be considered subverted. This is a 'postmodern revelry in popular television's often parodic play with form, with the notion of pleasure seemingly altogether divorced from the realm of social relations'.[41]

Television's music video programmes have been foregrounded by post-modernists as texts in which the postmodernist aesthetic is particularly displayed : 'postmodernists sometimes seem to be arguing that music video is not just beyond realism, but somehow outside the world of representation altogether'.[42] Music videos can be read as drawing on the history of popular music in ways which deny its capacity to celebrate particular historical occurrences. History is reduced to an unproblematically available set of stylistic images, cultural stereotypes of the past replayable at will in contemporary music. Kaplan's account of postmodernist music videos is in terms of their detachment of signifier from signified. Through 'the abandon-ment of the traditional narrational devices of most popular culture' post-modernist music video undermines the confirming of visual assumptions which elsewhere produces the veridical effect, a sense of reality.[43] But the radical edge of postmodernism's questioning of the references of a sign to 'mythic signifieds' (for example, in denying reality to sexist representation) is lost in the 'rapid flow' of a genre of music video whose ideological position is the refusal of political alignment.

In the 'culture of the simulacrum' the simulacrum constitutes the world in the textual displays and operations of television.[44] The reduction to the image occurs as an increasingly pervasive presence 'in what Sartre would have called the *derealization* of the whole surrounding world of everyday reality . . . [This] loses its depth and threatens to become a glossy skin, a stereoscopic illusion, a rush of filmic images without density.'[45] For postmodern theorists, 'reality' has dissolved into the image, there is 'no reality which is not itself already image, spectacle, simulacrum, gratuitous fiction'.[46] In the postmodern sequence the 'veridical' is dispossessed of the 'real'.

Like the postmodern image, television dream sequences do not contain images of reality. 'I'll tell you there was something odd about that journey, something not right, something I still dream about,' asserts Phillip Marlow (Michael Gambon) in voiceover, recovering his visual memory of the dream in the company of the audience ('Who Done It ?', *The Singing Detective*, BBC1, 9.05, 21.12.86, and subsequently ABC). To mark a set of images as representing the experience of a dream, however, is to imply that elsewhere on television there are sequences which are veridical presentations of an intersubjective world. Dream sequences may be said to be temporary 'experiments' with the non-representational, anticipating but not exemplifying the postmodern image which makes no 'pretence to be showing me, offering me sight of, the *Real* occurring elsewhere'.[47]

Postmodernism is generally understood to succeed modernism as the rejection of philosophical and aesthetic realism rather than their investigation. It asserts the omnipresence of the signifier in an endless 'play' of meaning, 'a world transformed into sheer images of itself . . . It is for such [images] that we may reserve Plato's conception of the "simulacrum" – the identical copy for which no original has ever existed.'[48] But the postmodernist aesthetic has also been read as attempting to resolve the very problem it has collaborated in generating, that of the rational defence and support of a world view in the face of a thesis which, as Giddens puts it, consists of 'dissolving epistemology altogether'.[49] This attempt at a solution is constituted by 'the postmodernist search for cultural tradition and continuity, which underlies all the radical rhetoric of rupture, discontinuity and epistemological breaks'.[50] It is as a contribution to this search that I offer a perspectival theory of truth in Chapter 7.

Postmodernism is correct in asserting the cultural centrality of the image, not least the televisual image. Its concern to assert the variety of discursive interpretations of the world and the difficulty of reconciling those interpretations is central to social theory.[51] Postmodernism's reduction of reality to the image cannot, however, be sustained. Discursive truth in a text depends (sooner or later) on a relationship to a television image presenting an intersubjective world to which individuals other than the viewer have direct access. In the next chapter I advance a perspectival theory of truth in which both visual and non-visual discourse relate to the world through asserting particular aspects of its reality.

Notes

1 MacCabe, 'Memory, Phantasy and Identity', p. 316.
2 MacCabe, 'Realism and the Cinema', pp. 216–35.

170 *Subverting the Veridical Image*

3 Ibid., p. 224.
4 Ibid., p. 221. MacCabe claims the classic realist text is using an 'empirical notion of truth'. It is difficult to know precisely to which philosophical theory of truth this is a reference. The phrase might describe a Correspondence Theory in which statements count as true if, and only if, they correspond to empirical reality. However, it might be taken to refer to the Foundationalist Theory : object language discourses are true if, and only if, they can be validated by reference to a foundation in visual metalinguistic discourse. Both theories of truth are distinct from what I shall later refer to as a Perspectival Theory of Truth in which statements are true if, and only if, they successfully describe an aspect of that to which they are intended to refer, reality.
5 Discourses offering contradictory definitions of a phenomenon may be present in a text either more or less simultaneously in montage, as MacCabe suggests, or evolve as the story unfolds.
6 MacCabe, 'Realism and the Cinema', p. 224.
7 MacCabe, 'Theory and Film', p. 24.
8 Eisenstein, 'A Dialectic Approach to Film Form', p. 52.
9 Eisenstein, 'The Cinematographic Principle and the Ideogram', pp. 94–6.
10 Eisenstein, 'A Dialectic Approach to Film Form', p. 46.
11 Ibid., p. 47.
12 Eisenstein, 'The Cinematographic Principle and the Ideogram', p. 91.
13 Eisenstein, 'Methods of Montage', p. 83.
14 Gadamer, *Truth and Method*, p. 236.
15 Caughie, 'Progressive Television and Documentary Drama', p. 350.
16 Jauss, *Toward an Aesthetic of Reception*, p. 23.
17 Kozloff, 'Narrative Theory and Television', p. 70.
18 Ricoeur, 'Hermeneutics and the Critique of Ideology', *Hermeneutics and the Human Sciences*, p. 93.
19 Schlesinger et al., *Televising 'Terrorism'*, p. 42.
20 Nicholls, *Ideology and the Image*, p. 172.
21 Hodge and Tripp, *Children and Television*, p. 104.
22 MacCabe, 'Theory and Film', p. 11.
23 Pritchard, 'Unrelenting Bias'.
24 Fiske, *Television Culture*, p. 163.
25 Schlesinger et al., *Televising 'Terrorism'*, p. 42.
26 Caughie, 'Progressive Television and Documentary Drama', p. 331.
27 Ibid., p. 346.
28 Ibid., p. 342.
29 McArthur, 'Historical Drama', p. 294.
30 P. Hockings, *Principles of Visual Anthropology* (Amsterdam, Mouton, 1975), p. 72, quoted in A. Kuhn, 'The Camera I, Observations on Documentary', p. 74.
31 Huyssen, 'The Search for Tradition', p. 33. (Cf. Seitz, 'The Televised and the Untelevised'.)
32 Zurbrugg, 'An interview with Baudrillard'.
33 C. Owens, 'The Allegorical Impulse (Part 2)', *October*, 13 (1980), pp. 79–80, quoted in Ulmer, 'The Object of Post-criticism', p. 95.

34   Connor, *Postmodernist Culture*, p. 168.
35   Kaplan, *Rocking around the Clock*, p. 44.
36   C. Owens, 'The Discourse of Others : Feminists and Postmodernism', in Foster, *Postmodern Culture*, p. 58.
37   Heller, and Feher, *The Postmodern Political Condition*, p. 1.
38   Baudrillard, 'The Ecstasy of Communication', pp. 126–7.
39   Pefanis, *Heterology and the Postmodern*, p. 115.
40   Caughie, 'Adorno's Reproach', p. 150.
41   Higson and Vincendeau, 'Melodrama', p. 2.
42   Goodwin, 'Music Video in the (Post)modern World', p. 42.
43   Kaplan, 'A Post-modern Play of the Signifier?', pp. 148, 155.
44   A postmodern television of simulacra and non-representational images, at least in its refusal of an 'external world', possesses similarities to Eco's 'Neo-TV'. (Cf. Eco, 'A Guide to the Neo-television of the 1980's', p. 19.)
45   Jameson, 'Postmodernism or the Cultural Logic of Late Capitalism', p. 76.
46   Eagleton, 'Capitalism, Modernism and Postmodernism', p. 62.
47   Wyver, 'Television and Postmodernism'.
48   Jameson, 'Postmodernism or the Cultural Logic of Late Capitalism', p. 66.
49   Giddens, *The Consequences of Modernity*, p. 150.
50   Huyssen, 'The Search for Tradition', p. 32.
51   A postmodernist discussion, for instance, of problems for the 'dominant culture' thesis raised by the discursive variety associated with 'the complexity of cultural production in de-centred cultures' is contained in J. Collins, *Uncommon Cultures*.

7

Towards an 'Epic' Television

Television's mechanisms of identification align the implied viewer in a hermeneutic role characterized by the construction of meaning and insight. As the intended audience, we identify with those who appear to speak the truth. Within the text there are particular forms of significance, to be acknowledged as valid perceptions of the way things are. In identification the solutions to enigmas provided by detectives are to be adopted as correct; insights in the narratives of guides, explorers and searchers after meaning are to be regarded as genuine.

Additionally, to ease the path of identification, subjects (characters, presenters) in possession of these truths are generally represented as, in some respect, already familiar presences in the audience's life-world. Recognition is an ever possible experience.

The discursive statement of this meaningful 'truth', in a form mediated through familiarity, is marked out as different from other apparently less valid positions in a programme (for example, a presenter's address is distinguished from an interviewee's). In this way a complex hierarchical arrangement of discourses is built up through the text, with those which articulate the truth providing a focus for identification.

In this chapter I shall analyse these discourses as hierarchies of 'meaning', 'truth' and 'familiarity'; they are discursive formations primarily involving the verbal dimension of programmes. The construction of these hierarchies is central to a text, operating across the distinction between 'factual' and 'fictional' television. As hierarchies they signify perspectival variations, different ways of conceptualizing the visual so that some aspects of what is seen are marginalized and others foregrounded.

Television, I shall indicate, mediates the world through familiar terms, often effacing as it does so the more unfamiliar dictions of political difference. In the second part of the chapter I make use of Brechtian theory of drama to explore a reflexive television which presents the familiar as the unfamiliar open to analysis by an audience.

7.1   The Programme as Hierarchy

7.1.1   *The hierarchy of meaning*

The hierarchy of meaning inscribed in a programme is the hierarchy of concepts around which the text can be read as organizing what it has to say. These constitute a framework in terms of which it interprets its subject matter, a 'focus' for the production of a coherent meaning. Such frameworks invariably act as general 'schemata' organizing more particular statements made by individual subjects in the text. In this sense the hierarchy of meaning, a hierarchy of horizons of understanding in the programme, extends from the general to the specific. Concepts around which the meaning of the text is organized are found in a discourse of truth (for example, belonging to a presenter).

Hierarchies of meaning often vary in how they are elaborated both between film and television, and between different forms of television. The hierarchizing of meaning may commence pre-textually. Concepts which later constitute the text's framework of meaning can occur in continuity announcements (for instance, in references to the enigmas of continuous serials) or within the programme's description in a broadcast journal (such as the UK *Radio Times*). These are signifiers of a text's selective horizons of understanding. In the programme itself particular organizing concepts will be found associated with particular types of text (for example, the idea of 'impartial' treatment in current affairs television). The meaning of a documentary may conform to the horizons of understanding provided by a voiceover.

The framework of meaning in a programme can consist of sets of concepts, of general assumptions (such as concerning what is 'important'), or take the form of typical narratives which occur in more than one text. Once these schemata are recognized by an audience, they will generate particular horizons of expectation. The categories of meaning which organize the significances of a text offer points of stability in the programme through which the world is seen and understood. Often familiar and therefore apparently inevitable, these categories are infrequently scrutinized. As such they provide a secure basis whereby particular points of view may be justified.[1] Horizons of meaning are often richly orchestrated, elaborated with verbal complexity and sophistication in the texts of both 'fact' and 'fiction'.

Everyman's 'The Mighty Quinn' (BBC1, 10.30, 4.2.86) was a UK documentary programme about alcoholism and its treatment at a Catholic centre in Detroit run by a priest. In this text, the priest interpreted the experience of the alcoholic through a complex framework of understanding drawing on traditional Christianity. Alcoholism was an experience of 'low self-esteem', of 'bleeding' from 'remorse', yet a 'pain' which was 'the greatest gift that any one of us was ever sent'. These categories of meaning permeated the documentary, directing, for instance, many individual discussions and interviews with clients.

On the other hand, a programme's horizons of meaning may be unspoken but nevertheless effective in organizing the content of a text. Sometimes the sense imposed is that of a 'structuring absence', a significant assumption which while never explicitly articulated has a powerful effect on the content of a programme. Knightly argues in a community television programme on journalism, *Open Space*, 'A Voyage Round the Monarchy' (BBC2, 7.50, 11.12.86), that 'there's some sort of unwritten little arrangement between Buckingham Palace and the British Press . . . "You can report as much trivia as you like about us . . . but you must not under any circumstances write stories querying whether or not we should continue to exist . . . Those stories are taboo, forbidden."'

In a similar way the concept of 'impartiality' may determine the distribution of meaning across a text and yet seldom be mentioned explicitly : 'the BBC regarded deference to the prime minister as impartiality' (*Television and Number 10*, BBC2, 5.40, 24.9.88). Particular interpretations of 'balance' and 'impartiality' may inflect the operation of television news and current affairs in unacknowledged directions. Hall et al. argue that the policy of 'equal' treatment for the representatives of parliamentary democracy is not extended to other political activists : 'the broadcaster is . . . partisan in terms of the maintenance of a certain mode and type of institutionalised power – namely the capitalist state as a parliamentary democracy'.[2]

Such 'balanced' treatment of the political meant that in the 1979 British general election, National Front candidates, as representatives of a political party, had to be treated as possessing a degree of legitimacy (even if subjected to substantial criticism). Anti-National Front organizations which had no parliamentary ambitions were often included in the news only as an issue of public order.[3]

In their analysis of media discourse around the 1987 UK general election Garton et al. refer to other organizing structures of meaning within news and current affairs. 'Narrative models' ('sedimented forms of "common-sense"') were used in programmes, according to their analysis, to interpret the sometimes elliptical utterances of particular politicians. During the campaign the media constructed Kinnock's assertions, as leader of the Labour Party, about a non-nuclear defence policy as a policy for defeat. This reconstruction was possible because it implicitly relied upon a widespread and 'common-sense' fear that a non-nuclear defence policy would lead to nuclear blackmail and subsequent occupation by hostile forces. While this 'common-sense' was not stated in the news, it 'is at least necessary to posit some such organization of [narrative] knowledge and background assumptions, in order to account for how "using all the resources you have got to make any occupation totally untenable" can come to be heard as, for example, "a policy of surrender"'.[4] Other organizing concepts in the news (such as the discussion of the election in the phraseology of a military campaign) were identified as having their source in the speeches of politicians : 'we have been struck by the way glossings which develop in the political sphere become incorporated into the discourse of news stories themselves'.[5]

Agenda setting in news and current affairs television is not best understood as establishing an agenda of items. It is, rather, the construction of a set of frameworks, hierarchically arranged in order of importance, through which news items are organized, represented and analysed. The day-to-day repetition of these frameworks establishes a hierarchy of meaning in programmes which is often familiar and apparently self-evident.

It is, for instance, not uncommon to find that any of a range of issues, including poor race relations, industrial conflict, unemployment and the collapse of traditional working-class communities, may be considered by a news commentator within a framework of concern for 'law and order'. Reducing these problems to a set of topics around the maintaining of law and order permits their source to be diagnosed as working-class 'crime and unruliness' rather than problems in capitalism. In London the 'Southall riot has thrust law and order into the election spotlight overnight' (Alistair Burnet, *News at Ten*, ITV, 10.00, 24.4.79). A privileging of the category of law and order in the list of items on the political agenda can indicate successful ideological work by the political Right.

Elsewhere on television other dominant horizons of understanding direct the viewer in coming to understand the content of a text. A documentary may announce itself to be an investigative recovery of 'the truth', the provision of objective insight rather than fanciful delusion. *QED*, 'The Science of Sexual Attraction' (BBC1, 9.25, 6.3.85), was 'a dispassionate appraisal of our more passionate feelings'.

A common feature of television documentaries is a structuring of meaning in terms of a cognitive horizon of concepts drawn from the processes of detection. The operations of the text are fundamentally conceived of as providing access to hidden knowledge, with other aspects of its meaning organized accordingly. Since this hierarchy of meaning occurs frequently across television, unlike other features of a documentary seen for the first time, its presence can be a source of recognition for the viewer. This in turn allows a hierarchy of familiarity to emerge within the programme (see section 7.1.3).

Organized in terms of the schemata of detection, a *World about Us* investigation reveals that the image of Australia as a 'great, beautiful, sunlit, European transplant' is 'one great Australian *myth*' ('Sacred Rights', BBC2, 8.10, 13.2.85). *Comrades* draws attention to the contradiction between the public wedding ritual and 'the reality of married life in the Soviet Union' (*Comrades: The Trial of Tamara Russo*, BBC2, 8.10, 8.12.85). The documentary *Brazil, Brazil* (BBC1, 11.00, 10.4.86) allows the viewer to discover that the 'postcard images' of Brazil are 'only the tip of the iceberg'. A John Pilger documentary series looks 'behind the popular images and stereotypes of Japan today' (*TV Times*), 'behind the mask of four important areas of Japanese life' (*Viewpoint 87*, 'Japan : Behind the Mask', ITV, 10.30, 13.1.87).

7.1.2　*The hierarchy of truth*

The texts of 'mainstream' television can be read as asserting a hierarchy of verbal discourses arranged on the basis of their degree of accord with the visual discourses of the programme, which in turn are to be taken as revealing the world. The relationship between verbal and visual discourses varies across texts. In news programmes, for instance, the visual can be indeterminate, open to a wide variety of different interpretations (for example, images of people arriving at a conference). Here, it serves only to corroborate the verbal at the most general level. Speech in these segments of text, often in voiceover, provides a discourse of interpretation for what is seen. It makes more precise the relationship and meaning of the visual layers of the programme, providing a 'verbal narrative that alone gives these images coherence'.[7] So open are such images to different readings that there is little probability of them undermining even elaborate verbal constructions of their meaning. In other texts, however, the specificity of the visual constrains the interpretations placed upon it.

The relationship of spoken discourse to the visual is perspectival.[8] Language 'catches' an aspect of the seen, marking out in it similarities to and differences from other signifieds. The verbal always asserts both more and less than can be justified by appealing to the visual discourse to which it 'corresponds'. A subject's speech may be apparently confirmed by the visual, only to turn out subsequently to be false : even words spoken at the close of a text can conflict with the visual discourse of a later programme. Yet a particular spoken discourse is always 'less than' the visual : the latter may always be described in other ways, using alternative horizons of understanding. In this sense events 'transcend' (Merleau-Ponty) their description, an excess always available to be appropriated through further signifiers. The visual in relation to the verbal is 'something transcendent standing in the wake of one's subjectivity'. The perspectival relationship between verbal and visual is repeated within the mediation of the world by what is seen. 'The thing and the world . . . transcend all perspectives because this chain is temporal and incomplete.'[9]

Like television, the filmic classic realist text employs a relationship to the visual as a criterion of linguistic 'truth'. I suggest this 'empirical' correspondence should be understood as perspectival. Language has a relevance to what is seen in terms of those aspects which, on the one hand, it emphasizes and, on the other, those which it marginalizes and about which it is silent. This 'is a picture of experience or cognition as a series of *prises* on a reality which, while it never eludes our grasp, is never fully within it either.[10] For both the verbal and the seen (the images of the film) appropriate only an aspect of that to which they 'point'. A subject's cognitive *prise* on reality often makes reference to the perspectives of others, evaluating them as truthful or otherwise : 'while each perspective offers a particular view of the intended object, it also opens up a view on the *other* perspectives'.[11]

A reader's and a text's horizons of understanding are cognitive frameworks through which events are 'focalized' (Genette). Perceptions of an object which regard it from different perspectives foreground different aspects. Likewise, in the perspectival relationship between the verbal and the visual by which truth is (at least temporarily) determined, competing interpretations of a single event draw on and emphasize alternative aspects of its character. The horizons of understanding brought to a text by its reader may draw attention to other aspects of its content from those marked out in the cognitive frameworks employed by the text itself. 'Fundamental to twentieth-century critical thought is the understanding, that, in a signifying system such as language, the signifier never coincides with the signified; one of these elements is always, so to speak, outstripping or in excess of the other.'[12]

A television text, often centrally verbal in character, frequently circulates a series of competing horizons of understanding in terms of which its subject matter can be interpreted and identified. Outside the non-veridical texts described in Chapter 6, these opposing cognitive frameworks can be read as occupying a hierarchy of truth. In some relatively open television texts (for example, the continuous serial) this hierarchy may temporarily appear to be absent, its presence nevertheless usually confirmed by a final ranking of discourses in the text. Until this point is reached in a programme, a 'regulated latitude of ideological positions' will, for a time, be available for appropriation and identification by a varied audience.'[13]. These positions may constitute points of rupture, sitting uneasily in the programme's flow of hegemonic 'sense'.

In dominant texts, where mechanisms of identification produce the (intended) viewer's identification with a subject, this carries with it the viewer's appropriation of reliable significance. At least as far as the text is concerned, the detective, journalist or whoever, has valid insights. Here a subject's horizons of understanding are privileged as truthful, as supporting an audience's projection of meaning into the text. In this way a character's discourses may be said to be 'protensive' (Husserl) or 'future-directed', the basis of valid anticipations by an audience concerning likely occurrences in a text.

But the interpretation of events through a subject's horizon of understanding may be evaluative as well as factual, drawing on discourses of morality or aesthetics. *Ladies in Charge* (ITV, 9.05, 27.8.85) was a single play on UK commercial television (subsequently followed by a series): 'Diana, Babs and Polly drove ambulances together during the Great War and found a sense of purpose. Back home in 1920, they feel that they are missing something, but are determined not to stagnate' (*TV Times*). The exercise of this 'determination' produces a series of activities systematically both understood and misunderstood from a range of different perspectives. Opening a 'social work' agency, they regard themselves as 'business women': 'we're business women, you know . . . we are trying to start up an agency for helping people . . . I'll have you know we're very serious business women.' But this display of economic independence is 'read' by the police as an assertion of feminine sexuality : 'these premises have been kept under observation and we have reason to believe that they may be used for immoral purposes'.

The visual discourses of this text become sufficiently determinate to allow a decision to be made by the viewer about which of these competing accounts of events is true. But the programme sustains to the end its interest in the ambiguity of the image. As one of the women comments in the closing segment, 'we've only been in business a week and this is the third time we've been taken for harlots'.

In the drama different ideological readings of the 'real' emerge, marginal-izing or foregrounding different aspects of what is seen, to constitute opposing identities. As Barthes writes, in the 'anchoring' of an image by the verbal the 'anchorage may be ideological and indeed this is its principal function ; the text directs the reader through the signifieds of the image, causing him to avoid some and receive others'.[14] Even the women's interpretation of events is contested : 'the day you lot get the vote I'll throw myself in the bleedin' river,' asserts a 'real' working-class 'harlot'. The discourse associated with these 'ladies in charge' appears to address a television audience occupying a life-world whose familiar needs and ration-alities are inflected by contemporary feminism.[15] Their speech is privileged as both a mediation of events in 1920 and a basis for identification in the present : 'times have changed, you know. It's 1920. Women aren't hothouse plants any more . . . We're not going to be taking anybody's job away. We just want to do something useful.'

Different cognitive horizons of understanding, then, ascribe different identities to 'reality'. These are open to revision in the face of the 'facts' : 'empirical concepts are changed by the continual admission of new attri-butes'.[16] Television comedy, like drama, may revolve around ambiguous identities or mistaken perceptions of identity resisting change. In *Fawlty Towers* Basil Fawlty's (John Cleese) obsessively held beliefs rarely measure up to reality. During one episode (BBC2, 9.05, 10.11.85, and subsequently on Australian ABC) 'Basil Fawlty tries to improve the class of the hotel's clientele with remarkable results' : a 'confidence-trickster' is treated as 'true upper class' (confirmed as such by his 'tatty cases') while the CID officer who comes to investigate is dismissed as 'that Cockney git'.

Identities are often more secure in 'factual' texts where the status of the voiceover is usually that of a privileged discourse of truth defining the nature of the 'real'. In the hierarchy of the text's 'knowledges', as I noted in Chapter 5, the voiceover articulates a cognitive perspective with which the intended viewer is to identify. In many television current affairs programmes it is reserved for the 'voice' of the media institution itself. This code of practice was not conformed to in a *Real Lives* programme on Northern Ireland, 'At the Edge of the Union' (BBC1, 9.25, 16.10.85) : its transmission was effectively prevented for a time by the UK government. In that text Martin McGuinness, 'accused by some of being the IRA's Chief of Staff'

(*Radio Times*), speaks in voiceover. This allows him a privileged commentary on, for instance, images of the army presence in Ulster. He is permitted to attribute to it a particular identity, that of an 'army of occupation': 'I believe that it's absolutely essential that Republicans express to the world in a very forcible fashion, that there is a big demand in Ireland for the removal of the British presence.' In other segments of the *Real Lives* programme the voiceover consists of the 'neutral' discourse of a BBC documentary presenter, defined as 'neutral' by its ideological position between the two 'extremes' for which it provides an introduction and initial commentary.

7.1.3. *The hierarchy of familiarity*

Television programmes frequently produce the experience of 'recognition' in the intended viewer. This may be the result of any one of a range of features in the text: its representation of the viewer's social roles, the recurring and hence familiar programme, attitude or character, or its engaging in conceptual or linguistic practices similar to those of the audience. All produce 'the televised illusion of familiarity'. While film actors are stars, television actors become 'personalities': 'personalities have a familiarity that offers their fans a much more intimate, equal relationship', a familiarity that may transfer itself to the character played by a particular actor.[17] An economically motivated repetition of forms of address, of camera angle and *mise en scène* support not only television's ordinariness but a pervasive sense of the recognizable.

Television's construction of audience 'recognition' generally works to deny a space in which differences of class, gender, race or generation explicitly confront the intended viewer. An apparent temporal and spatial contiguity in the discourse space between text and viewer implies a context in which familiarity is likely. The electronic immediacy of direct address suggests a conversational mode. Television abhors a distance, whether physical or cognitive, preferring instead to fill it with a content of semantic mediation. For the intended audience to experience conceptual difference is to inhibit its easy enjoyment of the programme. Difference may 'denaturalize' the text, prompting the viewer to examine its authority, to call into question its cognitive frameworks.

This cultivation of familiarity is a rhetorical dimension of television's address to the viewer in which, as for the first dialectician Plato, 'the arguments brought forward are always appropriate to the specific receptivity of the souls to which they are directed'.[18] Television's familiar address is occasioned by an entertainment-led need for the easily consumable, a need whose satisfaction requires that 'something *distant* has to be brought close, a certain strangeness overcome, a bridge built between the once and the now'.[19] Here conceptual distance between programme and intended audience is 'dissolved into a new and distinct familiarity in which [meaning] belongs to us and we to it'.[20]

The hierarchy of familiarity in a programme is constituted by television's translation of the unfamiliar by the familiar. In the economic phraseology of everyday life rather than the treasury, Queensland viewers of Channel Ten's *Brisbane with Anna McMahon* were informed one evening that Labour's first Queensland Budget in thirty-four years had 'kept out of the hip pockets of Queenslanders'. Mediation by the familiar occurs in both 'factual' and 'fictional' television, in texts which are in other respects very different. Indeed, this hierarchy replicates the way in which the non-televisual world presents itself to the individual. 'Structurisation by preacquaintedness and unacquaintedness is a fundamental feature of our consciousness of the world.'[21] In experience the unfamiliar is read in terms of the familiar. To retrieve reality for familiar modes of understanding is to emphasize certain aspects at the expense of others : 'nature programmes will often stress the "like us-ness" of the animals filmed, finding in their behaviour metaphoric equivalences with our own culture's way of organising its affairs'.[22]

The hierarchy of familiarity associated with 'factual' television such as documentary allows discourses intended for easy consumption by the viewer to occupy privileged epistemological positions in a voiceover or in direct address : from there they interpret the more difficult or unfamiliar discourses in the programme. In light entertainment shows the host's address to his or her audience is couched in terms of the unproblematic and easily consumable. Drama, as I indicated in Chapter 3, constructs for intended viewers the experience of familiar roles from which the content of the text can be read and interpreted. These provide points of entry to otherwise difficult discursive structures.

The two most popular forms of television drama, situation comedy and the continuous serial, both contain a hierarchical organization of textual discourses addressing to varying degrees the familiar experience of the intended viewer. The situation comedy is frequently set in a domestic context (familiar to the assumed audience) and contains images and individuals which are stereotypically common.

As with other television genres, so in the continuous serial the hierarchy of discursive familiarity replicates in the text aspects of the viewer's familiar life-world. This may range from the assertion of narratives already known to the audience (for example, of weddings or Christmas) to a statement of some of the ideas and assumptions which define the very identity of the viewers themselves. Contextualized by these familiarities the unfamiliar is located and discussed. Individuals belonging to the text can be experienced by the audience as 'friends', a friendship resting on a cognitive consensus between the extra- and intra-textual subjects concerned. The construction of these friendly relationships occurs through the same processes as in everyday life. In both text and life, knowledge about an individual is the product of the repeated encounter of another involved in the continuing activities of everyday living : 'the repetitiveness of day to day life, crosscut by the irreversibility of lifetime [*sic*], is continuously reproduced by these stories without beginning or ending'.[23]

Audience research on Scottish Television's serial *Take the High Road*, set in a village near Loch Lomond, confirms a successful soap opera to be one which constructs in a variety of ways the life-world of familiar experience belonging to its viewers. For the regular watcher of the 'High Road', its characters appear as friends in a community of the shared and known : 'it is as if friends came [*sic*] to call' ; 'they really must have studied *this* village'.[24]

Not only soap operas but other programmes such as ITV's breakfast television programme *Good Morning Britain* (discussed in section 1.2) construct the life-world of the implied viewer to an elaborate degree within the text. Discourses establishing familiar needs and values, recognizable social roles and cognitive horizons of experience, will all be present. The text has identified with its intended audience. And in its reproduction of the familiar it has established a context which in turn enables the viewer's identification with textual subjects to occur with ease.

Sometimes, as in the marginalizing of politics by the familiarities of the familial in *Good Morning Britain*, this identification will be reactionary in its effects. Elsewhere, the contributions of contestants in quiz shows, such as British television's *The Price Is Right* or the Australian *Perfect Match*, permit a female audience to identify with familiar, if transitory, challenges to ideological definitions of appropriate behaviour. 'If quiz shows are popular with women (and they are), they are so only because they bear not only the ideological voices of the dominant, but also the opportunity to resist, evade or negotiate with these voices'.[25]

As I have noted, the hierarchy of familiarity 'sets the mood' for identification, often articulating the roles, rules and relationships into which the viewer has already, pre-textually, entered. Some of these roles are to be defined in terms of their loss of power or social failure, others in terms of the powers and social status which accrue to their occupants. 'I run my estate and am also surrounded by wonderful characters,' asserts a viewer of *Take the High Road*, indicating recognition.[26] The attraction of a text's articulation of social roles is not only the construction of familiar points of identification but the experience of questioning and debating about them.

In the continuous serial the presentation of familiarity through the recurring character is important. The weekly repetition of some characters but not others, like the repetition of those who gather or report the news rather than those who make it, establishes a hierarchy of 'insiders' and 'outsiders' in the dramatic fiction, the 'deep-structural community basis of the soap opera'.[27] This is a hierarchy of the familiar/unfamiliar, a hierarchy not to be dissociated from those of meaning and truth. With the reappearance of a familiar soap opera character the viewer can anticipate just what frameworks of understanding are about to be rehearsed and with what credibility they are to be entertained.

Elsewhere on television, the hierarchy of familiarity relates to the viewer's hermeneutic processes of reading the text. It foregrounds a cognitive horizon of understanding which is not only recognized but likely to be regarded by the viewer as a discourse of truth and meaning in terms of which the programme's content may be rendered intelligible. The known news presenter, unlike some characters in the continuous serial, speaks the 'truth'. 'Dan Rather was trusted more on news issues than President Reagan.'

7.2   Subverting the Hierarchy

A veridical sequence allows its audience the transparent experience of the 'real'. Speech and activity in the sequence can articulate a range of social roles, each of which is associated with the discovery and knowledge of truth, with positions of cognitive insight which align the (implied) viewer. The discourses establishing these 'knowledges' are also likely to produce recognition, the viewer's experience of the already familiar. Situated within such a known horizon of understanding, information is rendered unproblematic. Newsreaders are both television friends and knowledgeable. Soap opera characters return week after week; and at least some offer moral insight.

A 'distanciated' reading of a television text, on the other hand, defamiliarizes the cognitively familiar, placing it in the inverted commas of 'estrangement'. The 'alienated' reader refuses the easy recognition of horizons of understanding on offer. The frequently encountered is no longer unproblematic but is open for questioning. In distanciation 'what was a process of knowing has become a piece of knowledge'.[28] To use a distinction from the Soviet writer Shklovsky, the viewer 'sees' rather than 'recognizes' the content of the text: 'a phenomenon, perceived many times, and no longer perceivable, or rather, the method of such dimmed perception, is what I call "recognition" as opposed to "seeing". The aim of imagery, the aim of creating new art is to return the object from "recognition" to "seeing".'[29]

To 'see' rather than 'recognize' the familiar is to resist involvement in the processes of identification associated with television or theatre. Instead of the audience adopting familiar social roles displayed in a text, it becomes the focus of critical attention. In this section I would like to examine whether techniques allowing the spectator to resist involvement in theatrical drama can be straightforwardly applied to television, encouraging its viewers to see familiar forms and content as if for the first time.

The dramatist Bertolt Brecht argued that his 'epic' theatre had the function of producing a 'critical' spectator, who, it might be said, could 'see', rather than become 'completely "entangled" in what is going on'.[30] The spectator of the epic theatre resists the mechanisms which seek to attain his or her identification with subjective perspectives in the text. To produce this detachment in the ideal audience, those subjective horizons must be 'made strange' through techniques and performances involving the 'A-effect (alienation effect)' of 'defamiliarization'. Through these 'dis-identificatory practices' (Wollen) the familiar and ordinary loses its appearance of inevitability and acquires the contingent status of that which might not have been : 'what is involved here is, briefly, a technique of taking the human social incidents to be portrayed and labelling them as something striking, something that calls for explanation, as not to be taken for granted, not just natural. The object of this "effect" is to allow the spectator to criticize constructively from a social point of view.'[31]

The alienation effect is a 'making strange' of the everyday so that its examination appears appropriate. For Brecht, this defamiliarization is cognitive, based on a need to examine or even replace the conceptual frameworks of the audience's familiar life-worlds. In this respect theatre studies agree with ethnomethodology : 'the member of the society uses background expectancies as a scheme of interpretation. With their use actual appearances are for him recognizable and intelligible as the appearances-of-familiar-events . . . For these background expectancies to come into view one must either be a stranger to the "life as usual" character of everyday scenes, or become estranged from them.'[32] The very familiarity of these horizons of understanding the world, according to Brecht, may efface an ideological content which should be contested.

Brecht's concept of 'distanciation' derives its sense from an opposition between traditional 'empathy', or Aristotelian theatre, and his own 'epic theatre' of alienation from the familiar. 'Empathy' theatre requires a 'passive' identification with the views of a dramatic subject : the actor 'does all he can to bring his spectator into the closest proximity to the events and the character he has to portray'.[33] Traditional theatre reconstructs social (class) contradiction as imaginary social coherence, allowing the spectator to 'swap a contradictory world for a consistent one, one that they scarcely know for one of which they can dream'.[34] This 'consistent' social universe has a structure which the individual is without power to alter or modify : 'the theatre as we know it shows the structure of society (represented on the stage) as incapable of being influenced by society (in the auditorium)'.[35]

The ideal spectators of traditional theatre have forgotten their class experience, remembering only a ' "common humanity" shared by all spectators alike'. Their identity as members of different social classes is not addressed, for 'the aesthetics of the day call for an impact that flattens out all social and other distinctions between individuals'.[36] The theatre of the bourgeoisie, while itself claiming to celebrate the individualistic, is a theatre of the general and non-specific : 'the central figures have to be kept general, so that it is easier for the onlooker to identify himself with them'.[37]

Brecht argues against a traditional theatre where the elements of the drama, as well as text and audience, are 'fused' together in an apparent unity supporting culturally dominant perceptions of its content : 'so long as the arts are supposed to be "fused" together, the various elements will all be equally degraded, and each will act as a mere "feed" to the rest. The process of fusion extends to the spectator, who gets thrown into the melting pot too and becomes a passive (suffering) part of the total work of art.'[38]

Brecht's theory and practice of distanciation is intended as a 'separation of the elements', 'prising open' the text and 'making distant' its familiarities. This releases a new pleasure for the audience, that of analysing the drama. 'Simple empathy with the characters in a play', an alignment with and confirmation of the familiar, is submitted to 'a process of alienation', 'the alienation that is necessary to all understanding. When something seems "the most obvious thing in the world" it means that any attempt to understand the world has been given up.'[39]

In epic dramas 'acceptance or rejection of [characters'] actions and utterances' is foregrounded for conscious examination.[40] Alienation devices make 'the incidents represented appear strange', supporting their critical scrutiny in what has become a theatre of reason. For in avoiding 'the passive empathy of the spectator',[41] 'the essential point of the epic theatre is perhaps that it appeals less to the feelings than to the spectator's reason'.[42] Brechtian theatre is intended as 'entertainment'[43] whose opportunities for social criticism allow the 'realism' of 'discovering the causal complexes of society/ unmasking the prevailing view of things as the view of those who are in power'.[44]

Brecht's mechanisms for alienating the spectator into an 'attitude of inquiry and criticism'[45] make use of a range of aspects of theatrical production and performance. An actor or actress looking directly at the audience from the stage undermines the spectator's illusion of watching an event in 'real life' without being seen. 'The audience can no longer have the illusion of being the unseen spectator at an event which is really taking place.'[46] Activities on the stage are in this way presented as a theatrical construct, permitting the audience to ask in respect of the cultural or social norms which guide the action, 'Why this rather than that ?' In an extension of the technique the actor or actress can talk to the audience, addressing its critical subjectivity through a commentary on the drama in 'the direct changeover from representation to commentary that is so characteristic of the epic theatre'.[47]

Particular techniques are used to subvert the processes of identification. An actor or actress can 'demonstrate' rather than act a part, delivering the character's lines as if 'quoting' them. This distance between 'demonstrator' and dramatic subject reminds the audience that the latter's speech is an authored construct. Identification is difficult where actors remain 'detached from the character they [are] playing and clearly [invite] criticism of him'.[48] The actor 'must not suppress the "*he* did that, *he* said that" element in his performance'.[49] If identification occurs in this theatre of detachment, it is with 'the actor as . . . an observer, and accordingly develops [the actor's] attitude of observing or looking on'.[50] Other aspects of the production may be used to produce this critical 'looking on' at a dramatic subject: 'documents which confirmed or contradicted what the characters said' can be projected on large screens.

In the epic theatre it is important not to hide the processes of rehearsal preceding the drama being performed, processes which, when examined, show its construction to embody particular perspectives on the world. The spectator's 'illusion of being present at a spontaneous, transitory, authentic, unrehearsed event'[51] must be undermined. By not pretending that the events taking place on the stage 'are now happening for the first and only time'[52] but are a rehearsed construction, the actor 'emphasizes that it is his own account, view, version of the incident'.[53] The spectator should also be reminded of the status of the dramatic artefact as a product synthesized together from many parts. This 'separation of the elements' may occur through presenting the drama as a series of 'episodes' in which distinctions between different locations and times are emphasized, making visible 'the knotting-together of the events'.[54] 'The episodes must not succeed one another indistinguishably but must give us a chance to interpose our judgment.'[55]

The status of the play as a particular construction from theatrical elements can be further underlined by other aspects of performance and production. Events which appear only to be present in the text to demonstrate general principles (for example, of a moral character) signify a degree of artificiality for the drama: 'the particular and unrepeatable incident acquires a disconcerting look, because it appears as something general, something that has become a principle'.[56] A 'heightened' or excessive stylization will similarly present the drama as artefact.[57] Attention can also be drawn to the text as construction by subverting viewers' expectations: A-effects 'include an expectation which is justified by experience but, in the event, disappointed . . . If one sees one's teacher hounded by the bailiffs an A-effect occurs: one is jerked out of a relationship in which the teacher seems big into one where he seems small.'[58]

The techniques of production and performance associated with distanciating the theatrical spectator, I would like to suggest, cannot be transferred unproblematically to television. Direct address to the viewer, as I have noted, is not an alienating device but a mark of familiarity. Nevertheless, some of Brecht's proposals for an epic theatre can be 'redirected' to subvert the hierarchies of meaning, truth and familiarity found in television drama, thereby undermining the discursive formations with which viewers align themselves in identification with a subject.

Direct address to the audience produces opposing readings in the different contexts of epic theatre and television. Brechtian theatre relies on it as a technique for defamiliarizing the content of the spectacle. But in the news, current affairs and light entertainment texts of television it invariably marks an assertion of the familiar. In television drama, however, unlike news and current affairs, direct address to the audience is unusual and therefore distancing. It produces not the audience which easily aligns itself with the direct address of 'truth' associated with news but an (ideal) viewer who is critically receptive of an unfamiliar communication. As the Open University television programme in their *Popular Culture* series, 'Politics of Drama' (BBC2, 1982), noted :

> in 1965 Dennis Potter used a character talking direct to camera, in this case Nigel Barton's Labour Party agent: 'Ah. Eh, my office. I'm sorry about all this but we in the Labour Party link drabness with idealism, see . . . the Conservative Central Office. Whew ! It's a very plush place that. Carpets plucking at your bleeding ankles. You see, they link drabness with idealism too.

In television, actors and actresses attempt to 'merge' with characters. Hobson, writing about the soap opera *Crossroads*, points out that 'script-writers actually pick up the personal mannerisms, attitudes and speech patterns of the performers and incorporate them into the personality of the character whom they are portraying'.[59] As I noted above, it is the contrary strategy of distancing actor or actress from character which allows, according to Brecht, a space for critique by both 'demonstrator' and theatre audience. A similar distancing is produced by a form of behavioural 'excess' associated with television situation comedy (though it is not normally used to heighten an audience's political consciousness). In one episode of *Fawlty Towers* (BBC2, 9.05, 15.12.85, and subsequently on ABC) 'a party of Germans and fire drill practice turn Fawlty Towers upside down'. John Cleese's performance in the role of Basil Fawlty separates actor from character in a construction of dramatic excess : Cleese goosesteps and salutes his way through a stereotypical caricature of the Teutonic. The actor 'demonstrates' rather than 'inhabits' the character. At this point the dramatic subject is not Fawlty, a character in a television series bearing the title *Fawlty Towers*, but the performer in and across many texts of different genres, John Cleese.

Here, *Fawlty Towers* can no longer function to provide the transparent disclosure of the apparently real presupposed in audience identification with a textual subject. The text has become a self-evident construction, with a content of uncertain reality. Its hierarchies of meaning and familiarity are, temporarily at least, associated with the performer Cleese. Fawlty, on the other hand, is dispossessed from his status as subject in a drama. Situation comedies provide other instances of distanciation : stereotyped or 'two-dimensional' characters inhibit an easy identification by the audience, alienating it from involvement in the text.

Many of the distanciation techniques employed in the epic theatre demand sustained attention from their intended audience. To become distanciated from a text as a result of experiencing it as excessively stylized presupposes an involvement which is more than casual. Transferred to television, these alienation devices continue to require a 'gaze' rather than a 'glance' and a continuous attention to the soundtrack. Only then will the artifice and artificiality of the text become apparent, with a consequent subverting of its easy accord with the 'real'.

Applying to television, for instance, the alienation techniques associated with emphasizing the differences of a text's spatio-temporal locations (in a 'separation of the elements') presupposes the concentrated attention of the viewer. In Scottish BBC's *The Story of a Recluse* (BBC2, 10.35, 25.12.87) the use of an abrupt segmentation of time and space is an important distanciation device. The programme is based on a short narrative begun by R.L. Stevenson and completed by Glasgow writer Alasdair Gray. Set in Edinburgh in the nineteenth century, the television drama opens in a woman's bedroom. Shot initially in monochrome, the corners of each image are tinged with blue, both signifying their status as subjective memory and undermining their transparent reference to the apparently real. In an inebriated stupor Jamie (Peter Capaldi) has mistaken Juliette's (Cristina Higueras) room for his own and he is hurriedly directed by her to the door. In the midst of these activities the music on the soundtrack slows and the camera cuts to the BBC2 caption for *The Story of a Recluse*. Alasdair Gray appears on screen seated against a white background, book in hand, and addresses the camera :

> Louis Stevenson stopped writing *The Story of a Recluse*, which is *not* the book you saw at the start behind the title, but just four pages in this collection of his unfinished stories. The only clues we have as to how Stevenson would have continued the tale are in the part you've just seen filmed. Scottish BBC employed me to give their film an *ending*, and the film makers think that you'll enjoy it more if I tell you how I worked it out. So first, the setting.

There follows a cut to images of builders at work with an uncompleted Forth Railway Bridge dominating the background. The period is Victorian Edinburgh in the 1880s ; the scene is shot in sepia.

To follow this shift through the divisions of time and space between the unidentified past of the drama, the present of authorial commentary on a document and the identified past of documentary requires the full attention of the viewer if it is to remain comprehensible. In this alienating of the audience other mechanisms of distanciation become apparent. Gray's comments foreground the construction and preparation of both the drama which has just been viewed and that which is about to be seen. In denying the status of the text as a transparent disclosure of the world, he authorizes a reading in which processes allowing identification are absent.

Brechtian mechanisms of distanciation subvert the audience's uncritical complicity in the experience of the subject. Applied to television drama, they qualify and restrict the veridical effect of the image. In undermining the status of the text as a transparent presenting of the real, they suspend its hierarchy of truth, allowing a critical intervention by the viewer. The familiarities of television practice are made strange. Those concepts which organize the meaning of the programme are delivered up for examination by the audience to whom the text is addressed.

Television documentary, as I have noted, can be read as an arrangement of discourses within a multiple hierarchy of meaning, truth and familiarity. Not all documentaries, however, organize their content by using the voiceover of a presenter with its claim to assert an objective, universal truth. Some articulate, unmediated, the subjective experiences of particular individuals (as in drama). One BBC programme about Belfast, *The Falls Road : A Kind of Limbo* (BBC2, 8.10, 5.6.86), is an account of life in the Falls Road from the point-of-view of its residents : 'the Falls Road, as I know it, or as I understand it, is more of an idea or an ideal in the people's minds who actually do live on the road'.

In one segment of the text the sounds of New Orleans jazz music accompany long camera pans showing the road and its inhabitants. Here, music and images appear at odds, not least because the former evokes associations with very different cultural communities from those of Belfast. Sound and vision play against each other, a separation of the elements in which a 'happy' music acts to distanciate the experience of poverty, exhibiting it for analysis rather than identification.

But other documentaries organize their hierarchies of truth, meaning and familiarity to privilege a voiceover. Identification is likely to be with presenter rather than character. Yet aspects of the text, in reminding the viewer of its status as construction, may render the processes of identification less than inevitable (for example, the subjective travelling shot).

While the alienation devices of drama undermine identification with the subjective horizons of experience of a particular individual, alienating the voiceover of a documentary subverts identification with a framework of understanding intended to be read as objective, as allowing a universal truth to emerge. Yet this opposition is not as total as it might appear. For even in drama, the universal is implicit in the particular. In interpreting their own experiences, individuals commit themselves to regarding their horizon of understanding as being universally valid for all in similar circumstances. In this sense the dramatic subject legislates ideologically, prescribing implicitly in an analogous way to that in which the documentary presenter prescribes explicitly for all.

However, a wider application of Brechtian techniques of distanciation to television confronts difficulties. As I noted earlier, aspects of television's construction of meaning may appear, erroneously, to possess a similarity to the alienation devices of the epic theatre. A 'separation of the elements' can characterize a drama production, with each section clearly separated from the others. Transferring this format to television, it might be argued, results in the serial, which prompts through its episodic structure a detached audience scrutiny of its several parts. But the operation of Brechtian distanciation techniques presupposes a difference between their use and the customary dramatic practices of the theatre. The episodic structure of the television serial represents not difference but its familiar and dependable construction of meaning. It is, as such, unlikely to alienate the viewer into a critical scrutiny of a text's assumptions. Likewise, the 'commercial interruptions that place the news "on hold" . . . are not pauses for reflection but breaks for manipulation'.[60]

A similar relationship obtains between forms of theatre and forms of television where their processes of construction are on public display. To demonstrate that the theatrical event is the culminating product of rehearsal and preparation was, for Brecht, to prevent identification and encourage criticism. When this practice is transferred to television, the open display of studio cameras and technology may signal not an attempt at distanciation, but television's cultivation of immediacy. Where the practice is frequently repeated (as for instance in the early evening 'trailer' for Scottish Television News), it constructs, as with any other form of repetition on television, a text which is simply familiar.

As I noted above, the use of Brechtian distanciation devices to 'alienate' the television audience into an active scrutiny of the text demands a certain type of audience and a certain style of viewing. This is an audience prepared to give a programme its undivided attention in a 'gaze' rather than a haphazard series of 'glances'. The use of these distanciation devices (ironically) presupposes adult concentration of a kind emulating that claimed by a nine-year-old male viewer of *Dynasty* : '*Dynasty*'s really good. Fridays, I just watch it. I say I want to get my eyes *stuck* into this telly, I don't want to move my eyes.'[61]

The gaze may characterize film spectatorship 'where we always have the time (and the space) to lose ourselves a little'.[62] But to gaze at the television screen is regarded by some (for example, Ellis) as untypical viewing, and by others (for example, Morley) as a form of television consumption restricted to the occupants of a particular gendered role. A heightened attention often appears, in any case, an inappropriate response to the 'constant dispersal of television's endless repetition'.[63] 'Indeed the "central fact" of television may be that it is designed to be watched intermittently, casually, and without full concentration.'[64]

Domestic television offers a 'socially acceptable means of "turning off" from direct social relations'.[65] But this may in practice be available only to male viewers, who, we are told, display a 'tendency to abandon their manager/parent role when viewing material of particular interest to them'.[66] For many women, other '"roles" interact with that of viewer' : watching television is combined with activities such as knitting, ironing, sewing or talking on the telephone.[67] Collett suggests on the basis of his empirical research that this multiple activity may arise from a sense of guilt about watching television, 'but it may also be related to the fact that [women] have more domestic work to do'.[68]

In the context of this evidence, the role of television viewer appears to be traversed by gendered difference.[69] On the one hand this produces a masculine 'look' at the screen, the attentive gaze 'in order not to miss anything'. On the other, there is a feminine 'glance', occupying time taken out from the performance of domestic duties. (Some women may have difficulty in identifying with the narrowly defined activities of, for instance, a television detective.) In the context of the intermittent glance, apparent narrative redundancy is useful repetition. Soap opera 'script writers, anticipating the housewife's distracted state, are careful to repeat important elements of the story several times', rewarding the return of the viewer with intelligible information.[70] The use of Brechtian theory and practice in distanciating the television audience presupposes what appears to be, then, a masculine gaze.[71]

But invoking Brechtian production techniques to distanciate the relationship between text and viewer faces a more fundamental (if not more important) difficulty. Its assumption is that the successful use of alienation devices will produce an 'active' audience. But the hermeneutic theory of reading I have proposed assumes that the viewer is already active in his or her creation of meaning for the text.

Moreover, the practices of Brechtian distanciation are an account of how to produce drama which supports the spectator's detached scrutiny of its content. Yet the use of these alienation devices is not related theoretically to the complex sense-building activities with which the reader approaches the play. Brechtian theory largely conceives of the process of reading in terms of a reductive opposition between passive 'identification' and active 'distanciation'.

Only in considering the alienation effect which results from 'disappointing' the viewer's expectations is the audience's pre-textual aesthetic and everyday knowledge explicitly taken into account by Brechtian analysis, allowing the possibility 'of continually unsettling the spectator's position'.[72] In this way *The Story of a Recluse* can be said to subvert its audience's anticipation of a unified space and time. In phenomenological hermeneutics, however, the function of a distanciation device can be theorized more thoroughly. Here 'alienation' is conceived of as undermining the complex and mutually confirming horizons of understanding and expectation in terms of which the viewer engages with a programme, producing in turn a defamiliarized 'seeing' of textual form and content.

Where a programme's playing out of social roles is inappropriate, distanciation results. In a Scottish Television dramatized documentary on the architect, *Charles Rennie Mackintosh: Dreams and Recollections* (C4, 8.30, 28.12.87), Tom Conti and Kara Wilson play the roles both of presenters and of artists, 'producing' the characters of Charles and Margaret Mackintosh. As presenters, it is with their work of investigation and their horizons of understanding the 'enigma' (*TV Times*) of 'Toshie' that the viewer, who is likewise attempting to construct a coherent sense for the text, can identify. As Kara Wilson says, 'I felt they [the documents] didn't tell me the whole story ... what puzzled me was why his success in Glasgow just slowly withered away, why he was forced to turn away from architecture to painting watercolours ... but I needed more information.' At the conclusion of this dramatized documentary the audience's sense of closure around a circle of understanding in the text is sustained by the thoughts of one of those who recollect (Mary Newbury). Her words at the beginning of *Dreams and Recollections* also bring it to an end : 'the tears come to my eyes and I feel *so* sad that this [pause] *genius* was wasted. I feel great, great sadness. For he really could have designed anything, but he *just* didn't get a chance.'

But in this dramatized documentary, audience identification resting on the similarities and differences of performing a role (reconstruction) is undermined when the investigators 'become' the artists themselves, and begin to 'play' according to new rules. In the third part of the drama Conti and Wilson conform to a new rationality and perceive new aspects of the world as relevant to their ambitions. Visually, they disappear as presenters and reappear as the 'Toshes'. Now they are artists involved in aesthetic practice, artists whose role-related problems and attempted solutions generate a sense for the 'texts' of their lives. 'Mackintosh's dreams are relived' (*TV Times*) in an articulation of meaning which looks towards the future rather than the past. Conti/Mackintosh can now assert : 'if I could just decide to start a new drawing of my rock, I'm sure it might be worth the effort . . . I find that each of my drawings has *something* in them, but none of them is everything. This must be remedied . . . You must not expect to see very much in the way of finished work. I go very slow because I still have so many problems to solve and the days of hit and miss or any such method are past, for me.'

In this shift from the rules of investigating a life to those of artistic activity the audience's alignment with subjects in the text, at least temporarily, is likely to become confused. In the face of this complexity of subjective discourse, the projection of a coherent meaning for the programme (as documentary) must be interrupted, a projection which supported the process of identification with the presenters. The viewer moves out of the documentary and returns to the role of reader.

Subsequently, there are two possibilities. The audience may re-enter the text, reading it as a drama. In a process of alignment through perceived similarities, the object of investigation becomes a subject of identification. Conti appears not as documentary presenter but as the architect Mackintosh : 'we find that France is not an expensive place for us . . . It was a lovely morning so I got up at six-thirty.' Alternatively, wholly displaced by the rules of a new game, the viewer can engage with the text in distanciated criticism.

The implied audience of Brechtian distanciation technique is an audience which has substituted an awareness of textuality for identification. But this condition of spectatorship also characterizes the television audience as, becoming conscious of difference, it moves out of the text and into the role of viewer. In the Conclusion I consider a hemeneutic theory of distanciated viewing which begins with audience rather than programme. This will provide a viewer-oriented account of readings which defamiliarize a text's hierarchies of meaning, truth and familiarity and 'acquire' (Gadamer) its horizons of understanding for analysis.

11 Tom Conti and Kara Wilson, here in the roles not of presenters but of Charles
and Margaret Mackintosh in *Charles Rennie Mackintosh*

Notes

1 My concern at this point is with cognitive horizons of understanding as frameworks of concepts in whose terms information is processed within a text. But they may also function to justify practices occurring throughout a life-world. In a belief system which supports and makes intelligible a way of life there are certain central concepts or horizons of experience whose function is, *inter alia*, to appear in any fundamental justification. It is within these horizons of understanding that ideology makes its presence felt in reason giving (cf. Chapter 1).

2 Hall et al., 'The "Unity" of Current Affairs Television', p. 93.

3 Clarke and Taylor, 'Vandals, Pickets and Muggers', p. 111.

4 Garton et al., 'Ideology, Scripts and Metaphors', p. 110.

5 Ibid., p. 113.

6 Clarke and Taylor, 'Vandals, Pickets and Muggers', p. 102.

7 R. Collins, 'Seeing Is Believing', p. 127.

8 For further elaboration of this point see T. Wilson, 'Reading the Postmodernist Image', p. 4.

9 Merleau-Ponty, *Phenomenology of Perception*, pp. 325, 333. (Cf. A. Rabil, *Merleau-Ponty*, New York, Columbia University Press, 1967, Ch.2.)

10 Carr, *Interpreting Husserl*, p. 36.

11 Iser, *The Act of Reading*, p. 96.

12 Freund, *The Return of the Reader*, p. 18. An instance of this principle as it relates to television is given by Lewis, 'Decoding Television News', pp. 208–12, where he argues that the viewer's pre-textual knowledge or 'channel of access' opens up 'only certain parts of the TV message'.

13 White, 'Ideological Analysis and Television', p. 160.

14 Barthes, *Image, Music, Text*, p. 40.

15 Here I define a viewer's 'life-world' as his or her familiar, everyday beliefs, action and experience. This phenomenological concept was further defined in Chapter 1.

16 Husserl, *Experience and Judgement*, p. 333.

17 Fiske, *Television Culture*, p. 150.

18 Gadamer, *Philosophical Hermeneutics*, p. 21.

19 Ibid., p. 22.

20 Ibid., p. 25.

21 Schutz, 'Type and Eidos in Husserl's Late Philosophy', p. 95.

22 Fiske and Hartley, *Reading Television*, p. 87.

23 Scannell, 'Radio Times', p. 22.

24 Quoted in Watt, *'Take the High Road'*.

25 Fiske, 'Women and Quiz Shows', p. 142.

26 Quoted in Watt, *'Take the High Road'*.

27 Allen, *Speaking of Soap Operas*, pp. 69–75.

28 Husserl, *Experience and Judgement*, p. 35.

29 Shklovsky, *Mayakovsky and His Circle* (London, Pluto, 1974), p. 114, quoted in Bennett, *Formalism and Marxism*, pp. 53–4.

30 B. Brecht, 'The German Drama : Pre-Hitler', in Willett, *Brecht on Theatre*, p. 78. Unless otherwise indicated, the essays by Brecht cited below are

published in *Brecht on Theatre*. Brecht's 'epic' theatre can be compared with Fish's 'dialectical text' : 'the dialectical text is not an end in itself – a transparent message – but rather the means of inducing and foregrounding the work of interpretation and understanding' (Freund, *The Return of the Reader*, p. 98.)

31 Brecht, 'The Street Scene: A Basic Model for an Epic Theatre', p. 125. 'Certain incidents in the play should be treated as self-contained scenes and raised . . . above the level of the everyday, the obvious, the expected (i.e. alienated)' ('Notes to *Die Rundköpfe und die Spitzköpfe*', p. 101).

32 Garfinkel, *Studies in Ethnomethodology*, pp. 36–7.

33 Brecht, 'Alienation Effects in Chinese Acting', p. 93.

34 Brecht, 'A Short Organum for the Theatre', p. 188.

35 Ibid., p. 189.

36 Brecht, 'Indirect Impact of the Epic Theatre', p. 60.

37 Brecht, 'A Short Organum for the Theatre', p. 188.

38 Brecht, 'The Modern Theatre is the Epic Theatre', p. 37.

39 Brecht, 'Theatre for Pleasure or Theatre for Instruction', p. 71.

40 Brecht, 'Alienation Effects in Chinese Acting', p. 91.

41 Brecht, 'Indirect Impact of the Epic Theatre', p. 57.

42 Brecht, 'The Epic Theatre and Its Difficulties', p. 23.

43 Brecht, 'A Short Organum for the Theatre', p. 180.

44 Brecht, 'Brecht against Lukács', in Taylor, *Aesthetics and Politics*, pp. 68–85.

45 Brecht, 'Short Description of a New Technique of Acting which Produces an Alienation Effect', p. 136.

46 Brecht, 'Alienation Effects in Chinese Acting', p. 92.

47 Brecht, 'The Street Scene', p. 126.

48 Brecht, 'Theatre for Pleasure or Instruction', p. 71.

49 Brecht, 'The Street Scene', p. 125.

50 Brecht, 'Alienation Effects in Chinese Acting', p. 93.

51 Brecht, 'Short Description of a New Technique of Acting', p. 141.

52 Brecht, 'A Short Organum for the Theatre', p. 194.

53 Brecht, 'Short Description of a New Technique of Acting', p. 139.

54 Brecht, 'A Short Organum for the Theatre', p. 194.

55 Ibid., p. 201.

56 Ibid.

57 Ibid., p. 204.

58 Brecht, 'Short Description of a New Technique of Acting', p. 144. There are similarities between this mechanism of distanciation and the example of Eisensteinian montage described by MacCabe in 'Realism and the Cinema', pp. 216–35. He suggests that in the Eisenstein case there is a 'shock' to the reader's expectations, producing an active spectator, when the woman in 'widow's weeds' turns out to be mourning a man other than her husband.

59 Hobson, *Crossroads*, p. 93.

60 Stam, 'Television News and Its Spectator', p. 37.

61 Buckingham, *Public Secrets*, p. 161.

62 Burch, *Theory of Film Practice*, p. 153.

63 Caughie, 'Popular Culture', p. 168.

64 Feuer, 'The Concept of Live Television', p. 15.
65 Lodziak, *The Power of Television*, p. 183.
66 Morley, 'Family Television', p. 26.
67 Connell, 'Commercial Broadcasting and the British Left', p. 78.
68 Collett, 'The Viewer Viewed', p. 9.
69 Lull's research suggests, however, that 'men also are working while they watch television – assuming an emotional and often physical involvement with their children, thinking about work, making plans, but also doing other "responsible" things like reading the newspaper or performing household tasks' ('Constructing Rituals of Extension', p. 253).
70 Modleski, 'The Rhythms of Reception', p. 73.
71 Further research on gendered viewing is required. The complex camera work during sports television suggests the intended viewer is exercising a gaze rather than a glance.
72 Caughie, 'Progressive Television and Documentary Drama', p. 349.

Conclusion : Resisting Television's Familiarity

Here there is nothing but Pepsi, and the mass compulsion to absorb it.
Mark Crispin Miller, 'Deride and Conquer'

Television hermeneutics attempts to describe the creative effort to under-stand, an effort sometimes continuous and sometimes interrupted, which, in a vast variety of ways, underwrites the television audience's response to its texts. A lapse in cognitive inquiry is a lapse in the hermeneutic circle of reading, of relating part to whole and whole to part.

Throughout this book I have argued that in identification a viewer is involved in sense-making. He or she appropriates a textual content mediated through a subject's horizons of understanding, perspectives usually in some respect already familiar and inevitably ideological. In the last chapter I argued that a distanciated reading resists this easy endorsement of a hierarchy of meaning, familiarity and apparent truth centred on a subject. It evades the position of the implied viewer. In a prolonged realizing of difference rather than similarity, the often stereotypical categories of the text are replaced by the particular 'knowledges' of the audience.

Distanciation precedes awareness and criticism of ideology, unpicking the 'imperfectly joined practices' of an 'ideological seam' (Radway). The multiple hierarchy of meaning, truth and familiarity exercises authority over both text and implied viewer. Where the relationship between programme and (real) viewer involves distanciated readings, this authority is under-mined. Images of the audience's life-worlds within the text can be resisted, yielding the difference between who you are and who television thinks you are. In an awareness of the distance between the text's conception of the audience and the real viewer, the equivocations of television's familiar address can be discerned. Under domestic conditions of viewing 'television comes to us, enters our cultural space, and becomes subject to our discourses'.[1] In 'our' discourses of criticism and awareness distanciation recovers the time and space of political differences effaced by familiarity. It resists their collapse in postmodernism.

My discussion below of the televisually familiar, and of distanciation from its processes of alignment, is limited in scope. It does not, for instance, enter into detailed examination of the 'cultural capital' (for example, education) which may allow some groups (less involved in their relationship with progamme content, perhaps) to entertain distanciated readings more easily than others. But the defamiliarized reading of a text is a significant political activity: for it is an attempt to counter the processes of reification, that 'naturalization of the present' which is 'domination'.[2]

The pleasures of resisting the dominant ideology of a text are twofold. On the one hand, they can involve viewers distancing themselves from a programme's familiar, stereotypical representations. This allows personal identity to be reasserted, a reclaiming of authenticity and the validity of particular experience in the face of the 'imposed generalities of an increasingly homogenised mass culture'.[3] On the other, audience pleasure can arise from reworking the text's narratives, applying them to the life of the individual viewer, 'liberating' them not only from their place in a text but from their otherwise reactionary implications. In the 'tactics of the subordinate', the manufacture of consumer delirium in *The Price Is Right* can be reread to celebrate everyday narratives of informed choice in the supermarket.[4] These are the limited pleasures of a tactical 'getting by'. In this response of selective recognition one claims membership of a life-world which does not quite conform to the dominant prescriptions of a text.[5]

As I indicate in what follows, Ricoeur's 'depth' hermeneutics is particularly suggestive in theorizing the recovery of ideology through the discovery of distance, through and despite the familiarizing operations of the text which disguise and naturalize its presence. In my discussion I shall refer to the reactionary pleasures on offer to the viewer of situation comedy as examined in a moment of television history in Channel Four's audience response programme *Right to Reply*. Although now itself a distant transmission, this televized discussion seems to me to constitute a salutary example of the processes of audience distanciation.

The discursive presentation of a programme such as ITV's *Good Morning Britain* or *Good Morning Australia* (Channel Ten) constructs the recognizability of the spoken; an illusion of face-to-face communication is maintained. Within the text's intense familiarity the viewer is allowed only the most marginal of opportunities to identify with interviewees' more unfamiliar perspectives on events. *Good Morning Britain* 'appropriates' reality, dissolving its cultural differences in a proposed identification with the familial.

Scientific analysis, asserts Burger, 'begins the moment one recognizes that the immediacy with which we perceive [the contents of a text] is illusory'.[6] Defamiliarizing a television programme such as *Good Morning Britain* 'recovers' semiotic difference, the distance between its ideological representation of its viewers' lives and those lives themselves, which is effaced in its communication. Distanciation is in philosophical terms a 'second order' practice aimed at discourses through which textual subjects construct accounts of reality. This practice operates at a meta-discursive level, calling into question otherwise seemingly natural points of view. It may rely upon wholly alternative conceptual schemas to provide alienated perceptions of a familiar object, 'turning the object of which one is to be made aware, to which one's attention is to be drawn, from something ordinary, familiar, immediately accessible, into something peculiar, striking and unexpected'.[7]

The familiar 'must be stripped of its inconspicuousness' through a re-presentation of its accustomed characteristics. By means of its redescription a particular aspect of the text's construction of the viewer's life-world is foregrounded for examination: 'the Eskimo definition "A car is a wing-less aircraft that crawls along the ground" is a way of alienating the car'.[8]

As I noted in Chapter 7, the television programme producing distanciation and 're-vision' is an unusual and difficult text to achieve. Television's spoken discourses generally constitute familiar forms of address. Its repetition of form and content mitigate against the 'alienation' of the viewer other than by boredom. Conditions of consumption typically involve group interaction and interruption rather than a sustained concentration by the individual spectator. Distanciation devices must therefore operate on the viewer's 'glance' rather than the 'gaze' of the theatre or cinema. Watching television is extensive, often the consumption of many texts in an evening, invariably casual and frequently undertaken in conjunction with other activities. Unlike the intensive experience of film spectatorship, it rarely takes the form of a heightened involvement which can be subverted by the specificities of a Brechtian 'A-effect'.

But it is exactly these extensive conditions of engaging with the text which permit viewers to retain a greater awareness of their own extra-textual subjectivity while watching television. A more prolonged sense of difference between self and textual subject results in commuting between identification and distanciation as a more likely response. Discourses of criticism can circulate while viewing television. Cinema demands an awareness more concentrated on a text. Criticism must find its own time, often subsequent to spectatorship.

In the time and space of watching, a television programme can be 'measured' against the audience's pre-textual experience, and the difference noted between its conception of the 'familiar' and the viewer's. 'Real-izing' this difference marks the beginning of a distanciated awareness of television's familiarities; 'they say they ask the questions that you'd like to know, but then again everybody's got different questions they'd like to ask'.[9] A failure to converge of needs, rules and rationalities in actual and implied life-worlds emerges for discussion.

At this point, then, a distanciated reading of television may be brought into play despite its avowedly familiar mode of address. This reading will be the product not of alienation devices in the text but of the reader's 'story'. The biographies of a text's creating ('authorial') and created subjects (characters), and its (real) viewer, are different. On the one hand, the manufacture and 'life-history' of the text, whether soap opera or news magazine, involves the appropriation of a range of concepts and inflection of their meaning in particular ways. On the other, the viewer's trajectory through the cultural differences of gender, class and race allow them to enter his or her reading of a programme, producing distinctive interpretations. The inevitable distance between the origins and 'life-histories' of text and reader permits the audience to engage in an alienated reading of a programme in which the familiar address of television can be reversed as the semiotically 'other'.

Brecht is aware of the relationship between spatio-temporal and cultural distance : 'social impulses . . . differ according to the period'.[10] He argues that traditional theatre, when presenting subjects from another era, attempts to deny historical and cultural distance between the life-worlds of textual subject and watching spectator : 'when our theatres perform plays of other periods they like to annihilate distance, fill in the gap, gloss over the differences'.[11]

His own epic theatre, however, must recognize historical distance. By presenting the contemporary culture of the audience as if it were the culture of a bygone age, Brecht argued, the theatre he was proposing could fulfil its task of defamiliarizing the 'obvious'. Perspectives expressed in the terms of such a historically distanced outlook would resist an audience's easy appropriation. Apparently now inessential to his or her everyday life in the present, aspects of the spectator's culture would become open to interrogation. Alienation of the audience is achieved here through the dramatized construction of historical distance : 'if we play works dealing with our own time as though they were historical, then perhaps the circumstances under which [the spectator] himself acts will strike him as equally odd ; and this is where the critical attitude begins'.[12] While arguing for the alienating potential of historical distance, Brecht clearly retains this as an aspect of a production-centred rather than reader-centred account of distanciation.

Whereas for Brecht distanciation is an artistic achievement originating in particular textual mechanisms, the philosopher Ricoeur argues that an alienated reading is made possible by virtue of spatio-temporal distance. The cultural experiences of 'otherness' and 'ownness' emerge from the different 'histories' of text and reader, allowing distanciation of textual meaning to occur.

Ricoeur's is a reader-centred theory which emphasizes the mediation of horizons at the heart of understanding. His conception of distanciation or 'cultural estrangement' is of the reader's 'recollecting' the distance between the cognitive horizons belonging to the text and those brought to its reading. These horizons of understanding are said to be associated temporally with the 'appearance' of the text and its 'use' by a reader :

> distance, then, is not simply a fact, a given, just the actual spatial and temporal gap between use and the appearance of such and such work of art or discourse. It is a dialectical trait, the principle of a struggle between the otherness that transforms all spatial and temporal distance into cultural estrangement and the ownness by which all understanding aims at the extension of self-understanding.[13]

In a hermeneutics of television, viewing is an overcoming of cognitive difference between horizons. As such it is a temporal as well as cultural process: 'appropriation is understanding at and through [temporal] distance'. The activities of viewing and coming to understand a programme for the first time mean a search for similarity between the cognitive horizons of text and audience rather than difference: 'reading is the *pharmakon*, the "remedy", by which the meaning of the text is "rescued" from the estrangement of distanciation and put in a new proximity, a proximity which suppresses and preserves the cultural distance and includes the otherness within the ownness'.[14]

The understanding of a text precedes its alienation. The difference between the cognitive horizons of the 'read' and the reader can be realized in an alienated rescrutinizing of the text. Distanciation as the beginning of critique and the analysis of an ideological aspect of the programme commences with the recovery, the resurfacing, of the 'cultural distance' between text and audience which the original process of reading 'suppresses'. 'Critique rests on the moment of distanciation': distanciation 'in all its forms and figures, constitutes *par excellence* the critical moment in understanding.'[15]

It is possible (and indeed necessary) to develop Ricoeur's account of the alienation of meaning. As I noted above, distanciation has its source in the different life-histories of the text, its 'authors' and its audience, their trajectories through different moments of class, gender and racial experience. This spatio-temporal distance allows concepts to emerge in a text whose particularity as modes of understanding reality can be recovered in an alienated reading by the audience. They offer themselves for an analysis founded on their unfamiliarity. Hermeneutics draws attention to the mediating process in which the reader appropriates the cognitive horizons given in the text, producing new meaning. In the context of distanciation, this productive difference between audience and textual perspectives is foregrounded for inspection.

Spatio-temporal distance, the distance of individual biography, is, as I first indicated in section 1.3, sufficient for cognitive difference to occur. But the biographies of textual subjects or 'authors' and the (actual) audience may be separated by opposing appropriations of dominant and subordinate hegemonies of class, gender or racial understanding. Here, the cultural distance between text and audience, open to 'recovery' despite the former's apparent familiarity, will be particularly great.

Brecht intends his theatrical apparatus of distanciation to operate in a political context. In the epic drama, since neither actor nor audience identifies with a character, a cognitive space is created which allows criticism of that subject's understanding of how things are. Features of the character's personality are shown to 'come within society's sphere', and the nature and malleability of these social conditions is examined. Dominant perceptions of human attributes and their origins are scrutinized and overturned, at least for a working-class audience: 'in this way [the actor's] performance becomes a discussion [about social conditions] with the audience he is addressing. He prompts the spectator to justify or abolish these conditions according to what class he belongs to.'[16] Brecht understands social situations to be processes subject to the Marxist laws of historical materialism, as containing contradictions and open to change. Epic theatre 'regards nothing as existing except in so far as it changes, in other words is in disharmony with itself'.[17]

The epic theatre relinquishes the traditional theatre's control of the spectator's emotions, a control exerted through constructing the audience's relationship with the text around identification. However, argues Brecht, those emotions which have been released as a result of the audience's new and critical insight into the social nature of human existence still require direction. The active spectator continues to be a spectator over whose behaviour the text exerts a 'decisive influence'; 'a considerable sacrifice of the spectator's empathy does not mean sacrificing all right to influence him'.[18]

Like Brecht, Ricoeur argues for the political effectivity of distanciated readings. 'Alienation' is for both a cognitive attitude preceding ideological critique. Ricoeur's conception of ideology locates it within a set of discourses (often referring to history) which function in a range of ways to unify a social group. Where, as is frequently the case, ideology supports a hierarchical organization within the group, it justifies this hierarchy of positions through attaching an 'over-value' or (in Ricoeur's sense) 'surplus-value' to those in power. One would want to argue that dominant ideology never succeeds in its call to unity; there is always a subordinate – and resisting – ideology of understanding. Nevertheless, its connection with sustaining power is unavoidable. Dominant ideology is '*meaning in the service of power*',[19] whether that power is gendered, racial, generational or class-related.

For Ricoeur, hermeneutics is critical hermeneutics, a distanciated, objectifying, scientific criticism of the ideological moment in culture and its texts. He acknowledges (drawing on Gadamer) that this criticism can never be 'total'. Critique is always from a place in a tradition, necessarily within the horizons of understanding which constitute that particular past and present. Consequently and unavoidably it is itself ideologically inflected.

Critical hermeneutics (and the textual readings for which it is responsible) transcends the hermeneutics associated with Gadamer. It is informed by a dialectical awareness of the possibility of both 'enjoying' a familiar culture and engaging with it in a critical awareness that its very familiarity effaces its ideological support for a hierarchical organization of society. A sense of 'belonging' is likely to characterize encounters of reader and subject matter. Distanciated criticism presupposes that this elimination of semiotic difference can itself be discarded. This is 'the destruction of the primordial relation of belonging – *Zugehörigkeit* – without which there would be no relation to the historical as such'.[20]

Critical hermeneutics is a response to traditions, to their continuities of belief and concept in which the reader is immersed. It is premissed upon an attitude of alienating distanciation, of *Verfremdung*, which allows the cultural distance (rather than the cultural proximity) between the viewing subject and the programme to assert its existence. Critical hermeneutics rereads the text 'in such a way that a certain dialectic between the experience of belonging and alienating distanciation becomes the mainspring, the key to inner life, of hermeneutics'.[21]

The 'methodological attitude' of distanciation realizes the fact of distance with its semiotic effects at the level of culture. 'Distance is a fact: placing at a distance is a methodological attitude.'[22] Television's familiarities (such as stereotyped characters) conceal, unless further examined, not only their underlying difference from the viewer's experience but their ideological operation on the audience. (Stereotypes of the old undervalue them and overvalue the young.) Distanciation prepares the ground for analysis, revealing the ideas through which an ideology is functioning in the text as it gains a purchase on the consciousness of the community of language users: 'distanciation, dialectically opposed to belonging, is the condition of possibility of the critique of ideology, not outside or against hermeneutics, but within hermeneutics'.[23]

Ricoeur argues for the recovery of the 'otherness' of the text, dislocating it from its apparent position within the familiar 'ownness' of the reader's experience. This is to discover its inflection through the hierarchical oppositions of gender, class, race and age, an inflection responsible for the distance of ideological images from the viewer's experience. Stereotype and self-image must be separated.

Television's construction of the familiar, the 'ownness' of the audience, was discussed in Chapter 1. The text's endeavour to draw upon the familiar cultural histories of its intended viewers means that it generally operates in what its audience can, without difficulty, regard as a received tradition of televisual genres and mediations of a given subject matter. Programmes easily disclose their status as examples of familiar forms of television which the viewer can be assumed to recognize. This structuring of discourse inhibits an 'alienated' reading and its subsequent use in textual criticism. Familiarity breeds in this instance not contempt but passive acquiescence in a content of the apparently normal and inevitable. In this respect the viewer finds unproblematic a text which also affirms horizons of expectation in respect of camera work and narrative development.

But television's self-definition as an integral element of the viewer's familiar culture and everyday life-worlds can be refused as ideological misrepresentation. What appears as an affirmation of the audience's identity may be rejected as disappropriating the viewer of valid subjective experience. In particular, it can be argued that in day-to-day viewing 'I exchange the *me, master* of itself, for the *self, disciple* of the text.'[24]

The horizons of understanding through which an audience mediates the texts of television are constantly present, articulated and rehearsed as the basis of discussion in what is frequently a familial context of 'watching the box'. It is these horizons which (whatever their limits) define for the viewer his or her perception of 'ownness', the position from which the distanciated 'otherness' of the text is to be discovered. This occasions not a fusion of horizons but the realization of their difference. A viewer-centred defamiliarization refuses the text's construction of familiarity, its foregrounding of 'easy' speech and direct address to the audience.

In the opposition which television (mistakenly) constructs between 'spoken' and 'written' discourse, distanciation is a rereading of the spoken discourses of the text as 'written', ascribing to them a life-history at a distance from the reader. In the attitude of distanciation, this speech has lost the ease of understanding which television, at least, regards as its defining characteristic. Distanciation materializes television's spoken discourse, 'realizing' its existence in an electronic medium and its invariable source in a written script.

As I noted in section 1.3, in the terms of this opposition between 'written' and 'spoken' discourse the meaning of a written text enjoys an autonomy from the 'intention of an author'. Unlike spoken discourse, no contributions from the source of the text restrict the determination of its sense. To distanciate a spoken discourse is to construct it as 'written' by depriving the speaker of authority over its meaning. Speech is distanciated from the speaker(s) to constitute the focus of 'alienated' rereadings by an 'audience': 'the emancipation of the text constitutes the most fundamental condition for the recognition of a critical instance at the heart of interpretation; for distanciation now belongs to the mediation itself'.[25]

This alienated rereading of the familiar is 'hermeneutical reflection' on the contents of pre-understanding, the assumptions of the life-world inhabited by the text's intended viewer: 'reflection on a given pre-understanding brings before me something that otherwise happens *behind my back* ... only through hermeneutical reflection am I no longer unfree over against myself but rather can deem freely what in my pre-understanding may be justified and what unjustifiable'.[26] For Habermas, equally, hermeneutical reflection is an exercise in revealing the latent power of familiar language and ideas 'to legitimate relations of organised force', a reflection which renders them the subject of rational criticism.[27]

The UK audience response programme on ageist television broadcasting in the *Right to Reply* series, 'A Certain Age' (C4, 6.00, 28.11.87), investigated the difference between television's familiar images of older people and the way they see their own lives. The individuals interviewed spoke of the cultural distance between the media construction of their identities and their own everyday experience. In a productive 'misrecognition', their distanciated rereadings of the images of age perceived them to be an expression of 'otherness' rather than 'ownness'. Re-viewings and discussions in 'A Certain Age' defamiliarized the media's attempts through a process of endless repetition to attain a familiar and naturalized status for an ideology of 'under-value' which 'limits people's lives'. Here there is a 'making strange' of television's production of the easily recognizable: 'we're shown as dependent, ill and *always* needing money'; 'the *endless* images of us freezing in winter perpetuate the myth that we're just a burden'; 'the *classic* stereotype of an older person on TV is stingy, boring, conservative, childish or just plain stupid'; 'when you retire . . . it *always* seems to be that life's at an end' (my italics).

Television's attempts, then, at producing a spoken discourse to reduce cognitive distance between text and viewer do not always succeed. The familiarity characterizing the 'neutral' diction of a presenter, for instance, may be alienated within a rereading of it as a classed and gendered discourse with a particular point of view. Where this is so, it will no longer be taken by the viewer to constitute an unproblematic framework of meaning within the text, the discourse of authoritative judgement. The programme's definition of the power of its subjects is rejected.

Yet 'as a matrix in which dominant and oppositional discourses do constant battle, television can never completely reduce the antagonistic dialogue of class voices to the reassuring hum of bourgeois hegemony'.[28] Television allows moments of recognition by marginalized social groups which are more generally without powers of public self-definition. The experience of similarity can occur within an awareness of difference. A sense of cultural proximity may be produced in the context of a prevailing awareness of cultural distance (for example, audience recognition of women's knowledge being rewarded within quiz shows).

At other times and confronted with other texts the practice of defamiliarization is central to providing a solution to (what Ricoeur refers to as) the problem of 'belonging', the experience of a familiar culture with its often elusive allocation of power. Audience distanciation allows the distance between perspectives on an issue to be revealed. For both Brecht and Ricoeur – that is, in the theory of the epic theatre and critical hermeneutics – a distanciated reading of a text discloses its ideological commitment. This is an ideological message which, in activating a meaning for the text, the reader has cooperated in producing (sustaining in turn their own mystification).

As I have noted, Ricoeur accepts that the analysis of historical or contemporary culture must be in the terms of contemporary culture itself; critical hermeneutics cannot arise from nowhere. 'Before any critical distance, we belong to a history, to a class, to a nation, to a culture, to one or several traditions.' However subversive a reading, it remains a reading from a position of *'belonging* upon which we can never entirely reflect'.[29] Ricoeur acknowledges that a critical or 'scientific' examination of a set of discourses cannot itself be entirely dissociated from 'the ideological condition of knowledge':[30] 'knowledge is always in the process of tearing itself away from ideology, but ideology always remains the grid, the code of interpretation'.[31]

The critique of dominant ideology must therefore be 'more modest'.[32] It cannot dissociate itself from the very concepts it needs in analysis. Such ideological purity would merely produce a hermeneutics of silence. The hermeneutics of cultural criticism must recognize the 'failure of the project of total reflection' as a consequence of the 'original and unsurpassable condition' that 'there is no zero point from which it could proceed'.

If ideological criticism is inevitably 'partial', never 'total', it is nevertheless not to be rejected as invalid. Rather it is a continuing process directed at assessing different aspects of a culture in turn. This process is made 'fundamentally possible in virtue of the factor of *distanciation*'.[33] Ideological critique 'strives to introduce so far as it can a factor of distanciation into the work that we constantly resume in order to reinterpret our cultural heritage'.[34]

This distanciated reading discloses the 'depth semantics' of a text, [35] its alignment with the ideological dimension of experience. Ricoeur's interest lies in the association between ideology and power, in the non-rational support which ideology provides for 'the permanent exercise of domination and violence'. This support is given through its presence in linguistic practices, 'the distortions of human communication'. Ricoeur's cultural hermeneutics is, consequently, a hermeneutics of discourse and the text. 'An eschatology of non-violence thus forms the ultimate philosophical horizon of a critique of ideology.'[36]

In its own critique of ideology 'A Certain Age' drew on distanciated readings of ageist images in accordance with the findings of 'self-reflection' (Thompson). Its subjects' self-conscious awareness as television viewers provides the distance enabling a deconstructive reading of comedy and other programmes. Deconstruction requires that attention be paid to textual discourses which 'do not easily fall into place'.[37] This edition of *Right to Reply* centres upon discursive arrangements which 'do not easily fall into place' for the studio audience. In this exploration of dissonance, popular television's cognitive horizons of understanding the world are foregrounded for discussion. Through a deconstruction which remembers the experience of those in the studio, television's ageism is clearly discerned : the hierarchical oppositions in its images of people are made plain (oppositions, for instance, between productive youth and non-productive age). A 'hegemonic viewpoint . . . defines within its terms the mental horizon, the universe, of possible meanings' in an area of cultural life.[38] Here such a 'mental horizon' is diagnosed and rejected.

This is not to argue that all distanciated readings are progressive, nor that all forms of recognition, of finding the content of a text familiar, are reactionary. Drama, as I indicated in an earlier chapter, can confirm a radical social identity for its audience. And as Tulloch notes, a 'resistance' reading of television can be produced by 'conservative prejudices of class, gender and reading formation'.[39]

I have tried in this book to give an account of the processes constituting 'identification', of its mechanisms, hierarchies and (to a limited degree) its dismantling by the real viewer. Much of my analysis has been directed at the complex 'negotiations' (Gledhill) of involvement in, identification with and distraction from a text. The relationship between television programme and audience is also 'playful'. This is a hermeneutic play in which in a to and fro movement across the dimensions of a text the viewer projects and often succeeds in constructing intelligible meaning not only for a programme but for his or her own life. Narratives are produced by the reader in a context of role-related needs and interests.

The pleasures of a viewer's active relaxing are those of recognition ('mutuality'):[40] 'popular pleasure is first and foremost a pleasure of recognition'.[41] But audience pleasure also derives from achieving coherency and the solution of indeterminacies (and indeed from surprise, when a horizon of expectations is not confirmed). Attaining a coherent understanding is a cognitive activity which, where supported and guided by the text, is often easier and more likely to meet with success than those offered by 'real life'.

The play of meaning between each viewer and a text produces a reading which is both similar to, and different from, those achieved by other members of an audience. Arriving at a coherent narrative for life or programme on the basis of information supplied by a dominant text bears an ambiguous relationship to ideology. The political horizons of a programme may be resisted or reinterpreted while 'incorporating' (Thompson) them into a life. But texts can 'so position the interpreter through their cues' that the very activity of producing their meaning can involve accepting presumptions which align a viewer in their ideological favour.[42]

Meaning is always constructed from a position, from a rule-governed inhabiting of a role whether within or outside the text. The movement back and forth over the distance between appropriation and disassociation from roles and their interest-related horizons of understanding in the text is a further aspect of the 'playful' relationship between programme and audience. This is a movement from the conditions of distanciation to those of identification, a movement whose fulcrum is the experience of the image as veridical and the recognition of similarity rather than difference. Reading is not to be conceived of as sustaining a position (being 'positioned') 'inside' or 'outside' a text. It is rather a continuous 'commuting' from one space and time (the programme's) to another (the reader's).

A reader aware of him- or herself as reader, of difference from the text, has satisfied the precondition of an ideological rereading. At this point the audience can begin to articulate 'its "own" ideological and cultural discourses ... [in] an eliciting of a partially submerged and fragmentary level of discourse'.[43] Here, a subordinate ideology emerges to assert the identity and suppressed powers of the dominated.

Of the theoretical tasks which remain one at least is central: a detailed investigation into how people speak about their experience of watching television, a scrutiny of discourses of viewing. The reception of textual operations becomes apparent in the viewer's response to a programme. Television transmits in the 'endlessly shifting, ever-evolving kaleidoscope of daily life'.[44] As Livingstone notes, further examination of the relative powers of 'the text to direct' and the viewer 'to create ... the resultant meanings' is needed.[45] Research must firmly establish a dual focus on both the text (its hierarchies and mechanisms of identification) and the audience response. My hope is that *Watching Television* contributes to the methodology of such investigations.

Questions need to be raised concerning the ways in which the text's prescriptions for its own reading (for example, in terms of a hierarchy of discourses) make it difficult for the viewer to produce particular extra-textual narratives of living. Under patriarchy, for instance, rereading a text may involve occupying different roles from those which it marks out as authoritative. A viewer's response may consist of generating insights into day-to-day existence on the basis of assuming a clearly subordinate outlook in the programme. Additionally, an extended survey of contextual or organizational discourses is required to establish the audience readings proposed by television institutions and journals for their particular pro-grammes, so that constraints on the intended viewer can be noted.

Only in this way can television's 'penetration into the warp and weft of everyday life'[46] be adequately explored as a televisual process of intervening and defining which in turn allows a viewer's tactical creativity. Creativity of this nature circulates around the viewer's construction of narratives in response to a role-related hermeneutic need for sense and identity. These stories may invoke resolutions to temporary or more continuing problems – may, that is, take a form akin to either series or serial. Whether or not such creativity is progressive or reactionary, an accommodation to (or rejection of) 'the sanitized world of a deodorant commercial where there's always a way to redemption'[47] can only be established through examining the individual case. Rereading and resistance are not essentially joined.

As the phenomenologist Iser indicates, 'the subjective processing of a text is generally still accessible to third parties, i.e. available for intersubjective analysis. This, however, is only possible if we pinpoint that which actually *happens* between text and reader.'[48] To allow Ricoeur the final word, 'hermeneutics without a project of liberation is blind, but a project of emancipation without historical experience [of the understanding of texts] is empty'.[49]

Notes

1 Fiske, *Television Culture*, p. 74.
2 Schole, 'Critical Studies', p. 32.
3 Silverstone, 'Television and Everyday Life', p. 173.
4 Fiske, '*Critical Response*', p. 249.
5 Brown, 'Motley Moments'.
6 Burger, *Theory of the Avant-Garde*, p. 4.
7 B. Brecht, 'Short Description of a New Technique of Acting which Produces an Alienation Effect', in Willett, *Brecht on Theatre*, p. 143. All the essays by Brecht cited below are published in *Brecht on Theatre*.

8   Ibid., p. 145.
9   Trainee metallurgist interviewed in Morley, *The 'Nationwide' Audience*, p. 46.
10 Brecht, 'A Short Organum for the Theatre', p. 190. 'It is up to the actor to treat present-day events and modes of behaviour with the same detachment as the historian adopts with regard to those of the past. He must alienate these characters and incidents from us' ('Short Description of a New Technique of Acting', p. 140).
11 Brecht, 'Appendices to the Short Organum', p. 276.
12 Brecht, 'A Short Organum for the Theatre', p. 190.
13 Ricoeur, *Interpretation Theory*, p. 43.
14 Ibid.
15 Ricoeur, 'Phenomenology and Hermeneutics', *Hermeneutics and the Human Sciences*, pp. 110, 113.
16 Brecht, 'Short Description of a New Technique of Acting', p. 139. 'The actress must not make the sentence her own affair, she must hand it over for criticism, she must help us to understand its causes and protest' ('Alienation Effects in Chinese Acting', p. 98).
17 Brecht, 'A Short Organum for the Theatre', p. 193.
18 Brecht, 'Notes to *Die Rundköpfe und die Spitzköpfe*', p. 101.
19 Thompson, *Ideology and Modern Culture*, p. 7.
20 Ricoeur, 'Hermeneutics and the Critique of Ideology', p. 64.
21 Ibid., p. 90.
22 Ibid., p. 74.
23 Ricoeur, 'Science and Ideology', *Hermeneutics and the Human Sciences*, p. 244.
24 Ricoeur, 'Phenomenology and Hermeneutics', p. 113.
25 Ricoeur, 'Hermeneutics and the Critique of Ideology', p. 91.
26 Gadamer, *Philosophical Hermeneutics*, p. 38.
27 J. Habermas, 'Zur Logik der Sozialwissenschaften', quoted in McCarthy, *Critical Theory of Jürgen Habermas*, p. 182.
28 Stam, 'Television News and Its Spectator', p. 40.
29 Ricoeur, 'Science and Ideology', p. 243.
30 Ibid., p. 224.
31 Ibid., p. 245.
32 Ibid., p. 224.
33 Ibid., p. 244.
34 Ibid., p. 224.
35 Ricoeur, 'Hermeneutics and the Critique of Ideology', p. 93.
36 Ibid., p. 87.
37 Carlshamre, *Language and Time*, p. 49.
38 Hall, 'Encoding/decoding', p. 137.
39 Tulloch, *Television Drama*, p. 217.
40 Ibid., p. 229.
41 Ang, *Watching 'Dallas'*, p. 20.
42 Fairclough, *Language and Power*, p. 85.
43 Jordin and Brunt, 'Constituting the Television Audience', pp. 245, 247.
44 Radway, 'Reception Study', p. 366.

45   Livingstone, *Making Sense of Television*, p. 193.
46   Silverstone, 'Let Us Then Return', p. 78.
47   Mellencamp, *Logics of Television*, p. 26.
48   Iser, *The Act of Reading*, p. 49.
49   Ricoeur, *Lectures on Ideology and Utopia*, p. 237.

Bibliography

Allen, R.C., *Channels of Discourse*, London, Methuen, 1987.
——, 'On Reading Soaps : A Semiotic Primer', in *Regarding Television*, edited by E.A. Kaplan, Los Angeles, American Film Institute, 1983.
——, *Speaking of Soap Operas*, Chapel Hill, University of North Carolina Press, 1985.
Althusser, L., *Essays on Ideology*, London, Verso, 1984.
——, *For Marx*, London, Allen Lane, 1971.
Ang, I., *Desperately Seeking the Audience*, London, Routledge, 1991.
——, 'Melodramatic Identifications : Television Fiction and Women's Fantasy', in *Television and Women's Culture*, edited by M.E. Brown, Sydney, Currency, 1990.
——, *Watching 'Dallas'*, London, Methuen, 1985.
Austin, J.L., 'How to Do Things with Words', Oxford, Oxford University Press, 1962.
——, *Sense and Sensibilia*, edited by G.J. Warnock, Oxford, Oxford University Press, 1962.

Barthes, R., *Image, Music, Text*, London, Fontana, 1977.
——, *Mythologies*, London, Cape, 1972.
——, *S/Z*, London, Cape, 1974.
Barwise, P., and Ehrenberg, A., *Television and Its Audience*, London, Sage, 1988.
——, 'Television as a Medium', paper presented at the British Film Institute/ University of London International Television Studies Conference, 1988.
Baudrillard, J., 'The Ecstasy of Communication', in *Postmodern Culture*, edited by H. Foster, London, Pluto, 1985.
Bennett, T., *Formalism and Marxism*, London, Methuen, 1979.
——, 'Texts in History : The Determinations of Readings and Their Texts', in *Post-structuralism and the Question of History*, edited by D. Attridge, G. Bennington and R. Young, Cambridge, Cambridge University Press, 1987.
Bennett, T., Boyd-Bowmann, S., Mercer, C., and Woollacott, J. (eds), *Popular*

Television and Film, London, British Film Institute/Open University Press, 1981.

Benson, D., and Hughes, J., *The Perspective of Ethnomethodology*, Harlow, Longman, 1983.

Benton, T., *Rise and Fall of Structural Marxism*, London, Macmillan, 1984.

Berman, R., *How Television Sees its Audience*, Newbury Park, Sage, 1987.

Bernstein, R.J. (ed.), *Habermas and Modernity*, Cambridge, Polity, 1985.

Berry, C., 'Meanings, Misunderstandings and Mental Models : Socio-cognitive Approaches to Perceived Bias in Broadcast Journalism', paper presented at the British Film Institute/University of London International Television Studies Conference, 1988.

Bordwell, D., 'Adventures in the Highlands of Theory', *Screen*, 29, 1 (1988), pp. 72–97.

——, *Narration in the Fiction Film*, London, Methuen, 1985.

Bordwell, D., Staiger, J., and Thompson, K., *Classical Hollywood Cinema*, London, Routledge and Kegan Paul, 1985.

Boyd-Bowmann, S., 'The MTM Phenomenon', *Screen*, 26, 6 (1985), pp. 75–87.

——, 'Open the Box', *Framework*, 32–3 (1986), pp. 146–9.

Brand, G., 'Intentionality, Reduction and Intentional Analysis in Husserl's Late Manuscripts', in *Phenomenology*, edited by J.J. Kockelmans, London, Anchor, 1967.

Branigan, E., 'Formal Permutations of the Point-of-view Shot', *Screen*, 16, 3 (1975), pp. 54–64.

——, *Point of View in the Cinema*, Amsterdam, Mouton, 1984.

——, 'The Spectator and Film Space : Two Theories', *Screen*, 22, 1 (1981), pp. 55–78.

Brewster, B., Halliday, J., Heath, S., Willemen, P., Cowie, E., Hanet, K., MacCabe, C., and Wollen, P., 'Reply', *Screen*, 17, 2 (1976–7), pp. 110–16.

Brown, M.E., 'Motley Moments : Soap Operas, Carnival, Gossip and the Power of the Utterance', *Television and Women's Culture*, Sydney, Currency, 1990.

Browne, N., *Rhetoric of Film Narration*, Ann Arbor, University of Michigan Press, 1982.

Brunsdon, C., '*Crossroads* : Notes on Soap Opera', in *Regarding Television*, edited by E.A. Kaplan, Los Angeles, American Film Institute, 1983.

Brunsdon, C., and Morley, D., *Everyday Television : 'Nationwide'*, London, British Film Institute, 1978.

Bruzina, R., *Logos and Eidos*, Amsterdam, Mouton, 1970.

Buckingham, D., *Public Secrets*, London, British Film Institute, 1987.

——, 'Television Literacy : A Critique', paper presented at the British Film Institute/University of London International Television Studies Conference, 1988.

Burch, N., *Theory of Film Practice*, London, Secker and Warburg, 1973.

Burger, P., *Theory of the Avant-garde*, Minneapolis, University of Minnesota Press, 1984.

Carlshamre, S., *Language and Time*, Gothenburg, Acta Universitatis Gothoburgensis, 1986.

Carr, D., *Interpreting Husserl*, The Hague, Nijhoff, 1987.

Caughie, J., 'Adorno's Reproach : Repetition, Difference and Television Genre', *Screen*, 32, 2 (1991), pp. 127–53.

——, 'Popular Culture : Notes and Revisions', in *High Theory/Low Culture*, edited by C. MacCabe, Manchester, Manchester University Press, 1986.

——, 'Progressive Television and Documentary Drama', in *Popular Television and Film*, edited by T. Bennett, S. Boyd-Bowmann, C. Mercer and J. Woollacott, London, British Film Institute/Open University Press, 1981.

——, 'Rhetoric, Pleasure and "Art Television"', *Screen*, 22, 4 (1981), pp. 9–31.

——, 'Scottish Television : What Would It Look Like ?', in *Scotch Reels*, edited by C. McArthur, London, British Film Institute, 1982.

——, 'Television Criticism : "A Discourse in Search of an Object"', *Screen*, 25, 4–5 (1984), pp. 109–20.

——, (ed.), *Theories of Authorship*, London, British Film Institute, 1981.

Chalmers, A.F., *What Is This Thing Called Science ?*, Milton Keynes, Open University Press, 1978.

Chambers, I., Clarke, J., Connell, I., Curti, L., Hall, S., and Jefferson, T., 'Marxism and Culture', *Screen*, 18, 4 (1977), pp. 109–19.

Chartier, R., *Cultural History*, Cambridge, Polity, 1988.

Clarke, A., and Taylor, I., 'Vandals, Pickets and Muggers', *Screen Education*, 36 (1980), pp. 99–111.

Clifford, J., and Marcus, G., *Writing Culture*, Berkeley and Los Angeles, University of California Press, 1986.

Collett, P., 'The Viewer Viewed', *Listener* (22 May 1986), p. 9.

——, 'Watching the TV Audience', paper presented at the British Film Institute/ University of London International Television Studies Conference, 1986.

Collins, J. *Uncommon Cultures*, London, Routledge, 1989.

Collins, R., 'Seeing Is Believing : The Ideology of Naturalism', in *Documentary and the Mass Media*, edited by J. Corner, London, Arnold, 1986.

Connell, I., 'Commercial Broadcasting and the British Left', *Screen*, 24, 6 (1983), pp. 70–80.

Connor, S., *Postmodernist Culture*, Oxford, Blackwell, 1989.

Cooke, L., *Psycho* (study notes), London, British Film Institute, 1984.

Corner, J., 'Documentary : Television's Language of Knowledge', *Media Education Journal*, 1, 7 (1989), pp. 17–24.

——, (ed.), *Documentary and the Mass Media*, London, Arnold, 1986.

Coward, R., 'Class, "Culture" and the Social Formation', *Screen*, 18, 1 (1977), pp. 75–105.

Coward, R., and Ellis, J., *Language and Materialism*, London, Routledge and Kegan Paul, 1977.

Crisell, A., *Understanding Radio*, London, Methuen, 1986.

Curti, L., 'Genre and Gender', paper presented at the British Film Institute/ University of London International Television Studies Conference, 1986.

Dahlgren, P., 'The Modes of Reception', in *Television in Transition*, edited by P. Drummond and R. Paterson, London, British Film Institute, 1985.

——, 'What's the Meaning of This ? Viewers' Plural Sense-making of TV News', *Media, Culture and Society*, 10 (1988), pp. 385–301.

Dallmayr, F.R., *Critical Encounters and Understanding*, Notre Dame, University of Notre Dame Press, 1987.
Dallmayr, F.R., and McCarthy, T., *Understanding and Social Inquiry*, Notre Dame, University of Notre Dame Press, 1977.
Davies, J., 'The Television Audience Revisited', *Australian Journal of Screen Theory*, 17–18 (1984), pp. 84–105.
Day-Lewis, S., *One Day in the Life of Television*, London, Grafton, 1989.
de Certeau, M., *The Practice of Everyday Life*, Berkeley, University of California Press, 1984.
De Lauretis, T., *Alice Doesn't*, London, Macmillan, 1984.
de Man, P., Introduction to *Toward an Aesthetic of Reception* by H.R. Jauss, Brighton, Harvester, 1982.
Deming, C., 'Control over Chaos : Hill Street Blues as Narrative', paper presented at the British Film Institute/University of London International Television Studies Conference, 1984.
Derrida, J., *Speech and Phenomena*, translated by D. B. Allison, Evanston, Northwestern University Press, 1973.
Drummond, P., and Paterson, R., *Television and Its Audience*, London, British Film Institute, 1988.
——, *Television in Transition*, British Film Institute, 1986.
Dyer, R., 'Victim : Hermeneutic Project', *Film Form*, 1, 2 (1977), pp. 3–22.

Eagleton, T., 'Capitalism, Modernism and Postmodernism', *New Left Review*, 152 (1986), pp. 60–73.
——, *Literary Theory : An Introduction*, Oxford, Blackwell, 1983.
Eco, U., 'A Guide to the Neo-television of the 1980s', *Framework*, 25 (1984), pp. 18–27.
——, *The Role of the Reader*, London, Hutchinson, 1981.
Eisenstein, S., 'The Cinematographic Principle and the Ideogram', in *Film Theory and Criticism*, edited by G. Mast and M. Cohen, Oxford, Oxford University Press, 1979.
——, 'A Dialectic Approach to Film Form', in *Film Form : Essays in Film Theory*, edited by J. Leyda, Durham, Dobson, 1951.
——, 'Methods of Montage', in *Film Form : Essays in Film Theory*, edited by J. Leyda, Durham, Dobson, 1951.
Ellis, J., *Visible Fictions*, London, Routledge and Kegan Paul, 1982.
Elsaesser, T., 'Narrative Cinema and Audience-oriented Aesthetics', in *Popular Television and Film*, edited by T. Bennett, S. Boyd-Bowmann, C. Mercer and J. Woollacott, London, British Film Institute/Open University Press, 1981.
Emmet, D., *Rules, Roles and Relations*, London, Macmillan, 1966.

Fairclough, N., *Language and Power*, Harlow, Longman, 1989.
Feuer, J., 'The Concept of Live Television : Ontology as Ideology', in *Regarding Television*, edited by E.A. Kaplan, Los Angeles, American Film Institute, 1983.
——, 'Narrative Form in American Network Television', in *High Theory/Low*

Culture, edited by C. MacCabe, Manchester, Manchester University Press, 1986.

Fiske, J., 'Critical Response: Meaningful Moments', *Critical Studies in Mass Communication*, 5 (1988), pp. 246–51.

——, *Introduction to Television Studies*, London, Methuen, 1982.

——, 'Popularity and Ideology', in *Interpreting Television*, edited by W.D. Rowland, Jr, and B. Watkins, London, Sage, 1984.

——, *Television Culture*, London, Methuen, 1987.

——, 'Women and Quiz Shows', in *Television and Women's Culture*, edited by M.E. Brown, Sydney, Currency, 1990.

Fiske, J., and Hartley, J., *Reading Television*, London, Methuen, 1978.

Fletcher, J., 'Melodrama: Versions of Masquerade', *Screen*, 29, 3 (1988), pp. 43–70.

Flitterman, S., 'The *Real* Soap Operas: TV Commercials', in *Regarding Television*, edited by E.A. Kaplan, Los Angeles, American Film Institute, 1983.

Flitterman-Lewis, S., 'Psychoanalysis, Film and Television', in *Channels of Discourse*, edited by R.C. Allen, London, Methuen, 1987.

Foster, H. (ed.), *Postmodern Culture*, London, Pluto, 1985.

Freund, E., *The Return of the Reader*, London, Methuen, 1987.

Gadamer, H.G., *Philosophical Hermeneutics*, Berkeley, University of California Press, 1976.

——, 'The Science of the Life-world', in *The Later Husserl and the Idea of Phenomenology*, edited by A. Tymieniecka, Norwell, Reidel, 1972.

——, *Truth and Method*, London, Sheed and Ward, 1979.

Garfinkel, H., *Studies in Ethnomethodology*, New York, Prentice-Hall, 1967.

Garton, G., Montgomery, M., and Tolson, A., 'Ideology, Scripts and Metaphors in the Public Sphere of a General Election', in *Broadcast Talk*, edited by P. Scannell, London, Sage, 1991.

Genette, G., *Narrative Discourse*, Oxford, Blackwell, 1980.

Giddens, A., *Consequences of Modernity*, Stanford, Stanford University Press, 1990.

——, 'Reason without Revolution', in *Habermas and Modernity*, edited by R.J. Bernstein, Cambridge, Polity, 1985

Gier, N.F., *Wittgenstein and Phenomenology*, New York, State University of New York Press, 1981.

Goodwin, A., 'Music Video in the (Post)modern World', *Screen*, 28, 3 (1987) pp. 16–33.

Gramsci, A., *Selections from the Prison Notebooks*, edited by Q. Hoare and G. Nowell-Smith, Oxford, Polity, 1985.

Gray, A., 'Reading the Readings', paper presented at the British Film Institute/University of London International Television Studies Conference, 1988.

Gripsrud, J., 'Watching versus Understanding *Dallas*', paper presented at the British Film Institute/University of London International Television Studies Conference, 1988.

Grondin, J., 'Hermeneutics and Relativism', in *Festivals of Interpretation*, edited by K. Wright, New York, State University of New York Press, 1990.

Grossberg, L., 'The In-difference of Television', *Screen*, 28, 2 (1987), pp. 35–51.
Gurwitsch, A., *Studies in Phenomenology and Psychology*, Evanston, North-western University Press, 1966.

Habermas, J., *Knowledge and Human Interests*, London, Heinemann, 1972.
——, *Legitimation Crisis*, Oxford, Heinemann, 1976.
——, *The Philosophical Discourse of Modernity*, Cambridge, Massachusetts Institute of Technology, 1987.
——, 'A Review of Gadamer's *Truth and Method*', in *Understanding and Social Inquiry*, edited by F. Dallmayr and T. McCarthy, Notre Dame, University of Notre Dame Press, 1977.
——, *Theory of Communicative Action*, vols. 1 and 2, Cambridge, Polity, 1987.
——, 'What is Universal Pragmatics ?', in *Communication and the Evolution of Society*, Oxford, Heinemann, 1979.
Hall, S., 'Encoding/decoding', in *Culture, Media, Language*, edited by S. Hall, D. Hobson, A. Lowe and P. Willis, Birmingham, University of Birmingham, 1980.
——, 'The Narrative Construction of Reality' (interview), *Southern Review*, 17 (1984), pp. 3–17.
Hall, S., Connell, I., and Curti, L., 'The "Unity" of Current Affairs Television', in *Popular Television and Film*, edited by T. Bennett, S. Boyd-Bowmann, C. Mercer and J. Woollacott, London, British Film Institute/Open University Press, 1981.
Hans, J.S., 'Hermeneutics, Play, Deconstruction', *Philosophy Today*, 24 (1980), pp. 305–23.
Harré, R., and Secord, P., *The Explanation of Social Behaviour*, Oxford, Blackwell, 1972.
Hayward, P., and Kerr, P., Introduction to *Screen*, 28, 2 (1987), pp. 3–7.
Heath, S., 'Screen Images, Film Memory', *Edinburgh Magazine*, 1 (1979), pp. 31–8.
Heath, S., and Skirrow, G., 'Television: A World in Action', *Screen*, 18, 2 (1977), pp. 7–59.
Hebdige, D., and Hurd, G., 'Reading and Realism', *Screen Education*, 28 (1978), pp. 68–78.
Heller, A., and Feher, F., *The Postmodern Political Condition*, Cambridge, Polity, 1988.
Hempel, C., *Aspects of Scientific Explanation*, New York, Freepress, 1965.
Hepburn, R.W., 'Vision and Choice in Morality', in *Christian Ethics and Contemporary Philosophy*, edited by I.T. Ramsay, London, SCM, 1966.
Higgins, C., 'Current Affairs, Consumers and Culture: A Case Study of *Brisbane with Anna McMahon*', paper presented at the Inaugural Australian Cultural Studies Conference, 1990.
Higson, A., and Vincendeau, G., 'Melodrama', *Screen*, 27, 6 (1986), pp. 2–5.
Hill, J., ' "Scotland Doesna Mean Much tae Glesca": Some Notes on *The Gorbals Story*', in *Scotch Reels*, edited by C. McArthur, London, British Film Institute, 1982.
Hobson, D., *Crossroads*, London, Methuen, 1982.
——, 'Soap Operas at Work', in *Remote Control: Television, Audiences, and*

Cultural Power, edited by E. Seiter, H. Borchers, G. Kreutzner and E.-M. Warth, London, Routledge, 1989.

Hodge, B., and Tripp, D., *Children and Television*, Cambridge, Polity, 1986.

Houston, B., 'Viewing Television: The Metapsychology of Endless Consumption', *Quarterly Review of Film Studies*, 9, 3 (1984), pp. 183–95.

Hurd, G., 'The Television Presentation of the Police', in *Popular Television and Film*, edited by T. Bennett, S. Boyd-Bowmann, C. Mercer and J. Woollacott, London, British Film Institute/Open University Press, 1981.

Husserl, E., *Cartesian Meditations*, translated by D. Cairns, The Hague, Nijhoff, 1970.

——, *Crisis of European Sciences and Transcendental Phenomenology*, edited by D. Carr, Evanston, Northwestern University Press, 1970.

——, *Experience and Judgement*, London, Routledge and Kegan Paul, 1973.

——, *Phenomenology and the Crisis of Philosophy*, translated by Q. Lauer, London, Harper and Row, 1965.

Huyssen, A., 'The Search for Tradition: Avant-garde and Postmodernism in the 1970s', *New German Critique*, 22 (1981), pp. 23–40.

Iser, W., *The Act of Reading*, Baltimore, Johns Hopkins University Press, 1978.

——, 'Interaction between Text and Reader', in *The Reader in the Text*, edited by S. Suleiman and I. Crosman, New Jersey, Princeton University Press, 1980.

Jameson, F., 'Postmodernism and Consumer Society', in *Postmodern Culture*, edited by H. Foster, London, Pluto, 1985.

——, 'Postmodernism or the Cultural Logic of Late Capitalism', *New Left Review*, 146 (1984), pp. 53–92.

Jauss, H.R., *Toward an Aesthetic of Reception*, Brighton, Harvester, 1982.

Johnston, L., 'Women, Popular Culture and the Question of Agency', paper presented at the Inaugural Australian Cultural Studies Conference, 1990.

Johnston, S., 'Film Narrative and the Structuralist Controversy', in *The Cinema Book*, edited by P. Cook, London, British Film Institute, 1985.

Jordin, M., and Brunt, R., 'Constituting the Television Audience: A Problem of Method', in *Television and its Audience*, edited by P. Drummond and R. Paterson, London, British Film Institute, 1988.

Kaplan, E.A., 'A Post-modern Play of the Signifier?', in *Television in Transition*, edited by P. Drummond and R. Paterson, London, British Film Institute, 1985.

——, *Rocking around the Clock*, London, Methuen, 1987.

——, (ed.), *Regarding Television*, Los Angeles, American Film Institute, 1983.

Kisiel, T., 'Repetition in Gadamer's Hermeneutics', in *The Later Husserl and the Idea of Phenomenology*, edited by A. Tymieniecka, Norwell, Reidel, 1972.

Kozloff, S.R., 'Narrative Theory and Television', in *Channels of Discourse*, edited by R.C. Allen, London, Methuen, 1987.

Kress, G., 'Language in the Media: The Construction of the Domains of Public and Private', *Media, Culture and Society*, 8 (1986), pp. 395–419.

Kuhn, A., 'The Camera I, Observations on Documentary', *Screen*, 19, 2 (1978), pp. 71–83.

——, 'History of Narrative Codes', in *The Cinema Book*, edited by P. Cook, London, British Film Institute, 1985.

Kuhn, H., 'The Phenomenological Concept of "Horizon"', in *Philosophical Essays in Memory of Edmund Husserl*, edited by M. Farber, Cambridge, Harvard University Press, 1940.

Kumar, K.J., 'Indian Families Watching Television: An Ethnographic Survey', paper presented at the British Film Institute/University of London International Television Studies Conference, 1988.

Leont'ev, A.N., *Activity, Consciousness, and Personality*, New York, Prentice-Hall, 1978.

Lewis, J., 'Decoding Television News', in *Television in Transition*, edited by P. Drummond and R. Paterson, London, British Film Institute, 1985.

Liebes, T., 'Cultural Differences in the Retelling of Television Fiction', *Critical Studies in Mass Communication*, 5 (1988), pp. 277–92.

Liebes, T., and Katz, E., 'On the Critical Abilities of Television Viewers', in *Remote Control: Television, Audiences, and Cultural Power*, edited by E. Seiter, H. Borchers, G. Kreutzner and E.-M. Warth, London, Routledge, 1989.

Lindlof, T.R., and Meyer, T.P., 'Mediated Communication as Ways of Seeing, Acting and Constructing Culture: The Tools and Foundations of Qualitative Research', in *Natural Audiences*, edited by T. R. Lindlof, New Jersey, Ablex, 1987.

Livingstone, S.M., *Making Sense of Television*, Oxford, Pergamon, 1990.

Lodziak, C., *The Power of Television*, London, Pinter, 1986.

Lovell, T., 'Ideology and *Coronation Street*', in *Coronation Street*, edited by R. Dyer, C. Geraghty, M. Jordan, T. Lovell, R. Paterson and J. Stewart, London, British Film Institute, 1981.

——, 'The Social Relations of Cultural Production: Absent Centre of a New Discourse', in *One-dimensional Marxism*, edited by S. Clarke, London, Allison and Busby, 1980.

Lukács, G., 'Realism in the Balance', in *Aesthetics and Politics*, edited by R. Taylor, London, Verso, 1980.

Lull, J., 'Constructing Rituals of Extension through Family Television Viewing', *World Families Watch Television*, London, Sage, 1988.

——, 'The Family and Television in World Cultures', *World Families Watch Television*, London, Sage, 1988.

——, 'How Families Select Television Programs: A Mass-observational Study', *Journal of Broadcasting*, 26, 4 (1982), pp. 802–3.

Lyotard, J.F., *The Postmodern Condition: A Report on Knowledge*, Manchester, Manchester University Press, 1987.

McArthur, C., 'Historical Drama', in *Popular Television and Film*, edited by T. Bennett, S. Boyd-Bowmann, C. Mercer and J. Woollacott, London, British Film Institute/Open University Press, 1981.

——, 'The Narrator as Guarantor of Truth', in *Communication Studies*, edited by J. Corner and J. Hawthorn, London, Arnold, 1980.

——, (ed.), *Scotch Reels*, London, British Film Institute, 1982.

MacCabe, C., 'The Discursive and the Ideological in Film: Notes on the Condition of Political Intervention', *Screen*, 19, 4 (1978), pp. 29–43.

——, 'Memory, Phantasy and Identity: *Days of Hope* and the Politics of the Past', in *Popular Television and Film*, edited by T. Bennett, S. Boyd-Bowmann, C. Mercer and J. Woollacott, London, British Film Institute/ Open University Press, 1981.

——, 'Realism and the Cinema: Notes on Some Brechtian Theses', in *Popular Television and Film*, edited by T. Bennett, S. Boyd-Bowmann, C. Mercer and J. Woollacott, London, British Film Institute/Open University Press, 1981.

——, 'Theory and Film: Principles of Realism and Pleasure', *Screen*, 17, 3 (1976), pp. 7–27.

McCarthy, T., *Critical Theory of Jürgen Habermas*, London, Hutchinson, 1978.

McDonnel, L., and Robins, K., 'Marxist Cultural Theory: The Althusserian Smokescreen', in *One-dimensional Marxism*, edited by S. Clarke, London, Allison and Busby, 1980.

MacShane, D., *Using the Media*, London, Pluto, 1979.

Mancini, P., 'Strategies of TV News Dramatization: An Attempt of [*sic*] Discourse Analysis', paper presented at the XI World Congress of Sociology, New Delhi, 1986.

Martin, W., *Recent Theories of Narrative*, Ithaca, Cornell University Press, 1986.

Massing, H., 'Decoding *Dallas*: Comparing American and German Viewers', in *Television and Society*, edited by A. Berger, New Brunswick, Transaction, 1987.

Mast, G., and Cohen, H., *Film Theory and Criticism*, Oxford, Oxford University Press, 1979.

Mayne, J., 'Response [on Feminism and the Audience]', *Camera Obscura*, 20–2 (1989), pp. 230–4.

Mellencamp, P. (ed.), *Logics of Television*, London, British Film Institute, 1990.

Merleau-Ponty, M., *Phenomenology of Perception*, translated by C. Smith, London, Routledge and Kegan Paul, 1962.

Metz, C., *Psychoanalysis and Cinema*, London, Macmillan, 1982.

Meyrowitz, J., *No Sense of Place*, Oxford, Oxford University Press, 1985.

Michaels, E., 'Hollywood Iconography: A Walpiri Reading', paper presented at the British Film Institute/University of London International Television Studies Conference, 1986.

Miller, M.C., 'Deride and Conquer', in *Watching Television*, edited by T. Gitlin, New York, Pantheon, 1986.

Millerson, G., *The Technique of Television Production*, Sevenoaks, Focal, 1979.

Modleski, T., 'The Rhythms of Reception: Daytime Television and Women's Work', in *Regarding Television*, edited by E. A. Kaplan, Los Angeles, American Film Institute, 1983.

——, 'The Search for Tomorrow in Today's Soap Operas: Notes on a Feminine Narrative Form', *Film Quarterly*, 33, 1 (1979), pp. 12–21; also in *Understanding Television*, edited by R.P. Adler, New York, Praeger, 1981.

Mohanty, J.H., '"Life-world" and "a priori" in Husserl's Later Thought', *The Possibility of Transcendental Philosophy*, The Hague, Nijhoff, 1985.

Morey, J., *The Space between Programmes: TV Continuity* (monograph), London, University of London Institute of Education, n.d.

Morley, D., 'Domestic Relations: The Framework of Family Viewing in Great Britain', in *World Families Watch Television*, edited by J. Lull, London, Sage, 1988.

——, *Family Television*, London, Comedia, 1986.

——, 'Family Television: Cultural Power and Domestic Leisure', paper presented at the British Film Institute/University of London International Television Studies Conference, 1986.

——, *The 'Nationwide' Audience*, London, British Film Institute, 1980.

——, 'The *Nationwide* Audience: A Critical Postscript', *Screen Education*, 39 (1981), pp. 3–14.

——, 'Texts, Readers, Subjects', in *Culture, Media, Language*, edited by S. Hall, D. Hobson, A. Lowe and P. Willis, Birmingham, University of Birmingham, 1980.

Morley, D., and Silverstone, R., 'Domestic Communication: Technologies and Meanings', *Media, Culture and Society*, 12 (1990), pp. 31–55.

Morse, M., 'Replay and Display', in *Regarding Television*, edited by E.A. Kaplan, Los Angeles, American Film Institute, 1983.

——, 'Talk, Talk, Talk', *Screen*, 26, 2 (1985), pp. 2–15.

Neale, S., *Genre*, London, British Film Institute, 1980.

Newcomb, H., 'Towards a Television Aesthetic', *Television: The Critical View*, Oxford, Oxford University Press, 1982.

Nicholls, B., *Ideology and the Image*, Bloomington, Indiana University Press, 1981.

Nightingale, V., 'What's "Ethnographic" about Ethnographic Research?', *Australian Journal of Communication*, 16 (1989), pp. 50–63.

O'Brien, M., *Coma* (study notes), London, British Film Institute, 1986.

Paterson, R., 'Restyling Masculinity: The Impact of *Boys from the Blackstuff*', in *Impacts and Influences*, edited by J. Curran, London, Methuen, 1987.

Pefanis, J., *Heterology and The Postmodern*, Sydney, Allen and Unwin, 1991.

Pietersma, H., 'The Concept of Horizon', in *The Later Husserl and the Idea of Phenomenology*, edited by A. Tymieniecka, Norwell, Reidel, 1972.

Plato, *The Republic*, London, Clarendon, 1961.

Press, A.L., 'Class and Gender in the Hegemonic Process: Class Differences in Women's Perceptions of Television Realism and Identification with Television Characters', paper presented at the British Film Institute/University of London International Television Studies Conference, 1988.

Press, A.L., *Women Watching Television*, Philadelphia, University of Pennsylvania Press, 1991.

Pritchard, G., 'Unrelenting Bias', *See 4*, 18 (spring 1988), pp. 3–14.

Radway, J., *Reading the Romance: Women, Patriarchy and Popular Literature*, Chapel Hill, University of North Carolina Press, 1984.
——, 'Reception Study: Ethnography and the Problems of Dispersed Audiences and Nomadic Subjects', *Cultural Studies*, 2, 3 (1988), pp. 359–76.
Rath, C.D., 'Live Television and Its Audiences: Challenges of Media Reality', in *Remote Control: Television, Audiences, and Cultural Power*, edited by E. Seiter, H. Borchers, G. Kreutzner and E.-M. Warth, London, Routledge, 1989.
Richards, J., and Sheridan, D., *Mass-observation at the Movies*, London, Routledge and Kegan Paul, 1987.
Richardson, K., and Corner, J., 'Reading Reception: Mediation and Transparency in Viewers' Accounts of a TV Programme', *Media, Culture and Society*, 8 (1986), pp. 485–508.
Ricoeur, P., 'Can There Be a Scientific Concept of Ideology?', in *Phenomenology and the Social Sciences*, edited by J. Bien, The Hague, Nijhoff, 1978.
——, *Hermeneutics and the Human Sciences*, edited by J.B. Thompson, Cambridge, Cambridge University Press, 1983.
——, *Interpretation Theory*, Fort Worth, Texas Christian University Press, 1976.
——, *Lectures on Ideology and Utopia*, edited by G.H. Taylor, New York, Columbia University Press, 1986.
Root, J., *Open the Box*, London, Comedia, 1986.
Rowland, W.D., Jr, and Watkins, B., *Interpreting Television*, London, Sage, 1984.

Sartre, J.P., *Sketch for a Theory of the Emotions*, London, Methuen, 1971.
Scannell, P., 'The Communicative Ethos of Broadcasting', paper presented at the British Film Institute/University of London International Television Studies Conference, 1988.
——, 'Radio Times: The Temporal Arrangements of Broadcasting in the Modern World', in *Television and Its Audience*, edited by P. Drummond and R. Paterson, London, British Film Institute, 1988.
Schenck, D., 'Merleau-Ponty on Perspectivism', in *Philosophy and Phenomenological Research*, 46 (1985), pp. 302–23.
Schlesinger, P., Murdock, G., and Elliott, P., *Televising 'Terrorism'*, London, Comedia, 1983.
Schole, D., 'Critical Studies: From the Theory of Ideology to Power/Knowledge', *Critical Studies in Mass Communication*, 5 (1988), pp. 16–41.
Schroder, K., 'Cultural Quality: Search for a Phantom?', paper presented at the British Film Institute/University of London International Television Studies Conference, 1988.
——, 'The Pleasure of *Dynasty*', in *Television and Its Audience*, edited by P. Drummond and R. Paterson, London, British Film Institute, 1988.
Schutz, A., *Collected Papers*, vol. 2, edited by A. Brodersen, The Hague, Nijhoff, 1976; vol. 3, edited by I. Schutz, The Hague, Nijhoff, 1978.
——, *On Phenomenology and Social Relations*, edited by H. R. Wagner, Chicago, University of Chicago Press, 1970.

——, 'Type and Eidos in Husserl's Late Philosophy', *Collected Papers*, vol. 1, edited by M. Natanson, The Hague, Nijhoff, 1962.

Schutz, A., and Luckmann, T., *The Structures of the Life-world*, Evanston, Northwestern University Press, 1973.

Seiter, E., 'Making Distinctions in TV Audience Research: Case Study of a Troubling Interview', *Cultural Studies*, 4, 1 (1990), pp. 61–84.

——, 'Semiotics and Television', in *Channels of Discourse*, edited by R.C. Allen, London, Methuen, 1987.

Seiter, E., Borchers, H., Kreutzner, G., and Warth, E.-M. (eds), *Remote Control: Television, Audiences and Cultural Power*, London, Routledge, 1989.

Seitz, B., 'The Televised and the Untelevised: Keeping an Eye On/off the Tube', in *Postmodernism: Philosophy and the Arts*, edited by H.J. Silverman, London, Routledge, 1990.

Sharma, A., 'Do They Think We're Uloo?', in *The Neglected Audience*, edited by J. Willis and T. Wollen, London, British Film Institute, 1990.

Sharrock, W., and Watson, R., 'Autonomy among Social Theories', in *Actions and Structure*, edited by N.G. Fielding, Newbury Park, Sage, 1988.

Silverman, H.J. (ed.), *Postmodernism: Philosophy and the Arts*, London, Routledge, 1990.

Silverstone, R., 'The Agonistic Narratives of Television Science', in *Documentary and the Mass Media*, edited by J. Corner, London, Arnold, 1986.

——, 'Let Us Then Return to the Murmuring of Everyday Practices: A Note on Michel de Certeau, Television and Everyday Life', *Theory, Culture and Society*, 6 (1989), pp. 77–94.

——, 'Narrative Strategies and Television Science: A Case Study', *Media, Culture and Society*, 6 (1984), pp. 380–91,

——, 'The Right to Speak: On a Poetic for Television Documentary', *Media, Culture and Society*, 5 (1983), pp. 133–48.

——, 'Television and Everyday Life: Towards an Anthropology of the Television Audience', in *Public Communication*, edited by M. Ferguson, London, Sage, 1990.

Spurling, L., *Phenomenology and the Social World*, London, Routledge and Kegan Paul, 1977.

Stam, R., 'Television News and Its Spectator', in *Regarding Television*, edited by E.A. Kaplan, Los Angeles, American Film Institute, 1983.

Stevens, T., 'Reading the Realist Film', *Screen Education*, 26 (1978), pp. 13–34.

Taylor, R. (ed.), *Aesthetics and Politics*, London, Verso, 1977.

Thompson, J.B., *Ideology and Modern Culture*, Cambridge, Polity, 1990.

——, *Studies in the Theory of Ideology*, Cambridge, Polity, 1984.

Tolson, A., 'Anecdotal Television', *Screen*, 26, 2 (1985), pp. 60–4.

Tulloch, J., 'Approaching the Audience: The Elderly', in *Remote Control: Television, Audiences, and Cultural Power*, edited by E. Seiter, H. Borchers, G. Kreutzner and E.-M. Warth, London, Routledge, 1989.

——, *Television Drama*, London, Routledge, 1990.

Tulloch, J., and Moran, A., *A Country Practice*, Sydney, Currency, 1986.

Tymieniecka, A. (ed.), *The Later Husserl and the Idea of Phenomenology*, Norwell, Reidel, 1972.

Ulmer, G., 'The Object of Post-criticism', in *Postmodern Culture*, edited by H. Foster, London, Pluto, 1985.

Volosinov, V.N., *Marxism and the Philosophy of Language*, Moscow, Seminar, 1973.

Walkerdine, V., 'Video Replay : Families, Films and Fantasy', in *Formations of Fantasy*, edited by V. Burgin, J. Donald and C. Kaplan, London, Methuen, 1986.
Warnke, G., *Gadamer: Hermeneutics, Tradition and Reason*, Cambridge, Polity, 1987.
Watt, J., 'Take the High Road : A Case Study', Ph.D. diss., Open University, 1988.
Watts, H., *On Camera*, London, BBC, 1984.
Weinsheimer, J.C., *Gadamer's Hermeneutics*, New Haven, Yale University Press, 1985.
White, M., 'Ideological Analysis and Television', in *Channels of Discourse*, edited by R.C. Allen, London, Methuen, 1987.
Willemen, P., 'Notes on Subjectivity', *Screen*, 19, 1 (1978), pp. 41–69.
Willett, J. (ed. and trans.), *Brecht on Theatre*, London, Methuen, 1979.
Williams, L., 'Feminist Film Theory : *Mildred Pierce* and the Second World War', in *Female Spectators: Looking at Film and Television*, edited by E. D. Pribram, London, Verso, 1988.
Williams, R., *Keywords*, London, Fontana, 1976.
——, *Television: Technology and Cultural Form*, London, Fontana, 1974.
Willis, J., and Wollen, T. (eds), *The Neglected Audience*, London, British Film Institute, 1990.
Wilson, E., 'All in the Family', in *Television Mythologies*, edited by L. Masterman, London, Comedia, 1986.
Wilson, T., 'Depressing Stories with Inconclusive Endings ?', *Journal of the Association for Media Education in Scotland*, 1 (1984), pp. 7–28.
——, 'Reading the Postmodernist Image : A "Cognitive Mapping"', *Screen*, 31, 4 (1990), pp. 390–407.
——, 'TV-am and the Politics of Caring', *Media, Culture and Society*, 12 (1990), pp. 125–37.
Winch, P., *The Idea of a Social Science and Its Relation to Philosophy*, London, Routledge and Kegan Paul, 1965.
Wyver, J., 'Television and Postmodernism', *Postmodern ICA Documents 4*, London, Institute of Contemporary Art, 1986.

Zukin, C., 'Mass Communication and Public Opinion', *Handbook of Political Communication*, edited by D.D. Nimmo and K.R. Saunders, London, Sage, 1981.
Zurbrugg, N., 'An Interview with Baudrillard', *Eyeline* (Brisbane), 11 (1990), pp. 4–7.

Index

Harré, R., 106
Heath, S., 85, 127
hegemony, 10, 37, 67, 72, 158, 177, 204–5
Hempel, C., 90–1
hermeneutic
    activity, 126, 137, 181; circle, 51, 72, 75, 80; critical, 201; paradox, 67; reflection, 38, 203; role, 54, 83, 85, 115, 158; of suspicion, 153; theory, 111, 190–1; of understanding, 3, 5–7, 15, 36, 44–68, 71–100, 106
hierarchy, 23, 31, 91
    absence of, 97; of discourses, 155, 163, 167, 172–82, 207; of familiarity, 23, 175, 179–82; of meaning, 173–5; of narrative, 119; of organization, 201; of truth, 176–9
Hobson, D., 7, 89
holism, 14, 24, 75, 77
horizon, 13, 15–17, 19, 47, 68, 128–9
    of caring, 17; of categories, 32; of common understanding, 19; of everyday life, 5; of existence, 10; of expectancies, 183; of expectation, 7, 16, 50, 61, 72, 81, 104–14, 134, 173, 202–6; of experience, 15–16, 18, 20, 26, 40, 129, 150; of familiarity, 182; of fellow men, 14; of gender, 64; of horizons, 20; of interpretation, 46; of leisure, 31, 57; of life-world, 22; of meaning, 173–4; of need, 53; of ordinary, 25; of other person, 49; of presuppositions, 19, 48; of programme, 46; of relevance, 31; of retention, 15; of scepticism, 161; of suspicion, 23–4, 162; of uncertainty, 161; of understanding, 3, 6, 9–10, 15–16, 18–19, 27, 38, 47–8, 90, 105, 114, 138, 144, 150,

156, 173, 175–7, 182, 188, 190, 196, 201–2, 205; of viewer, 46; of viewing, 30
horizon
    cognitive, 4, 16, 32, 37, 61, 128, 167, 178, 193; interest-related, 30, 38, 44–5, 56, 206; internal and external, 16, 39; mental, 205; moral, 26; moving, 15; practical, 5; pretextual, 47; as selective, 173; structure, 129; subjective, 188; world, 40
horizons
    competing, 177; as cultural competences, 48; as frameworks, 46; hierarchy of, 172–82; as normative background, 25; political, 206
horizons, fusion of, 21, 23, 44–7, 49–50, 62, 128, 131, 137, 144, 149, 199
Husserl, E., 14–19, 81, 177
hypothesis
    of meaning, 80; testing, 73

identification, 4–7, 27, 32, 49–71, 76, 78–80, 83–92, 98, 104–5, 114–18, 153, 156, 160, 162, 166–8, 178, 181, 201, 205–6
    counterfactual, 45, 55; disturbed, 88; forgetting in, 5; imperfect, 63; intellectualism in, 71; mechanisms of, 20, 115, 126–51, 172, 177, 182; multiple, 6; and ontology, 115; subverting of, 182–92; and the theatre, 182
identity
    ambiguous, 178; contradictory, 153–8; of viewer, 180, 207; of visual with truth, 163
ideology, 2–5, 10, 18, 37, 46–8, 56, 65–7, 79, 86, 112, 163, 175, 177–9, 181, 183, 188, 196–7, 200–6
    and challenge, 154; competing, 155; and typology, 15

separation of the elements,
184–8
serial, 76, 78–82, 92–100, 105–6,
188, 207
continuous, 5, 7–8, 31, 36, 48,
61, 64–5, 72, 81, 87–8, 90,
107, 110–11, 113, 115, 159,
168, 173, 180–1, 190;
investigative, 66
serial/series, 98–9
series, 76, 81, 98, 105–6, 168,
186, 207
detective, 106; police, 98
sexism, 47, 94, 99
Silverstone, R., 9, 13, 24, 45, 82,
118
similarity, 110, 176, 200, 204,
206
cognitive, 131; and difference,
84, 87, 191; of emotions,
131; and identification,
53–4, 64–5, 83–93
simulacrum, 166–9
single play, 36, 164
situation comedy, 5, 88, 109,
111, 115, 159, 178, 180, 186
stereotype, 38–9, 168, 175, 186,
197–202
structuralism, 1–4, 7, 9, 47,
56–7, 63, 65–6, 70, 111
subject, 24, 34, 44, 50, 52, 56–7,
63, 76, 83, 92, 199
definition of, 10; embodied,
111; extra-textual, 149, 198;
of gaze, 134–6; intra-
textual, 127, 137, 149; male,
167; nomadic, 86, 92; and
phenomenology, 13–18; and
return look, 132; split, 139;
transcendental, 15; unified,
2; and voiceover, 145
subject en famille, 27
subjective/objective look, 135
subjective
discourse, 191; and presenter,
162; pseudo-unity of, 153;
as source of meaning, 164;
travelling shot, 121, 134–6;
and truth, 176

television, professional practice,
117
textual shifter, 36, 94
theatre, 199, 201, 204
Thompson, J. B., 205–6
tilt, camera, 113, 116, 127–8,
134, 136
to and fro movement, 8, 51, 81,
92, 116–17, 206
tracking shot, 111, 113, 116, 120,
127, 134–5, 145
transparency, 108–14, 186–7
absence of, 115–16; counter-
to-factual, 116; of image,
65, 104, 116–18, 121, 132,
153–69
Tulloch, J., 88–9, 205
TV Times, 57, 82, 85, 97, 99
typical
form, 19–20, 24, 39; motives,
50; patterns of activity, 106

understanding, 45–9; identity of,
38; immediacy of, 37
unified
meaning, 79, 87, 144, 165;
space and time, 190
unit of meaning, 86, 107, 110
uses and gratifications, 8, 30

Verfremdung, 21, 202
veridical
effect, 6, 104–22, 126, 132,
135, 141, 153–69, 182, 187,
206; myth of, 162
viewer, *see* audience
viewpoint, 83
personal, 158–66; political,
160; wandering, 76
voiceover, 34–5, 82, 109, 114,
116, 120–2, 126, 131,
136–48, 173, 176, 178, 188
authorial, 164; contradictory,
153–8; and identity, 179

Williams, R., 107, 112
Wittgenstein, L., 19, 27

zoom, 111, 116, 134–5